Anglo-American Encounters

ANGLO-AMERICAN ENCOUNTERS

ENGLAND AND THE RISE OF AMERICAN LITERATURE

BENJAMIN LEASE

Professor of English
Northeastern Illinois University

CAMBRIDGE UNIVERSITY PRESS

Cambridge
London   New York   New Rochelle
Melbourne   Sydney

Published by the Press Syndicate of the University of Cambridge
The Pitt Building, Trumpington Street, Cambridge CB2 1RP
32 East 57th Street, New York, NY 10022, USA
296 Beaconsfield Parade, Middle Park, Melbourne 3206, Australia

First published 1981

Printed in Great Britain by
Western Printing Services Ltd, Bristol

Library of Congress catalogue card number: 81-3914

British Library Cataloguing in Publication Data
Lease, Benjamin
Anglo-American encounters.
1. American literature–History and criticism
1. Title
810'.9   PS88
ISBN 0 521 23666 5

To my son, Joseph Lease

Contents

Preface

The half-decade of 1850–5 was marked in England by the publication of a number of remarkable books: Elizabeth Browning's *Sonnets from the Portuguese,* Tennyson's *In Memoriam,* Wordsworth's *Prelude,* Dickens' *David Copperfield* and *Bleak House,* Thackeray's *Pendennis,* Robert Browning's *Men and Women.* It was a very distinguished period – but not one startlingly richer than the preceding half-decade or the one immediately following; that England's literature should flourish was a predictable phenomenon. But the extraordinary half-decade of 1850–5 in which five American books were produced that are now universally recognized as world classics was an unprecedented and not-to-be repeated phenomenon. The millenarian role of America as the redeemer nation of the Western world was, in a sense, fulfilled in the realm of literature when *The Scarlet Letter* (1850), *Moby-Dick* (1851), *Uncle Tom's Cabin* (1852), *Walden* (1854), *Leaves of Grass* (1855) made their appearance with a rapidity and authority that – except for Stowe's novel – were little noted then but seem miraculous now. This book attempts to shed light on that half-decade and on the rise of American literature during the several decades that preceded it – a rise initiated and signalled by a British critic's taunt, in 1820: "Who reads an American book?"

Sydney Smith's infuriating question appeared in the January number of the *Edinburgh Review.* An "Advertisement" added by Washington Irving to the British edition of *The Sketch Book* the following month pleads for "courtesy and candour" for his "desultory" papers from the British critics – a gentle monition to Sydney Smith and his countrymen. In 1850 – three decades after Smith's taunt and Irving's gentle rejoinder – Herman Melville, still smoldering, uttered a pronouncement designed to atomize from the American landscape the hovering shade of

Smith: "And the day will come [wrote Melville], when you shall say who reads a book by an Englishman that is a modern?"

In successive chapters – after a short one devoted to Sydney Smith – ten American writers, from Irving to Whitman, are discussed in terms of their involvement with England. Our old home, as Hawthorne called it, was a significant force in shaping the literary careers of each of these writers. The distinctive nature of American literature was forged during these decades in the crucible of Anglo-American love–hate encounters; the process and product are more clearly visible and intelligible when the British experiences and involvements of these American writers are placed in the foreground for detailed examination.

Individual biographies, book-length treatments of American writers abroad (most notably, by Robert Spiller, Clarence Gohdes and Ernest Earnest), and numerous articles provide valuable insights into what it meant to be in England for Irving, Cooper, Neal, Poe, Hawthorne, Melville, Stowe, Emerson – and what England meant to Thoreau and Whitman. But I have been out for more elusive game – for answers to a more slippery question: How does the British connection (through books, magazines, visits, visitors – and transatlantic friendships) clarify the career, the quest for nationality, the imaginative world of each of these major contributors to the shaping of an American literature?

A foray is a sudden raid or military advance; a second meaning moves away from the battlefield to any venture or initial attempt in some unspecified field. Part one of this book, Forays (chapters 1–7), deals with – after a short chapter on "the paper war" initiated by Sydney Smith's famous insult – the ventures into British terrain of six American writers of fiction (Irving, Cooper, Neal, Poe, Hawthorne, Melville) in their strivings toward a distinctively American voice. Part two, Forays and Friendships (chapters 8–11), also describes forays – the campaigns of Harriet Beecher Stowe, Emerson, Thoreau, Whitman for cultural independence; and there is added a significant new dimension: a series of intense relationships with British friends that has no parallel in the first part of the book. The significant alliances between Mrs Stowe and Lady Byron, Emerson and Carlyle, Thoreau and Thomas Cholmondeley, Whitman and Anne Gilchrist – each of these Anglo-American friendships sheds valuable new light on the persons involved and the two cultures they represent.

My ten chapters in search of ten authors vary greatly in length and approach. To illustrate, in the Irving chapter the answer could emerge only by sketching the shape of an entire career; for Poe, glimpses into his obsession with a British journal, and with the English village of his childhood, provided illumination for some important truths about the man and his art; the beginning point of the Hawthorne chapter was his revelatory religious experience at the bedside of his dying mother – a liberating experience that enabled him to produce, in rapid succession, three great American romances (and that led him, soon after, to an obsessive search for ancestral footsteps in England); my account of Harriet Beecher Stowe's mission as God's ambassador deals at length with her triumphal tour of England – and its stormy aftermath; Carlyle is a central figure in the chapter on Emerson – and he also looms large in the chapters dealing with Thoreau and Whitman.

All of us who seek a better understanding of the emergence and rise of an authentic American literature are deeply indebted to Benjamin T. Spencer's comprehensive and definitive *The Quest for Nationality: An American Literary Campaign* (1957). Spencer's Foreword calls attention to a difficulty and paradox: the nationalistic or antinationalistic views that might be inferred from the imaginative writings of such important writers as Irving, Hawthorne and Melville seem to contradict their explicit pronouncements; and some major American writers " . . . left scant record of their participation in the quest for nationality." Spencer's book is crowded with forgotten figures and he charts, in his massive study, the shifting currents of American thought concerning the nature of nationality in our emerging American literature as conveyed by these shadowy figures. My own concern has been, in contrast, less with the nature of nationality in American literature than with a better understanding of our most important early writers. (The relatively unknown John Neal is included as a significant forerunner of Poe, Hawthorne, Melville and Mark Twain.) The ten writers on whom this book is centered were profound and courageous explorers of the truths of the human heart. Of some of these explorers it might be said (as Alexander Cowie wrote of Neal) that they wrote "during the difficult days when American writers were just beginning to *be* American" – during the difficult days (as Joseph Conrad somewhat inaccurately wrote of Cooper) " . . . before the great American language was born." England was the prism through which some important truths about these American writers and their art were refracted. In the episodes charting the rise of American literature that comprise the eleven chapters of this book, I have offered up some glimpses of these truths.

Acknowledgments

Professor Benjamin T. Spencer of Ohio Wesleyan University generously made available to me a xerox copy of about seventy-five pages of unpublished footnotes (omitted from his monumental *The Quest for Nationality*); these manuscript notes were a great help to my research for this book and it is a pleasure to take this opportunity to thank him.

I wish also to thank the Committee on Organized Research of Northeastern Illinois University for several grants that facilitated my research and financed, in part, my typing expenses. A sabbatical leave granted by the University Educational Policy Council gave me the leisure to complete a first draft of this book. My work at the British Library was made easier by the staff of the Reading Room and North Library; and by the many kindnesses of Mr George Goosens, Deputy Superintendent of the Newspaper Library at Colindale, and his staff. I am indebted to the staffs of the three American libraries that provided me with invaluable assistance: the Newberry Library (Chicago); the Northwestern University Library; and my own library at Northeastern Illinois University. I am also indebted to Professor Earl John Clark, my colleague and department chairman, and to Dean Frank Dobbs for assistance of various kinds; and to Mrs Birdie Serlin and Mrs Katherine Snyder for preparing part one of the final typescript.

The longstanding interest and encouragement of Professor Hans-Joachim Lang of the University of Erlangen helped me to write this book. On two occasions, he invited me to Erlangen to lecture on aspects of the work-in-progress; and Professor Lang also kindly paved the way for similar lectures (in May–June 1978) at a number of other German universities. To my hosts and to my audiences in English and American Studies departments in the universities at Münster, Kiel, Tübingen, Stuttgart (also Amerika-Haus Stuttgart), Frankfort/Main, Regensburg and Erlangen I am deeply grateful.

Part 1

FORAYS

"Who reads an American book?"

According to Frank Luther Mott, the United States has fought three wars with England: the Revolution; the War of 1812; and "the Paper War, which lasted for more than a hundred years after the Revolution, and which still breaks out occasionally."[1] (According to the foremost British authority on Anglo-American relations in our own time, "it is not without significance that in 1951 Britain, with only a third of the population, produced eighteen thousand book titles to America's ten thousand.")[2] The animosities that smoldered after the Revolution broke out with fresh force in 1812. In that year Poet Laureate Robert Southey summed up his feelings in a letter to his friend Landor: "They [the Americans] have in the course of twenty years acquired a distinct national character for low and lying knavery; and so well do they deserve it that no man ever had any dealings with them without having proofs of its truth."[3] An ardent antagonist on the American side, James Kirke Paulding, suggested that "one could not help laughing to see John Bull, who ten times a day called Jonathan a lying, cheating, spitting, gouging, guessing, drinking republican sinner, complaining of him for an ungrateful rascal, because he did not love his daddy."[4]

The frenzy of patriotic pride that swept over America at the victorious conclusion of the War of 1812 intensified these antagonisms and introduced a more strident clamor for a native literature. In January of 1816, *The Portico* announced in the "Advertisement" prefacing its first number that "Dependence, whether literary or political, is a state of degradation, fraught with disgrace; and to be dependent on a foreign mind, for what we can ourselves produce, is to add to the crime of indolence, the weakness of stupidity." In the same vein (and at the same time), another newly-founded magazine, *The Port-Folio*, proclaimed that, despite the military victories: "We are yet without a name distinguished in letters." The writer urged American men of letters to emulate the drive and persistence of its military forces; if they did, America would soon become "as renowned in literature, as she is in arms."[5]

In such a climate, it was not surprising that, just a year later, a long poem entitled *Crystalina, A Fairy Tale*, by "an American," should be pronounced by a *Portico* reviewer as "one of the most splendid productions of the age," with passages in it unsurpassed by Shakespeare, Spenser, Dryden or Milton. In a similar vein, another review suggested that John Pierpont's *Airs of Palestine*, an eight-hundred-line tribute in verse to sacred music, would bring "a transport of delight, unfelt before, to the patriotic American critic, who has had to depend upon imported materials for the exercise of his trade."[6] And in such a climate it was not surprising that the British critics should respond with ridicule. *The Quarterly Review*, in 1814, sounded a characteristic note when it pointed out that "the states of America can never have a native literature any more than they can have a native character." Even the magnificent wilderness regions would not encourage the production of imaginative writing, the British commentator argued, because they are being invaded, for the most part, by "hordes of discontented Democrats . . . or desperate adventurers."[7] Such rhetoric can be dismissed as wartime rhodomontade, but the second peace with England, such as it was, seemed to intensify rather than allay the bitterness. Blasts and counterblasts filled the columns of newspapers and magazines on both sides of the Atlantic until a caustic and witty British critic, the Reverend Mr Sydney Smith, brought it all to a climax with a single overwhelming question: "In the four quarters of the globe, who reads an American book?" "Few other single sentences," observes William B. Cairns, "have aroused so many international heart-burnings and caused so much harm."[8] It may also have caused much good.

Sydney Smith's burning question appeared in the pages of the *Edinburgh Review*, founded in 1802 by Smith in association with Francis Jeffrey and several other Edinburgh intellectuals.[9] Smith and Jeffrey were close friends and associates but they did not, by any means, look at America and American literature in the same way. Both were extraordinary men whose distinctive personalities shed light on the *Edinburgh Review* and its important involvement with Anglo-American literary relations.

Mr Jeffrey of Edinburgh

Writing to his sister in Edinburgh from Queen's College, Oxford (which he heartily detested and fled from after a year), young Francis Jeffrey proclaimed: "I feel I shall never be a great man unless it be as a poet; for, though I have a boundless ambition, I am too much a slave of my heart."[10] A week later, he discoursed at length about the magical transformation of the college by moonlight – "the deep and romantic shades on the sculptured towers – the sparkle of their gilded vanes – their black and pointed shadows upon the smooth green turf of our courts – the strong shades of the statues over the library – the yellow and trembling heads of the trees beyond them!" Unfortunately, he can find no kindred spirit to share his vision; his fellow students "are all drunkards, or pedants, or coxcombs."[11] Like many other aspiring young poets, Francis Jeffrey was later to achieve a measure of greatness not as a poet but in more prosaic endeavors, as a critic and lawyer. In the early years of his law practice he complained to a friend that "I lose all my originalities, and ecstasies, and romances, and am far advanced already upon that dirty highway called the way of the world."[12] But Jeffrey retained the poet's eye and feeling for nature all of his life. "The contemplation of the glories of the external world [reports his friend and biographer Cockburn] was one of his habitual delights."[13] When Jeffrey met Thomas Moore on the field of honor after being challenged for what the Irish poet regarded as an insulting critique, the first words that passed between them (Moore later recalled) "was Jeffrey's saying . . . 'What a beautiful morning it is!'" (The police intervened before a shot could be fired and the two men, who had taken an instant fancy to each other, became lifelong friends.)[14]

Jeffrey's intense dislike for his fellow students at Oxford may have stemmed in part from an acute sense of social insecurity. All of his life, reports Cockburn, he was extremely dependent on the presence of old familiar friends and "scarcely ever took even a professional journey of a day or two alone without helplessness and discomfort."[15] Contributing to his dreamy romanticism and social uneasiness might have been his youthful sensitivity concerning his short stature. "His robes, God knows, will cost him little," Smith wrote to John Murray when Jeffrey became Dean of the Faculty of Advocates; "one buck rabbit will clothe him to the heels."[16]

Despite – perhaps because of – Jeffrey's diminutive stature and social insecurity, he had a pronounced proclivity for flirtatiousness throughout his lifetime. Shortly after the death of the first Mrs Jeffrey, Sydney Smith reported to Lady Holland the "great scandal about Jeffrey and the Dutchess of Gordon." "He is a very amorous little gentleman," observed Smith, "and her disposition is not I fancy wholly dissimilar; it is probable therefore they will build a nest."[17] Smith was mistaken about the Duchess, but several years later, when Jeffrey fell in love deeply enough to propose, he crossed the Atlantic in time of war to claim his American fiancée. Cockburn regarded this dangerous voyage "as one of the greatest achievements of love" and tactfully ignored the tendency towards flirtation that by no means came to a halt after Jeffrey's marriage.[18] William Charvat has suggested that Jeffrey's romantic wartime voyage was made possible by the record of friendship he had established in the pages of the *Edinburgh Review*. "Realizing, perhaps, that British Whiggism and American Federalism were intellectually and socially on about the same level," suggests Charvat, "Jeffrey courted and won American readers for his periodical, which within a few decades gained a circulation in the United States as large as that of our own *North American Review*."[19] But the pro-American tone of the *Edinburgh Review* was not nearly so pronounced and consistent as has been suggested by Charvat. According to a more recent commentator, John Clive, "the *Review* took it as axiomatic that in the realm of culture and intellect nothing better than the mediocre could, for the time being, emerge from America."[20] The conflicting views of Charvat and Clive and the circumstances leading to Sydney Smith's explosive taunt in the January 1820 number of the *Edinburgh Review* can best be understood by a closer look at the man who penned that burning question.

The Smith of Smiths

In Emerson's "Each and All," a humble sexton tolls his bell, unaware that the great Napoleon "Stops his horse, and lists with delight, / Whilst his files sweep round yon Alpine height . . . " But when Napoleon's files swept round the Continent in the fall of 1797, a British country squire took note and altered his plans for his son's university education in Germany, sending him instead to Edinburgh. Accompanying young Michael Hicks-Beach as tutor–companion was a young clergyman named Sydney Smith. Smith's five-year stay in Edinburgh was eventful. "Never," he wrote years later, "shall I forget the happy days I passed there, amidst odious smells, barbarous sounds, bad suppers, excellent hearts, and most enlightened and cultivated understandings!"[21] Most notable among the results of his Edinburgh years – aside from a long and happy marriage – was the successful launching of the *Edinburgh Review*.

Smith had a warm regard for Jeffrey, nominated him to the editorship and persuaded him to accept the post. But these two men were temperamentally and intellectually very different and the precarious balance they maintained is revealed by a letter Smith wrote to Jeffrey in 1819: "You must consider that Edinburgh is a very grave place, and that you live with Philosophers – who are very intolerant of nonsense. I write for the London, not for the Scotch market, and perhaps more people read my nonsense than your sense."[22] Smith's playfulness persisted throughout his twenty-five-year association with the *Review*. Here, for example, is the opening paragraph of his review of the Rev. Dr W. Langford's *Anniversary Sermon of the Royal Humane Society*:

An Accident which happened to the gentleman engaged in reviewing this Sermon, proves, in the most striking manner, the importance of this charity for restoring to life persons in whom the vital power is suspended. He was discovered, with Dr. Langford's discourse lying open before him, in a state of the most profound sleep; from which he could not, by any means, be awakened for a great length of time. By attending, however, to the rules prescribed by the Humane Society, flinging in the smoke of tobacco, applying hot flannels, and carefully removing the discourse itself to a great distance, the critic was restored to his disconsolate brothers.[23]

In matters relating to America, the temperamental differences between them resulted in appeals for restraint and caution by Jeffrey when he was confronted by what he believed to be Smith's reckless expressions of animosity. In reviewing several books of travel in America by Englishmen, Smith conveyed a vehemence that Jeffrey tried to restrain; Jeffrey's letter has not survived but we have Smith's response. "I entirely agree with you respecting the Americans," he wrote ,"and believe that I am to the full as much of a Philoyankeist as you are." Protesting his basic admiration for the way in which this new people was conducting itself, Smith nevertheless assented to the changes suggested by Jeffrey ("your caution was proper and I am obliged to you for it").[24] What survived in print after the agreed-upon changes, however, can scarcely be labeled "Philoyankeist":

Literature the Americans have none – no native literature, we mean. They had a Franklin indeed; and may afford to live for half a century on his fame. There is, or was, a Mr. Dwight, who wrote some poems; and his baptismal name was Timothy. There is also a small account of Virginia by Jefferson, and an Epic by Joel Barlow – and some pieces of pleasantry by Mr. Irving. But why should the Americans write books, when a six weeks' passage brings them, in their own tongue, our sense, science and genius, in bales and hogsheads? Prairies, steam-boats, grist-mills, are their natural objects for centuries to come. Then, when they have got to the Pacific Ocean – epic poems, plays, pleasures of memory, and all the elegant gratifications of an ancient people who have tamed the wild earth, and set down to amuse themselves. – This is the natural march of human affairs.[25]

It should be noted that there were also sharp criticisms of British shortcomings. And the most passionate animadversions on America have to do with the institution of slavery ("the consummation of wickedness").

But these observations were only a preparation for the long and explosive paragraph published in the *Review* in January 1820. In it, Smith argued that the chief claim to glory of the Americans is their British heritage. The great sages and heroes of the Revolution, their Franklins and Washingtons, were born and brought up as subjects of the King of England; during the following decades a large proportion of their statesmen and artists have been foreigners. Smith then lists numerous distinguished Britons in the period of American independence and inquires about their counterparts among "this self-adulating race." "In the four quarters of the globe," he asks, "who reads an American book? or goes to an American play? or looks at an American picture or statue?"[26]

Robert E. Spiller has suggested that the "lurking antipathies" of Sydney Smith were less characteristic than the "instinctive sympathy" he felt for America – a sympathy that made him "an often misguided but frequently penetrating critic and friend."[27] But Sydney Smith's explosive paragraph – and the notorious taunt that concluded it – reflected a point of view prevalent throughout Smith's lifetime. Jeffrey attempted, on occasion, to deal with these antipathies. In a letter of 1822, Smith complained that he could not comply with Jeffrey's request that he (Smith) curb his raillery in a nearly-completed review: "There are many passages in my review which would make the Americans very angry, and – which is more to my immediate purpose – make you very loath to publish it; and therefore to avoid putting you in the awkward predicament of printing what you disapprove or disappointing me I withdraw my pretensions." Smith insisted that he admired Americans and wished to praise America, while laughing "at her little defects."[28]

In 1824, when Smith again reviewed several travel books about America, he found much to praise concerning American egalitarian institutions and customs – using them as a springboard for his criticisms of British inequities ("If a man finds a partridge upon his ground eating his corn, in any part of Kentucky or Indiana, he may kill it, even if his father is not a Doctor of Divinity"). But, responding to the anger aroused by his 1820 review, he also chastised the "sensitive and touchy" Americans ("We really thought at one time they would have fitted out an armament against the Edinburgh and Quarterly Reviews, and burnt down Mr. Murray's and Mr. Constable's shops, as we did the American Capitol"). Smith will confess to no other anti-American crime "than preference of Shakespeare and Milton over Joel Barlow and Timothy Dwight."[29]

James Fenimore Cooper, incensed over a hostile criticism of his *Notions of the Americans*, was convinced that Smith was responsible ("I think I see the stale witticisms of Sydney Smith in the article"). The reviewer actually was William Empson,[30] but Cooper's misattribution was symptomatic of a widespread American hostility toward Smith and a pervasive skepticism concerning his professed admiration for America. That this skepticism was not merely a sign of American "touchiness" is made clear by the controversy surrounding the repudiation by the State of Pennsylvania, in 1843, of its interest payments on bonds invested in by Smith. After venting his spleen (and splenetic wit) in a petition to Congress, Smith addressed several letters on the subject to the *Morning Chronicle*. In one of them, Smith asserted that if he were an American, "[he] would fly to Newgate for greater purity of thought, and seek in the prisons of England for better rules of life."[31] In 1819, when George Ticknor met Sydney Smith in London, he found him "the soul of the society" – one whose "plain good-sense" he valued as much as his "admirable humor." As an old and loyal friend, the American initially defended Smith's position in his petition to Congress. But when Smith's letters to the *Chronicle* appeared, Ticknor complained to Charles Lyell: "How foolish, then, is Sydney Smith in his last letter, to treat us all as pick-pockets!"[32]

One of the most perceptive of American literary critics in the 1840s, E. P. Whipple, praised Smith's gift as a wit and satirist ("every thing that comes from his mind seems to be original, even when it is old"). "The only points at which he lashes us," Whipple observed, "are slavery and national vanity, – one awaking his indignation and the other his ridicule." And he pointed out that the same essay in which appeared the insuffer-able, unforgettable taunt ("who reads an American book?") also featured a satiric blast at the British system of taxation known, in 1844, to every schoolboy. But Whipple nevertheless deplored Smith's *Letters on American Debts* as unworthy of its author.[33]

Sydney Smith died in 1845, but his presence was still felt in America in 1856, when Evert A. Duyckinck edited the *Wit and Wisdom of the Rev. Sydney Smith*, prefaced by a lengthy bio-graphical memoir. For Duyckinck, Smith was not only a great and memorable wit but also a defender of America in days "when America had been in need of English opinion . . . " His *Letters on American Debts* "did good service," for: "The cause was just, and his wit was trenchant." To an excerpt from Smith's famous review (headed "WHO READS AN AMERICAN BOOK?") Duyckinck provided an explanatory footnote: "This is the famous passage which has been the peg to hang many wearisome dissertations upon. Not needed to excite rapid American invention, it has become simply an historical landmark, from which to date extensive national achievements. Its questions in politics, art, science, literature, are an index to American triumphs."[34] Duyckinck's conciliatory tone, in 1856, is far removed from the aggressive nationalism of Melville's 1850 essay on Hawthorne with its climactic question (parodying Smith's old taunt): "And the day will come [wrote Melville], when you shall say who reads a book by an Englishman that is a modern?"[35] When Duyckinck edited Melville's essay for publication in the *Literary World* he made numerous changes. The major ones, reports Perry Miller after examining Melville's manuscript among the Duyckinck papers, "are all of a single tendency: they cut down or restrain the exuberant nationalism of [Melville's] draft." Miller sees Duyckinck's revisions as "obvious efforts to accommodate Melville's rage to the new, conciliatory tone Duyckinck had imparted to the *Literary World*."[36]

Duyckinck's eagerness to smooth over Anglo-American hostilities is in evidence throughout his Sydney Smith anthology. It was a point of view shared by many other Americans. In the same year that the Duyckinck compilation appeared (1856), H. T. Tuckerman was observing in the pages of the *North American Review* that "Notwithstanding the deserved rebuke [Sydney Smith] administered to our national delinquency in his American letters, he vindicates his claim to the title of Philo-Yankeeist. No British writer has better appreciated the institutions and destiny of the United States."[37] But many other Americans – Herman Melville among them – resented Sydney Smith's taunt and, even worse, his dismissal of the possibility of an emerging American literature "for centuries to come."

In the four decades following Sydney Smith's taunt – an era that culminated, in the half-decade between 1850 and 1855, in the publication of *The Scarlet Letter, Moby-Dick, Uncle Tom's Cabin, Walden* and *Leaves of Grass* – Anglo-American attitudes and encounters have much to tell us about the rise of American literature. Let us begin with a closer look at the gentle Washington Irving who, according to Thackeray, taught millions of his countrymen "to love England, and why to love her."[38]

2

Washington Irving: uneasy ambassador

"Ambassador of the New World to the Old"

In an "Advertisement" added to the British edition of *The Sketch Book*, the author informs his readers that his "desultory" papers can be interesting only to Americans; he reprints them reluctantly, with an awareness of "the austerity with which the writings of his countrymen have hitherto been treated by British critics . . . " He can only hope that these critics, if they find his sketches worthy of attention, give them "that courtesy and candour which a stranger has some right to claim, who presents himself at the threshold of a hospitable nation."[1] Irving's advertisement is dated February 1820, and it seems certain that Sydney Smith, whose provocative taunt had appeared in print just a month before, was very much in his mind.

Irving's hesitant, diffident approach was not an affectation. In October of 1820, several months after the enormous success of *The Sketch Book*, Irving seems still to be pinching himself in disbelief as he writes to his British publisher, John Murray: "I am astonished at the success of my writings in England, and can hardly persuade myself that it is not all a dream. Had any one told me a few years since in America, that any thing I could write would interest such men as Gifford and Byron I should have as readily believed a fairy tale."[2] He had indeed, after a fashion, become Geoffrey Crayon, Esq., an affable and modest American visitor, ready and willing to gratify the prevailing demand for the picturesque and sentimental and to build a comfortable and comforting bridge between two embittered peoples. The second installment of *The Sketch Book*, sent from England on April 1 1819, opened with "English Writers on America," an essay which a recent commentator on Irving finds "almost unreadable."[3] But if read in the context of its composition, "English Writers" is an eminently readable and revealing piece of writing, one in which Irving establishes himself – at a time when Anglo-American animosity was most pronounced – as a loyal American keenly conscious of the sensitivity of his countrymen to British rancor and slander; keenly aware of the growing strength and glowing possibilities of his youthful native land. Without excusing the British slanderers of America, Irving pleads for an end to retorts in kind that can only prolong the bitterness and inhibit American literary progress. Let us, he says, by all means respond with "prompt and spirited vindication of our country" and with "the keenest castigation of her slanderers"; but, he reminds his compatriots, "the retort of abuse and sarcasm" is necessarily self-defeating. Not only are such retorts futile because they are never republished in England; even worse, "they foster a querulous and peevish temper among our writers" and "sour the sweet flow of our early literature . . . " Our national existence is rooted in an enlightened and philosophic age. It is knowledge and enlightenment that strengthen our youthful nation and literature; national prejudices can only sap the foundations of our growing strength. Irving closes with a plea for the rejection of both indiscriminate animosity and adulation, substituting in their place a creative interaction:

It should be the endeavour of our writers, therefore, discarding all feelings of irritation, and disdaining to be affected by the illiberality of British authors, to speak of the nation dispassionately, and with determined candour. While they rebuke the indiscriminating bigotry with which some of their countrymen admire and imitate every thing English, merely because it is English, they should point out what is really worthy of approbation. We may thus place England before us as a perpetual volume of reference, wherein the sound deductions of ages and experiences are recorded; and while we avoid the errors and absurdities which may have crept into the page, we may draw from thence golden maxims of practical wisdom, wherewith to strengthen and embellish our national character.[4]

This rarely reprinted essay provides a central clue to Irving's dilemma as an artist seeking approval from both of the two warring camps. He paid a price for a success that, in the eyes of some American and British critics, was actually a defeat. He was temperamentally suited for the mediator's role. But it must also be remembered that the author of the lively and satiric *Salma-gundi* papers and of Knickerbocker's ebullient *History* had, in the nationalistic climate of the War of 1812, uttered fervent sentiments that sounded more like James Kirke Paulding and John Neal than the genteel Geoffrey Crayon of *The Sketch Book*:

We would rather hear our victories celebrated in the merest dog-gerel that sprang from native invention, than beg, borrow, or steal from others, the thoughts and words in which to express our exaltation. By tasking our own powers, and relying entirely on ourselves, we shall gradually improve and rise to poetical independence.[5]

These words are a far cry from the conciliatory and moderate stance Irving later adopted in "English Authors on America." That he should have written them at all is significant for they represent a point of view that was pervasive before, during, and after the war – one that he had constantly to take into account even at the time Geoffrey Crayon had apparently left it far behind.

Patriot and Officer

At the outbreak of the second war with England in June 1812, Washington Irving was as little affected as his friend Henry Brevoort, who was then traveling through Great Britain, meeting with Scott and Jeffrey, and presenting copies of *A History of New York* "to everyone that mattered." But as the hostilities intensified, Irving's warlike emotions were increasingly aroused. "He who fancies he can stand aloof in interest [he wrote in *The Analectic*], and by condemning the present war, can exonerate himself from the shame of its disasters, is woe-fully mistaken." "The disgrace of defeat," he added, "will not be confined to the contrivers of the war, nor the party in power, or the conductors of the battle; but will extend to the whole nation, and come home to every individual."[6] When the news broke of the British occupation of the nation's capital – and of the widespread burning and destruction – Irving was in the darkened cabin of a Hudson River steamboat. A passenger boarding at Poughkeepsie gave his account of the disaster, and a derisive voice out of the darkness "wondered what *Jimmy* Madison would say now." "Let me tell you, sir," was Irving's response (as he told it many years later to his nephew), "it is not now a question about *Jimmy* Madison, or *Jimmy* Armstrong. The pride and honor of the nation are wounded; the country is insulted and disgraced by this barbarous success, and every local citizen would feel the ignominy and be earnest to avenge it."[7]

Soon after his arrival in New York City, Irving volunteered his services to Governor Daniel D. Tompkins and, as the city prepared to stand siege against the British, was commissioned as the governor's aid and military secretary with the rank of Colonel in the Iron Greys of the New York State Militia. Irving traveled extensively with Tompkins but, though he longed to witness a military engagement, saw no fighting. His letters in this period do, however, provide some vivid descriptions of the preparations for the expected onslaught at Sackett's Harbor. But even more striking and characteristic is this account of a forest ride en route to the harbor:

While I was jogging thus pensively on, my horse scarce dragging a snail's pace, and seemingly, like his rider, sunk into a reverie, I was suddenly startled by a loud rustling on the right; a beautiful doe came bounding through the thickets, leaped lightly over a fallen pine, and alighted in the road just before me. The poor animal seemed transfixed with astonishment at beholding another tenant of these solitudes; it gazed at me for an instant with the most picturesque surprise, and then launching away to the left, I presently heard it plunge into the river.[8]

Several months later, in February 1815, the treaty of peace with Great Britain was ratified by President Madison. There followed a series of wild demonstrations that elicited in Irving a lack of enthusiasm – even a distaste for these chauvinistic displays. "This," Irving said sadly of the war shortly after it ended, "was the first thing that roused and stimulated me, but it did not last long."[9] His forays into patriotism now gave way to an even greater desire for conciliation with Britain and British culture.

Geoffrey Crayon and "a Mr Paulding"

Washington Irving had first gained wide attention through the publication of the *Salmagundi* papers (1807–8), a series of satirical sketches written in collaboration with James Kirke

Paulding and Washington's brother William. (That Paulding was a close friend of Washington Irving, early and late, is well known; less well known is the fact that he was William Irving's brother-in-law.)[10] The *Salmagundi* papers were (and still are) usually characterized as clever imitations of Addison and Steele – but they also parody their models and poke fun at supercilious British travelers in America.[11] It is this satiric side of *Salmagundi* that helps us better understand the imminent arrival (in 1809) of a new satiric *persona*, the eccentric and "extravagant" Diedrich Knickerbocker. It also clarifies the early literary kinship of Irving and James Kirke Paulding, a staunch and unequivocal battler for American cultural independence throughout his long life.

On the publication of one of his anti-British satires, *The Diverting History of John Bull and Brother Jonathan* (1812), Paulding sent a copy to Irving (along with a reference to a new collaborative work, "our contemplated undertaking," that seems to have been abandoned).[12] A year later, in September, 1813, Irving reviewed Paulding's *The Lay of the Scottish Fiddle*, for the most part praising this parody of Scott's *Lay of the Last Minstrel* with, however, expressions of regret for some touches of political satire "calculated to awaken angry feelings in some bosoms."[13]

Irving must have found himself in a peculiarly equivocal position in reviewing this spoof on Scott by his old friend and collaborator. Just a short time before, he had received a letter from another close friend, Henry Brevoort. Writing from London (on June 24, 1813), Brevoort tells of presenting a copy of Irving's *Knickerbocker's History of New York* to Walter Scott while visiting Edinburgh; and he encloses Scott's letter of praise – a response that was everything an aspiring writer could hope for: "I am sensible [wrote Scott], that as a stranger to American parties and politics, I must lose much of the concealed satire of the piece, but I must own that looking at the simple and obvious meaning only, I have never read any thing so closely resembling the style of Dean Swift, as the annals of Diedrich Knickerbocker." Other passages reminded Scott of Sterne and he urged Brevoort "to let me know when Mr. Irvine takes pen in hand again, for assuredly I shall expect a very great treat."[14]

Such praise from the great man of the north must have been extremely gratifying to Irving; it probably emboldened him when, four years later, during a visit to Scotland (the land of his forebears), he made a pilgrimage to Abbotsford, where he spent four days with Scott that he remembered and valued all his life. Scott, in turn was favorably impressed by the American ("one of the best and pleasantest acquaintances I have made this many a day").[15] When Henry Murray decided against publishing *The Sketch Book*, Irving turned to Scott for assistance. Scott expended considerable effort on Irving's behalf and was finally able to persuade Murray to reconsider. As finally brought out by Murray, *The Sketch Book* was appropriately dedicated "To Sir Walter Scott, Bart. . . . in testimony of the admiration and affection of the author."

Under these circumstances, it was especially aggravating to Irving to be charged, several months later, with the authorship of Paulding's parody of Scott. "As I wish to be answerable to no one's sins but my own [Irving wrote to his publisher Murray] I would take it as a particular favour if you would contradict it in your next advertisement of the Sketch Book &c. The work in question was written by a Mr Paulding." Irving is especially annoyed at being held responsible for "a burlesque on the writings of Sir Walter Scott for whom I have so perfect an esteem & affection, and beside it contained political and national reflections of a different nature from those I have entertained."[16] A long-time friend and literary collaborator becomes, for the occasion, "a Mr Paulding." It is unlikely that the genteel and gracious Irving would similarly disclaim Paulding if his friend were to make an appearance (a most unlikely event) at one of Murray's fashionable literary soirées.

Paulding, with all his anti-British sentiment and flamboyant nationalism, was sensitive to Irving's feelings about Scott. When Irving praised Paulding's *Koningsmarke* (1823), Paulding explained his satiric thrusts at Scott and other British writers in terms that try to take into account his friend's point of view:

My motives for "tilting" as you term it, at some of the fashionable English writers, are altogether national, and devoid of any personal feeling. We Americans are treated so scurvily by the English press that my feelings often arise against this persevering ill-nature, and I am prompted to retaliate. However, I learn from all quarters that

Sir Walter is a fine liberal fellow, and his being your friend, shall in the future, as it ought to have been in the past, render him sacred to me. As the gnat said to the eagle, "I'll spare him hereafter."[17]

Though they differed widely in their conceptions of American literature and Anglo-American relations, they remained good friends all of their lives. (Paulding called Irving, in 1840, "my oldest friend.")[18] But on at least one occasion, during the first months of widespread acclaim for *The Sketch Book*, Irving was moved to refer to one of his closest friends as "a Mr Paulding."

" . . . but Mr. Washington Irving is an American."

In "The Author's Farewell," appended to *Bracebridge Hall* (1822), Irving called attention to "the unexpected sympathy and approbation" with which his remarks on Anglo-American animosity (in "English Writers on America") had been received on both sides of the Atlantic. A twenty-one-line paragraph added to the second English edition suggests further that "the time of the slanderer is gone by; the ribald jokes, the stale common places, which have so long passed current when America was the theme, are now banished to the ignorant and vulgar, or only perpetuated by the hireling scribblers and traditional jesters of the press."[19] But just a short time after expressing this hope, Irving found himself at the center of a controversy between British and American journalists. The Shakespeare Committee controversy has only recently come to light a century and a half after it erupted and subsided. It was, in retrospect, a tempest in a teacup, but the passions it aroused tell us much about the problems of the aspiring American writer in this period, and of Irving's uneasy position as the first American writer to achieve fame in Britain.

It was *The Sketch Book* that admitted Irving to London literary society. At first rather diffidently but with increasing confidence, Geoffrey Crayon entered the literary world of the House of Murray and the fashionable world of Lord and Lady Holland. London society made him very welcome, but the precariousness of his status as an American and an outsider can be gauged by what happened when Irving was nominated to be a member of a Shakespeare Memorial Committee.

In 1820 the actor Charles Mathews conceived a plan to

honor Shakespeare by erecting a monument in Stratford-upon-
Avon.[20] Mathews was well acquainted with the glowing
eloquence of Irving's tribute to Shakespeare in his *Sketch Book*
essay "Stratford-on-Avon"; and Irving's passion for the
English drama had led to a close friendship with Mathews and
other theatrical people. It was natural, therefore, that Mathews
should propose his American friend for membership on the
committee that would carry through his plan. But Irving's
nomination seemed most unnatural to Theodore Hook's *John
Bull*; on July 7, 1822, this London weekly devoted three-fourths
of a column to the proposed Shakespeare monument, concluding with an expression of surprised dismay:

MR. WASHINGTON IRVING is the author of a publication called the
Sketch Book, (Which, under the auspices of that Lord Chamberlain
of the Muses, MR. MURRAY, who regulated its costume of wove
paper and wide margin, and introduced it to the Beau-monde, after
it had lain mouldering for months unnoticed in minor shops, has
been very popular with light readers at the west end of town,) and
of a work called "KNICKERBOCKER'S" History of New York, very
full of fun and quaintness; and moreover, MR. WASHINGTON IRVING
is a very pleasant and gentlemanly man, modest, quiet, and un-
assuming, and therefore it is painful to find him published in this
list; but Mr. Washington Irving is an American; at least, all the
success of his works has arisen from the wonderment excited that
a Yankee could have written so well. Now, really, what an American
Sketcher can have to do in a London Committee, formed to com-
memorate SHAKESPEARE, we cannot see. If it is meant as a compliment to the Americans, which we suspect it to be, it is paid at too
great a sacrifice. We repeat, we have no personal feeling against
MR. IRVING; far from it – we are prepossessed in his favour; but as a
general question, we certainly must say, that it does appear that a
national monument could have been raised to SHAKESPEARE without
selecting as a Committee-man, a member of a republic which has
denationalized itself.[21]

Several months later, in November, *John Bull* describes with
amusement the angry response of American newspapers to its
criticism of Irving's nomination; an extract from the *Baltimore
Chronicle* is offered to illustrate Jonathan's rage and illogic:

"It seems that offence has been taken in England," (says the
"Baltimore Chronicle," "that WASHINGTON IRVINE [*sic*] should have
been appointed a member of a committee to devise the form of a

proper monument to the memory of Shakespeare. The ground of objection is, that this gentleman is a native of America – he is not an Englishman. Perhaps it may be new to those snarling cynics, to learn, *that Shakespeare was one of our own countrymen.* What were the Americans in the day of Shakespeare? English subjects. Yes, the Americans claim for their countrymen, Hampden and Sydney, and Newton, and Locke, and Shakespeare, and Milton, and Pope, and all those literary, and martial, and civil, and legislative, and scientific luminaries . . . and we can say these are our countrymen, in the same sense precisely as they are your countrymen."[22]

Such reasoning, suggests *John Bull*, enables one to conclude with equal cogency that Voltaire was an American, since prior to 1800 the King of England was "styled" King of France.

That these heated exchanges represented more than journalistic animosity is made clear by a letter concerning the affair from Sir Robert Liston, a retired British diplomat, to one of Washington Irving's London society friends. In his letter (dated February 10, 1823 from Milbourn, near Edinburgh), Sir Robert tells of reading in a London newspaper "sometime ago" that Mr Irving had been proposed as a member of the Committee planning the construction of a Shakespeare monument; he urgently requests his correspondent, Miss Rebecca Bond, "to tell me all you know." His admiration for the author of *The Sketch Book* is unbounded but, "The time alas! is not yet come" for an American to serve on such a Committee.

In June 1823 Irving – despite the objections of Sir Robert Liston and *John Bull* – was designated an official member of the Shakespeare Committee.[23] When he met Theodore Hook in Paris in March 1824, the American writer entered in his journal no more than a brief comment on the "excellent story" Hook told about a classical scholar; he was apparently unaware of Hook's connection with *John Bull*.[24] Meanwhile the pages of *John Bull* continued to crackle with ill-will toward Washington Irving and America. On July 18, 1824, a vitriolic essay on "Traits of America" concluded with a peevish reference to Irving: "[He] is to be sure an American, yet we confess, with every respect for his talent, that we do not think him superior to CAMPBELL, or the HERMIT IN LONDON, Captain Somebody, now in jail, waiting for trial for stealing a pocket book."[25]

Despite these persistent cracklings, Irving's membership was not countermanded – but Mathews' project ran into difficulties and was eventually abandoned. It was a minor episode, to be sure, but the controversy sheds important light on Irving's literary career at a time of acute Anglo-American distrust.

From Diedrich Knickerbocker to Geoffrey Crayon

In the "Author's Account of Himself" introduction to *The Sketch Book*, Irving explains the pull of Europe to an American: "There were to be seen the masterpieces of art, the refinements of highly cultivated society, the quaint peculiarities of ancient and local custom. My native country was full of youthful promise; Europe was rich in the accumulated treasure of the age."[26] Here Irving sounds a note that would be repeated, with variations, throughout the nineteenth century, culminating in Henry James' famous catalog of the "items of high civilization" missing in Hawthorne's America.[27] *The Sketch Book* was to be a guide book to England for Americans yearning, as did the author, for "the Charms of storied and poetical association." Such a book must charm not only the Americans but the British, who would take double pleasure in the pleasure an American visitor takes in English customs and architectural splendors. (According to Ben Harris McClary, Irving's essays relating to Shakespeare in *The Sketch Book* were accepted in England "as a kind of tourist guide for the Shakespeare country.")[28] But Geoffrey Crayon was a shrewd guide, for he adds an ironic note on the great men of Europe ("I will visit this land of wonders, therefore, thought I, and see the gigantic race from which I have degenerated") – a note that would certainly elicit a sympathetic response from compatriots smarting at British condescension. Such condescension, wedded to the friendliest of intentions, was to find characteristic expression in Francis Jeffrey's praise of *The Sketch Book* as the first American literary production "written throughout with the greatest care and accuracy, and worked up to great purity and beauty of diction, on the model of the most elegant and polished of our native writers."[29]

Geoffrey Crayon was reaching out to readers on both sides of the Atlantic; in this, he had considerable success. But there were critics, both American and British, who valued Washington Irving much more in the role of Diedrich Knickerbocker than as Geoffrey Crayon. Yankee John Neal's highest praise was for *Knickerbocker's History*, a bold and original work far superior to the "timid, beautiful" *Sketch Book*.[30] In this opinion Neal was anticipated by the Scottish critic John Gibson Lockhart, who insisted, in 1824, that *Knickerbocker's History* was by far Irving's best work and that, to make for himself an enduring reputation, Irving must

at once cut all ideas of writing about European matters. He can never be anything but an imitator of our Goldsmiths here, – on his own soil he *may* rear a name and a monument, *aere perennius*, for himself. No, he must allow his mind to dwell upon the only images which it can give back with embellished and strengthened hues. He must riot in pumpkin pies, grinning negroes, smoking skippers, plump jolly little Dutch maidens, and their grizzly-periwigged papas. This is his world, and he must stick to it.[31]

Another British critic, Marcus Cunliffe, arrived at a similar conclusion 130 years later. *Knickerbocker's History*, observed Cunliffe, "is an uneven book, half fact, half fancy; yet it has a cocksure irreverent quality that makes everything Irving wrote afterwards seem by comparison sadly insipid." Cunliffe praises the Twainian flavor of the *History* and suggests that Irving abandoned Knickerbocker for Geoffrey Crayon because truly American prose "could not survive until conditions were more favourable."[32]

What these and other critics (in Irving's and our own time) valued in *Knickerbocker's History* was an exuberant vitality most clearly revealed in its numerous satiric thrusts at the Yankees, a race of Americans whom Irving cordially despised. Something of Diedrich Knickerbocker's characteristic bravura and ribaldry is conveyed in his account of Antony Van Corlear journeying through Connecticut:

solacing himself by the way according to his wont – twanging his trumpet like a very devil . . . ogling and winking at the women, and making aerial wind-mills from the end of his nose at their husbands – and stopping occasionally in the villages to eat pumpkin-pies, dance at country frolics, and bundle with the Yankee lasses – whom he rejoiced exceedingly with his soul-stirring instrument.[33]

The colloquial extravagance and tall-tale hyperbole of later native American humorists are anticipated in Knickerbocker's description of Antony leaning over the side of a Hudson River ship as the sun comes out from behind the clouds: a sunbeam bounces off his giant red nose, shooting down, "hissing hot, into the water" to kill "a mighty sturgeon that was sporting beside the vessel."[34]

The racy exuberance of 1809 gave way, in *The Sketch Book*, to a dreamier, more sentimental style. "The Author's Account of Himself" opens with an inscription from Lyly's *Euphues*: " . . . the traveller that stragleth from his owne country is in a short time transformed into so monstrous a shape, that he is faine to alter his mansion with his manners, and to live where he can, not where he would." The potency of Crayon's spell is intensified by the *persona* he creates of the alienated observer, whose self-deprecatory touches suggest that he is not really at home in England or in his own land (or with himself). Crayon's wanderings through the old streets, courtyards, gateways, taverns, abbeys of England convey a sense of melancholy and loneliness that anticipate the studies in isolation of Hawthorne and Melville.

It is significant that Geoffrey Crayon resurrects Diedrich Knickerbocker to tell the tales for which Irving is best remembered: "Rip Van Winkle" and "The Legend of Sleepy Hollow." Both of these tales drew heavily on German folklore, but these sources are transmuted into American materials – and Rip Van Winkle and Ichabod Crane have become typical and recurrent figures in American literary mythology. Significantly, both these folk heroes are outsiders – Rip escaping from his workaday world (and the terrors of Dame Van Winkle) through his long sleep, Ichabod dreaming the impossible dream of the blooming Katrina and her father's prosperous farm. We laugh with Crayon at Rip and Ichabod – but sense that the vividness of these characters derive in considerable part from Crayon's stance: he mocks them – but reaches out to them into an American past as shadowy and evocative as England's. Rip and Ichabod become ludicrous counterparts of Crayon himself – all of them, in a sense, travelers that straggle from their own country.

According to Stanley T. Williams, "never was a book of Irving's so damned as was *Tales of a Traveller*." The public rejection of the book left its author, during the autumn of 1824, "sleepless, anguished, beaten."[35] He had begun studying Spanish seriously about this time and was planning a series of essays on American life. He was making progress on his American sketchbook, but was somewhat gloomy about the hostile reception of *Tales of a Traveller* and his increasingly precarious financial situation. In January of 1826, Irving was greatly cheered by his appointment to the American Legation in Madrid.[36] A new world awaited him and he was to write, during the next few years, four new books based on Spanish materials and experiences.

Ambassador Alexander Everett's invitation to Spain was accompanied by a proposal that Irving consider translating Navarrete's study of Columbus' voyages, the first volumes of which were about to be published in Madrid.[37] Irving promptly set aside his American essays to journey with quickened spirits to Madrid, where he wrote with great rapidity *The Life and Voyages of Columbus*, a "translation" of Navarrete so free that William L. Hedges calls it "as much as any American novel – a romance."[38] For *The Conquest of Granada* Irving created a Spanish version of Diedrich Knickerbocker in Fray Antonio Agapida, an imaginary historian who enables Irving "to tell the story in whichever way it sounds best, without having to worry about refined criteria for testing the reliability of evidence." The historian Agapida reminds us of Geoffrey Crayon in his romantic stance and his retreat from the routine duties and cares of the everyday world.[39]

But even while Irving was working on his *Life of Columbus* in Madrid, his thoughts were of America, and he wrote Henry Brevoort that "the longer I remain from home the greater charm it has in my eyes and all the colouring that the imagination once gave to distant Europe now gathers about the scenes of my native country."[40] And shortly before leaving Granada for England, he wrote his brother that his Spanish writings must not keep him too long from America. He had acquired source materials that would enable him to continue these chronicles at home; "I feel the importance, however, and I may say the duty of producing some writings relating to our own country which would be of a decidedly national character."[41]

In the summer of 1829 Irving left the Alhambra and Spain to accept another diplomatic post, the secretaryship of the American Legation in London. He resumed the rounds of his old social and literary sets and was acclaimed wherever he went. Public recognition took the form, in 1830, of a medal from the Royal Society of Literature and an honorary LL.D. from Oxford. But he was restive and dissatisfied; his diplomatic duties left him too little time for writing. Further, these duties gave him a new perspective on Anglo-American relations and he was, according to Williams, "jolted out of his sentimental theories of transatlantic brotherhood and stung by the real enmity of Englishmen toward America."[42] When, in addition, Murray made it unmistakably clear that he was losing money on Irving's books and had little interest in continuing their relationship, Irving began thinking very seriously about returning to his native land. But before he left England, Irving – seeking to help a fellow American and writer – made a decision that was to have unforeseen and unpleasant consequences in America.

William Cullen Bryant, unaware of Irving's difficulties with Murray, attempted to interest the publisher in bringing out a collection of his poems. "I hope you will pardon a countryman of yours, who relies on the known kindness of your disposition to plead his excuse," Bryant wrote Irving, asking for whatever helpful influence the American writer could bring to bear.[43] Murray turned down the book but Irving was able to persuade another London publisher, John Andrews, to bring it out. There was, however, an obstacle. Andrews was horrified by two lines in Bryant's "Song of Marion's Men": "The British soldier trembles" and "Wo to the English soldiery." Pressed for a quick decision under difficult circumstances (Bryant was an ocean away), Irving altered the offending lines to read: "The foeman trembles in his camp" and "Wo to the heedless soldiery." On receiving a copy of the London edition of his poems, Bryant expressed gratitude for the honor Irving had done him in facilitating its publication and improving its chances (by a laudatory introduction) for a favorable British reception.[44] He made no mention of Irving's emendations in "Marion's Men" but angry charges (by others) of editorial high-handedness and moral cowardice were to surface at a later date.

Geoffrey Crayon on the frontier

On May 21, 1832, Washington Irving – after seventeen years abroad – caught his first glimpse of his native land. He was, for the most part, greeted enthusiastically as a famous man of letters. The prominent citizens and city fathers of New York City welcomed him with a great public dinner – "a grandilo-quent dinner, done soundly on the old manner, with honest pomp and prodigious cheers."[45] There were more than three hundred guests and almost as many speeches and toasts in honor of an American writer whose "celebrity has been of a nature so unalloyed and universal, as to rank him with Addison, Goldsmith, and Steele."[46] Seated at Irving's right hand throughout the long proceedings was an old friend, James Kirke Paulding. Among the numerous toasts to Irving were several directed to others: to "The memory of Washington"; to Bryant; to Samuel Rogers, "the friend and admirer of American literature." The ardent nationalist William Leggett may have been sounding a slightly hostile note in his toast, without embellishments, to "James Fenimore Cooper." M. M. Noah directed his tribute to "'The Dutchman's Fireside' and its able and patriotic author," Paulding. Paulding himself settled for a brief toast: "Old times, old friends, and old associations."

But all was not sweetness and adulation among the American critics. "His literature is not national," complained a spokesman for the *North American Review*, " – it is not peculiarly the literature of America." The critic complained further that Irving wrote mostly "in England, on English subjects, and for an English public"; he never loses the opportunity to praise all aspects of British life.[47] "What would Irving's fame have been compared with what it is," asked a writer in the *New-York Mirror*, "had it not been sanctioned by the infallible conclave of British reviewers?"[48] A Philadelphia critic blasted the "slovenly and insipid productions" of Sir Walter Scott and the imitative-ness of Geoffrey Crayon; Irving's popularity, he argued, could be attributed to "the bribery and corruption of the Edinburgh and London reviewers, by the booksellers, to help Irving along!"[49]

Such attacks had long been in the air; he had been accused in the early 1820s of writing "of and for England, rather than his own country."[50] But the nationalistic tide was higher than ever and rising. Even at the great dinner in his honor, there had been expressions of hope that Irving would eventually write a book rooted in his native land. In his toast, Professor James Renwick had proudly recalled an unforgettable question and the answer Irving had provided to it: "We can all of us remember when it was tauntingly asked: 'Who reads an American Book?' The success of the Sketch Book of Geoffrey Crayon has furnished a triumphant answer to this question."[51] But in his opening address Chancellor James Kent had suggested that, despite Geoffrey Crayon's consummate skill in depicting "the beautiful scenes of English rural life, and the magnificent remains of Gothic grandeur," he (Kent) must confess to "a far deeper interest in those enchanting visions which brought us back to the borders of the romantic Hudson" and to other native settings.

Irving had begun and abandoned an American sketchbook while in Europe; now, in the early summer of 1832, he felt an urgent need to explore his native country, to travel westward and write a book about it: "He would wander with a notebook; the method which had served him in the Black Forest and the Alpujarras would aid him in the timberlands of Ohio."[52] During a preliminary journey in upper New York, Irving fortuitously encountered Henry Leavitt Ellsworth, a government commissioner to the Indians. Irving had little affection for Yankees, as mentioned earlier, but he took a liking to this Connecticut lawyer and was quickly persuaded to join him on an expedition to Arkansas. For a long month and more, Geoffrey Crayon, lover of cities, roughed it through a thousand miles of forest, prairies and Pawnee territory. Out of this experience came a long narrative, "A Tour on the Prairies" that – buttressed by writings on British and Spanish subjects – resulted in Irving's first book written and published in America since 1809: "After twenty-six years he was again an American author, living in his own country and writing of her."[53] In England the three-volume book was titled *Miscellanies* ("By the author of 'The sketch-book'"); in the United States the title was *The Crayon Miscellany*. As if to hedge his bet in writing an American book, Irving reached into his notebooks and manuscripts to round out his book – volume II, "Abbotsford" and "Newstead Abbey"; volume III, "Legends of the conquest of Spain."[54]

Prefacing the American edition of *A Tour on the Prairies* was a long emotional account of his extended absence from home. At those times, Irving informed his fellow Americans, "when I was supposed to be beguiled by the pleasures and splendours of Europe, and 'treading the primrose path of dalliance,' I was in fact shut up from society, battling with cares and perplexities, and almost struggling for subsistence." He had come back to America and his native city with trepidation – and found his surroundings so transformed that "The saddening conviction stole over my heart that I was a stranger in my own home!" But the warm welcome he received from friends ("now scattered widely asunder over a splendid metropolis") soon dispelled all doubts and fears. It was this reception that emboldened him to make these confessions. Now, "I look round with delightful exultation upon my native land, and feel that, after all my ramblings about the world, I can be happiest at home." In response to many requests for an account of his tour to the far west, he presented what follows in these pages – "a simple statement of facts, pretending no high-wrought effect." If the response was favorable, "he may be tempted to give further sketches of American life."[55]

A Tour on the Prairies was a popular success. Writing in his diary, New Yorker Philip Hone observed that Irving's account of killing buffaloes, hunting wild horses, sleeping on the ground for a whole month, subsisting on wild game – all such experiences must be

matters of thrilling interest to comfortable citizens who read of them in their green slippers, seated before a shining grate, the neatly printed page illuminated by a bronze astral lamp; or to the sensitive young lady, who drawing up her little feet on the crimson damask sofa, shudders at the hardships which the adventurous tourist has undergone, "and loves him for the dangers he has passed."[56]

Hone's shrewd assessment is given support by a reviewer for the *American Ladies' Magazine* who exclaimed: "Oh, for the reality of a free-forest life – or a Tour on the Prairies! – To ride days and weeks on a wild fiery horse – to dash into Savage life, 'and boldly' scour the hunting grounds, – there is rapture *in the very thought* – and what would not be the reality!"[57] In a more serious and prophetic vein, Edward Everett called Irving "the best living writer of English prose" and saw *The Tour* as a harbinger of an advancing indigenous literature. Everett's pride in Irving's sketches of English life had been transformed to rapture at the poetical treasures he had brought back from the primitive wilderness; Irving had earned America's gratitude by "joining his inspiration to that of Cooper, in breathing life and fire into a circle of imagery, for the purposes of imagination."[58]

The British response was less enthusiastic. A writer for the *Quarterly Review* expressed amusement at the spectacle of Geoffrey Crayon on the prairies ("Clad in his leather jerkin, mounted on his fiery steed, and armed with his huge blunderbuss"). Another critic used Irving's book as a springboard for an extended comparison between the "sad butchery" of an American buffalo hunt and the "fair play – straight forward, manly, dauntless work" involved in an English fox hunt.[59]

Irving's four weeks on the prairies released his imagination in new ways; but, basically, Geoffrey Crayon was exploiting his new American materials in familiar picturesque ways. Here, for example is Irving's characteristic evocation of a Gothic cathedral in the midst of a description of a great American forest:

We were overshadowed by lofty trees, with straight, smooth trunks, like stately columns; and as the glancing rays of the sun shone through the transparent leaves, tinted with the many-colored hues of autumn, I was reminded of the effect of sunshine among the stained windows and clustering columns of a Gothic cathedral. Indeed there is a grandeur and solemnity in our spacious forest of the West, that awaken in me the same feeling I have experienced in those vast and venerable piles, and the sound of the wind sweeping through them supplies occasionally the deep breathings of the organ.[60]

Nonetheless, Geoffrey Crayon on the frontier also exhibited an ear for native American speech that aroused a reviewer of *Astoria*, in 1837, to complain about its barbarous Americanisms and deviations from pure English vocabulary.[61] Irving's frontier books provide a significant record of western and northwestern speech; many colloquial words and phrases found their way into print for the first time in them.[62] Irving was, further, a meticulous observer of prairie plant and animal life, Indian and white hunter customs and numerous other particularized details that suggest that he took himself seriously as an observer and interpreter of the far west.[63] Whatever Geoffrey Crayon's deficiencies as an observer and recorder of the frontier, he is by no means the inconsequential dilettante so frequently evoked by commentators old and new. His western books are a significant milestone in the rise of American literature.

A dying fall

Shortly after his return from his western tour, Irving purchased and rebuilt a house near Tarrytown, overlooking the Hudson – "Sunnyside, solitary yet near mankind, that he might live serenely in this bewildering country."[64] He was one of America's most famous authors; and he was now, after long years abroad, putting down new roots into his native soil. But there were discordant notes. Irving's chief rival, Fenimore Cooper, was suspicious and downright hostile; in a letter to his publisher, in 1883, Cooper conveyed his disdain for a writer who would contribute to *The Quarterly Review*, a British journal notorious for its anti-American bias.[65] Cooper's acute distrust was shared by others.

In January 1837 the tranquility of Sunnyside was rudely disturbed by an ugly controversy prominently featured in a New York newspaper. William Leggett, editor of *The Plain-dealer* and close friend of Bryant, suddenly leveled a double-barreled blast:

When Mr. Irving, in publishing a book of his own, prepares one preface for his countrymen, full of *amor patriae* and professions of American feeling, and another for the London market, in which all such professions are studiously omitted, he does what he has an undoubted right to do, whatever we may say of its spirit. But when, at the suggestion of a species of literary pusillanimity, he changes the language of poems, every word of which, as written by the author, will live long after even Bracebridge Hall and Knickerbocker are forgotten, he shows a deficiency of manliness, not calculated to raise him in our opinion, to say the least of it.[66]

Irving abhorred and usually avoided controversy, but wrote, on this occasion, a long and patient explanation of the special circumstances that had induced a preface to *A Tour on the Prairies* directed expressly at his fellow Americans – one that would have been entirely inappropriate to the British edition. As for the change in the language of Bryant's poems, an offending phrase was removed in "a spirit of friendship to Mr. Bryant, and with a view to his success, for it was suggested that this passage might be felt as a taunt or bravado, and might awaken a prejudice in the work, before its merits could be appreciated." Shortly after, Irving wrote Bryant to apologize for the liberty he had taken with the text of his poem, "a liberty, I freely acknowledge, the least excusable with writings like yours, in which it is difficult to alter a word without marring a beauty."[67]

Decades later, in the midst of an obituary tribute to Irving, Bryant took time to summarize at considerable length the Irving–Leggett controversy over his "Song of Marion's Men." Bryant treats Irving's editorial changes gently and generously, but at the same time recalls two alterations in lines allegedly anti-British. In the heat of the controversy, Leggett and Irving had mentioned only one of the offending lines ("The British soldier trembles"), but in 1860 the poet still remembers that there were "two lines" tampered with ("The other alteration was of a similar character").[68] Bryant's vivid recollection thirty years after the event surprises us less when set alongside his 1843 prophecy of an imminent struggle for a decision as to "which power holds and governs the world – the mind of England, old and knit by years and wisdom into strength, or America, roused to new duties in its youth, and in the van with opinions born of the hour."[69]

The Leggett controversy and its attendant aggravations were more than counterbalanced by an extraordinary expression of admiration from a rising young English writer named Charles Dickens. In response to a letter from Irving (in March of 1841) praising *The Old Curiosity Shop*, Dickens poured out his gratitude with a warmth that attested to a longstanding admiration for the American. "There is no living writer," wrote Dickens, "and there are very few among the dead, whose approbation I should feel so proud to earn." All of Irving's writings, he added "are upon my shelves, and in my thoughts, and in my heart of hearts." The rest of his long letter is given over to the hope that Irving would again visit England and provide Dickens with the opportunity of visiting in his company those places that *The Sketch Book* has made dear to him; and to a demonstration of his familiarity with and love for Irving's other books ("Diedrich Knickerbocker['s *History*] I have worn to death in my pocket – and yet I should shew you his mutilated carcass – with a joy past all expression").[70] But it was Dickens who came to America in the following year and his desire to meet Washington Irving was prominent among the motives that led to his visit.[71]

Soon after Dickens' triumphal tour of America began, the two writers met in New York. For Dickens, Irving remained an admired writer and warm friend ("Washington Irving is a *great fellow*. We have laughed most heartily together. He is just the man he ought to be").[72] But Irving's feelings for Dickens cooled perceptibly in response to the Englishman's savagely satiric pictures of America and Americans in *American Notes* (1842) and *Martin Chuzzlewit* (1843). After a visit to Sunnyside in 1859, Evert A. Duyckinck recorded in his diary what Irving said and felt about his British admirer:

He spoke of Dickens and of his liking for his writings in spite of his disapproval of his ungenerous treatment of the Americans in his books, who had given him so extraordinary a reception simply on the score of his talents and genius. When he was last in London, dining with the artist Leslie, he refused to accompany him, though specially sent for, to one of Dickens' private theatricals. He would not visit a man who had proved so insensible to American kindness.[73]

Irving's idyllic life at Sunnyside was shadowed and complicated by the financial crises of 1837 and 1840–3; these were hard times for most Americans, especially so for American authors.[74] The market for books was suddenly inhospitable and Irving turned to the magazines – always a precarious source of income. Irving, wrote Longfellow, "is writing away *like fury*, in the Knickerbocker; – *he had better* not; old remnants – odds and ends, – about Sleepy Hollow and Granada. What a pity."[75] In February 1842 Irving accepted with gratitude an appointment as Envoy Extraordinary and Minister Plenipotentiary to the Court of Spain, a post he served with considerable distinction for four years.[76]

On his return, Irving busied himself with workmen to re-model and enlarge Sunnyside. A small book close to his heart was culled from the sketches and tales of Diedrich Knicker-bocker; Geoffrey Crayon's introduction to *A Book of the Hudson* opens: "I thank God that I was born on the banks of the Hudson."[77] His final writings were biographical – the cul-minating achievement his five-volume *Life of George Washington*. According to Stanley T. Williams, this work has the gift (not found in the sources from whom Irving borrowed) of simpli-city. "The reader of Sparks will learn nothing new from Irving's biography," observes Williams, but the great American hero is presented for the first time "not as a marble statue but as a man." Irving was delighted to hear that parts of the book had been read to children. "Ah," he exclaimed, "that's it: that is what I write it for. I want it so clear that anybody can understand it. I want the action to shine through the style. No style, indeed; no encumbrance of ornament."[78]

This statement about his last work may help explain Haw-thorne's extraordinary tribute to Irving, conveyed in a letter of 1852 accompanying a gift copy of *The Blithedale Romance*:

Ever since I began to write, I have kept it among my cherished hopes to obtain such a word [praise from Irving]; nor did I ever publish a book without debating within myself whether to offer it to your notice. Nevertheless, the idea of introducing myself to you as an author, while unrecognized by the public, was not quite agree-able, and I saw too many faults in each of my books to be altogether willing to obtrude it beneath your eye. At last, I sent you "The Wonder Book," because, being meant for children, it seemed to reach a higher point, in its own way, than anything I had written for grown people.

Pray do not think it necessary to praise my "Blithedale Romance" – or even to acknowledge the receipt of it. From my own little experience, I can partly judge how dearly purchased are books that come to you on such terms. It affords me – and I ask no more – an opportunity of expressing the affectionate admiration which I have felt so long; a feeling, by the way, common to all our country-men, in reference to Washington Irving, and which, I think, you can hardly appreciate, because there is no writer with the qualities to awaken in yourself precisely the same intellectual and heart-felt recognition.[79]

From Diedrich Knickerbocker's satirical *History*, Irving moved to the emotional world of Geoffrey Crayon, a thoughtful and sentimental (and gently ironic) American adrift between two worlds – sketching pictures of England and America that are fresh and engrossing because the reader is always aware of the sketcher's shadowy presence. Crayon's sketches foreshadow Hawthorne's tales; Hawthorne's remarkable tribute reflects a feeling of kinship, a sympathetic identification with an American literary artist of an earlier generation who struggled early and late to come to terms with "Our Old Home" and with America – and with what Hawthorne called "the truth of the human heart."

3

Homeward Bound:
the two voices of Fenimore Cooper

Cooper versus Irving and Scott

On August 6, 1842, Rufus Wilmot Griswold wrote a long letter to James Fenimore Cooper in an attempt to smooth over the novelist's longstanding hostility toward Washington Irving. Irving's high esteem for Cooper's genius, Griswold reported, had been forcefully expressed in several recent conversations with literary friends. Griswold conveyed the hope that the letter he was now writing might "lead to some pleasant consequences" in bringing his two friends closer together. In the reply that he fired off the following day, Cooper made it clear that his evaluation of Irving was quite "independent of what that gentleman might have said of me, or my writings, or character." Indeed: "A published eulogy from Irving's pen could not change my opinion of his career." Irving's faults, wrote Cooper, are similar to those of Scott:

They were all meannesses, and I confess I can sooner pardon crimes, if they are manly errors. I have never had any quarrel with Mr. Irving, and give him full credit as a writer. Still, I believe him to be below the ordinary level, in moral qualities, instead of being above them, as he [is] cried up to be. I believe the same to have been the case with Scott, whom I know for a double dealer.[1]

A decade earlier, Cooper had conveyed similar sentiments in a letter to his publisher denouncing Irving as: "A man who takes the money of the U. States with one hand, and that of the Editor of the Quarterly Review with the other." (Editor William Gifford was notorious for his acrimonious attacks on American writers and Irving incurred Cooper's wrath by contributing to his journal.) Cooper's contempt for Irving and his writings are summed up in a sentence: "One grain of plain, healthful principle goes further with me, than any quantity of sentimentality in fine words."[2]

In Cooper's mind, sentimentality was equated with insincerity – a cardinal sin; his dissatisfaction with Irving on this score was sounded very early. In one of Cooper's rare excursions into literary criticism, an 1822 review of *Bracebridge Hall*, Irving is given somewhat less than "full credit as a writer." His love scenes are described as "puerile and mawkish; characterized by a morbid sensibility, and by a fastidious and artificial arrangement of common place details, language, and scenery."[3] In another review written about the same time, a laudatory criticism of Catharine Maria Sedgwick's *A New-England Tale*, Cooper reflects on the rarity with which "our domestic manners" and "the multitude of local peculiarities, which form our distinctive features" are depicted in American fiction. In his *History of New York*, "Rip Van Winkle," and "The Legend of Sleepy Hollow," Irving had given us ludicrous and picturesque subjects that did not tell the essential truth about "the diversities of passion, sentiment, and behaviour" in American communities. *A New-England Tale* was much more rewarding in this regard and its author deserved to be ranked among the authentic historians of "the characters of communities, the local peculiarities of separated regions, the traits marked by grades of station, and the influence of passions and interests, operating at different periods, and under various events of life."[4]

In 1820, just two years before paying tribute to Sedgwick's authentic American tale, Cooper had launched his own literary career with *Precaution*, a novel of British manners inspired by a British novel – probably Jane Austen's *Persuasion*.[5] Many British reviewers had no suspicion that the author was an American, and the *Gentleman's Magazine* praised its edifying scenes of domestic life;[6] an 1830 criticism in the *Spirit of Literature*, however, more accurately reflects the prevailing sentiment. Cooper's first novel, the commentator complained, failed to follow the Walter Scott pattern of his following productions, was "decidedly *Miss Burneyish*," badly put together, "excessively dull," and, most surprising of all, "there is no trace of the writer's being a Yankee."[7]

Beginning with *The Spy*, however, Cooper's career took a

new turn – one that soon led to his being labeled "the American Scott." It was a label he disliked because he greatly valued his sense of independence and could, at best, pay only grudging tribute to Scott's literary achievement.

Scott's "intimate knowledge of the corrupt workings of the human heart," Cooper observed, "enabled him to render in a pleasing manner much that would otherwise seem obnoxious to the right-minded and just."[8] It was Scott's "*tact* in throwing a high degree of grace around all he did" that was his most distinctive characteristic as a writer. Cooper ridiculed Lockhart's "pretension" that Scott's novels were a significant advance over "the sickly sentimentalism" of earlier fiction, insisting that numerous writers – Maria Edgeworth and Jane Austen among them – had supplanted the sentimentalists long before Scott made his appearance. "Still [Cooper observes] he was vastly their superior, for he raised the novel, as near as might be, to the dignity of the epic." Alongside this commendable aspect of Scott's narrative art, Cooper noted further, was another that pervaded not only his writings but every part of the man himself: "It was, in truth, the art of seemliness, of *vraisemblance* in delineation, of appearances in practice . . . "

These strengths were counterbalanced by what was, in Cooper's view, a central flaw: Scott characteristically alternated bardic inspiration and deflating comedy, "a combination of ironic comedy with the grimly serious."[9] The pervasive strain of irony in Scott helps explain Scott's enthusiasm for Irving and Cooper's lack of enthusiasm for both these writers. Both Scott and Irving were deeply involved with German concepts of romantic irony – concepts that encouraged ambivalence as man's only possible response to a chaotic and incomprehensible universe. In contrast, Cooper's universe rested on an unwavering Christian faith – the foundation on which he created American epics of the land and sea and an American epic hero, Leatherstocking, "A man who keeps his moral integrity hard and intact."[10]

Declarations of "mental independence"

In his polemical novel of manners, *Home as Found*, Cooper (speaking through the character Paul Powis) conveys his impatience with American subservience to the Old World:

Miss Effingham, you and I have seen Europe, have stood in the presence of its wisest, its noblest, and its best; and what have they to boast beyond the immediate results of their factitious and labored political systems, that is denied to the American – or rather would be denied to the American, had the latter the manliness and mental independence to be equal to his fortunes?[11]

Americans are never truly independent, complains Powis, unless moved by financial considerations. Early and late, Cooper campaigned for intellectual independence, insisting that "unless a 'manly, independent literature' in harmony with American facts were forthcoming, the very '*safety*' of the people and their institutions was in danger."[12] He did not underestimate the dangers and difficulties of such a campaign, echoing the complaints of literary nationalists after the War of 1812: "Alas! [wrote Cooper] it is much easier to declare war, and gain victories in the field, and establish a political independence, than to emancipate the mind."[13] In an 1831 letter, Cooper summed up his lifelong credo: "Her [America's] mental independence is my object, and if I can go down to the grave with the reflection that I have done a little towards it, I shall have the consolation of knowing that I have not been useless in my generation."[14]

The struggle for cultural independence among American writers was complicated by the absence of international copyright protection: "The fact that an American publisher can get an English work without money must for a few years longer . . . have a tendency to repress a national literature. No man will pay a writer for an epic, a tragedy, a sonnet, a history, or a romance, when he can get a work of equal merit for nothing."[15] When Cooper published this observation in 1828, he was supporting himself by his pen; but he was the only American author who could make this claim (Irving had been driven out of authorship into one of several periods of government service).[16]

There was, in Cooper's view, an even more formidable obstacle – the poverty of materials available to the American writer:

There is [wrote Cooper (disguised as an Englishman) in *Notions of the Americans*] scarcely an ore which contributes to the wealth of the author, that is found, here, in veins as rich as in Europe. There are no annals for the historian; no follies (beyond the most vulgar and commonplace) for the satirist; no manners for the dramatist; no obscure fictions for the writer of romance; no gross and hardy offences against decorum for the moralist . . . The weakest hand can extract a spark from the flint, but it would baffle the strength of a giant to attempt kindling a flame with a pudding-stone.[17]

Irving had complained in much the same way in "The Author's Account of Himself" introductory to *The Sketch Book*; Hawthorne and James were to present similar negative catalogs of American civilization.

Cooper had already refuted the Englishman he had invented for *Notions* through his production, by 1828, of such novels as *The Spy, The Pioneers, The Last of the Mohicans* and *The Prairie*. And he had demonstrated his own sense of achievement in dealing with native materials by referring to himself as "the author of a series of tales, which were intended to elucidate the history, manners, usages, and scenery of his native country."[18] That this was an achievement resulting from a carefully executed plan is made clear by Cooper's announcement to his friends about "his intention of writing a series of works illustrative of the physical aspect of his native country, of revolutionary occurrences, and of the red man of the western world."[19] (In 1859, eight years after Cooper's death, a British commentator conveyed his sense of Cooper's success in carrying out his plan: "We prophesy no short existence for Cooper's novels. In years, perhaps centuries to come . . . Cooper's works will be read as giving the clearest, happiest insight into the early life of American settlers and aborigines.")[20]

The central question about Cooper's literary career has less to do with the poverty of materials in America than with Cooper's unresolved and ambivalent feelings about those materials. Cooper produced romance after romance celebrating the awe-inspiring and unique wonders of the American wilderness (and deploring through his most eloquent spokesman, Natty Bumppo, the rapid disappearance of that wilderness); he was also capable of celebrating American progress and the advance of civilization in terms that would scarcely give comfort to the hero of the Leatherstocking tales:

The American axe! It has made more real and lasting conquests than the sword of any warlike people that ever lived; but they have been conquests that have left civilization in their train instead of havoc and desolation. More than a million square miles of territory have been opened up from the shades of the virgin forest, to admit the warmth of the sun; and culture and abundance have been spread where the beast of the forest so lately roamed, hunted by the savage ... A brief quarter of a century has seen these wonderful changes wrought; and at the bottom of them all lies this beautiful, well-prized, ready and efficient implement, the American axe![21]

In *The Prairie* (1827), old Natty, driven westward by the "march of civilization," conveys his opinion of the American axe in somewhat different terms:

They scourge the very 'arth with their axes. Such hills and hunting grounds as I have seen stripped of the gifts of the Lord, without remorse or shame! I tarried till the mouths of my hounds were deafened by the blows of the chopper, and then I came west in search of quiet. It was a grievous journey that I made; a grievous toil to pass through falling timber and to breathe the thick air of smoky clearings, week after week, as I did! ... Look around you men; what will the Yankee choppers say, when they have cut their path from the eastern to the western waters, and find that a hand, which can lay the 'arth bare at a blow, has been here and swept the country in the very mockery of their wickedness. They will turn on their tracks like a fox that doubles, and then the rank smell of their own footsteps will show them the madness of their waste.[22]

The depth and power of Cooper's characterization of Leather-stocking, suggests Henry Nash Smith, derive from the author's sympathetic response to "the ideal of forest freedom despite his own commitment to the ideal of an ordered, stratified society based on the secure ownership of land by a leisure class."[23]

This "clash of irreconcilable values" is most powerfully dramatized in the earliest (and perhaps best) novel in the Leatherstocking saga, *The Pioneers* (1823). Subtitled "A Descriptive Tale," this was the first of many romances celebrating the American landscape with a passionate pictorialism which, in Balzac's view, was "quite inimitable" – a pictorialism "that literary landscape-painters ought to study; all the secrets of the art are here."[24] Significantly, one of the most moving descriptions of the wilderness is put into the mouth of Judge Temple: "The leaves were fallen, and I mounted a tree, and sat for an hour looking on the silent wilderness."[25] Temple gazes at the impenetrable forest, the mirror of glass that is the lake, the birds and animals; in all these vast surroundings there is no trace of man or of his works. He meditates on this scene "with a mingled feeling of pleasure and desolation." It is fitting that he finds shelter that night in Natty Bumppo's rough cabin – and cannot comprehend Leatherstocking's displeasure when he learns of the Judge's plans for a settlement in this location.

If Judge Temple were indifferent to the great wonders of unspoiled nature, he would not have spent an hour reflecting on its grandeur. But his pleasure in the sublimity of the scene is mingled with a sense of desolation; his vision of America is incomplete without Americans shaping a settlement out of the wilderness, a settlement governed by law. In an earlier part of the century, Natty would respond (for it was in a novel yet unwritten) to the unspoiled beauty of the same place with different sentiments: "This is grand! – 'Tis solemn! – 'Tis an edication itself to look upon! . . . not a tree disturbed even by redskin hand, as I can discover, but everything left in the ordering of the Lord to live and die according to his own designs and laws!"[26] And when Natty is sentenced to imprisonment for taking the law into his own hands, he appeals in vain to a principle of natural law that can have no force in Templeton: "Have you forgot the time you came on to the lake-shore, when there wasn't even a jail to lodge in; and didn't I give you my own bear-skin to sleep on, and the fat of a noble buck to satisfy the cravings of your hunger? Yes, yes – you thought it no sin then to kill a deer!"[27]

To Leslie Fiedler, Cooper's ambivalence reflects a basic philistinism – a point of view that the American novelist shared with Scott:

Scott would not, of course, have wanted to leave Abbotsford for a medieval castle or a Highland hide-away, any more than Cooper would have wanted to abandon his Westchester County home or his Paris hotel for a wigwam; they felt free to create fantasies of flight from civilized comfort to primitive simplicity because they were sure that no one would believe them any more than they believed themselves.[28]

But Fiedler's strictures fail to do justice to the vision of the wilderness presented by both Scott and Cooper – a complex vision that emphasizes the impracticability of the wilderness ideal. What separates Cooper from Scott is the way in which the American novelist pulls his hero out of society – and out of time: Natty's world is a timeless one and his death, like his life, is in harmony with the forces of nature and the universe.[29] Through Natty, Cooper evoked an American wilderness – and wildness – far removed from Irving's genteel descriptions of the prairie. Through Natty, Cooper evoked a mythic American asserting a "mental independence" that has no counterpart in Scott.

Cooper's emphasis on the importance of "manliness" and "mental independence" in American writers did not preclude Cooper's responsiveness to Shakespeare, Milton, Austen, Scott and, on occasion, Byron. Unlike the ardent nationalists calling for total cultural independence, Cooper felt that the literatures of England and America had a single foundation, and that Americans had as much claim to the British classics as the British:

It is quite obvious, that, so far as taste and forms alone are concerned, the literature of England and that of America must be fashioned after the same models. The authors, previously to the revolution, are common property, and it is quite idle to say that the American had not just as good a right to claim Milton, and Shakespeare, and all the old masters of the language, for his countrymen, as an Englishman. The Americans having continued to cultivate, and to cultivate extensively, an acquaintance with the writers of the mother country, since the separation, it is evident they must have kept pace with the trifling changes of the day. The only peculiarity that can, or ought to be expected in their literature, is that which is connected with the promulgation of their distinctive political opinions.[30]

Cooper's conception of "distinctive political opinions," it must be emphasized, was broad and deep. It encompassed the view that the sturdy manliness and independence he valued so highly in men are of central importance everywhere – and have the greatest possibility for realization in the United States. He assessed men – British or American – in terms of their "moral qualities," their "meannesses," the presence or absence in their behavior of "plain, healthful principle." Cooper saw no distinction between morality and politics.[31]

In the concluding pages of *England* (1837), Cooper summarized his findings concerning the essential differences between the two cultures. The systems under which Englishmen and Americans lived were so completely "the converse of each other" that it was surprising so many resemblances survived. Cooper thought the extreme deference of subordinate classes toward their superiors was the overriding characteristic of the English system; and that the opposite was true among Americans. But an unfortunate concomitancy of American egalitarianism was "the moral cowardice by which men are led to truckle to what is called public opinion." Cooper found "more honesty of public sentiment in England than in America."[32]

It is not surprising that the Englishman for whom Cooper felt the keenest admiration was Lord Grey, whose manner was characterized by an unaffected simplicity and "masculine" directness. Lord Grey's house was one of the few in England in which Cooper was put completely at his ease – where nothing occurred "to make me feel that I was not only a foreigner but *an American*."[33] In sharp contrast to Lord Grey was Sir Walter Scott, who earned Cooper's disdain by backing out of an excursion to Hampton Court because of "a summons from the King to dine at Windsor; a command of this sort superseding all other engagements." The Newberry Library copy of *England*, bound together with *Recollections of Europe*, is sprinkled with the pencilled marginalia (added in 1837) of an indignant English reader. Alongside Cooper's unsympathetic account of Scott's postponement of their trip to Hampton Court, the English annotator works off his spleen with ten exclamation marks (in two rows of five each) – and this comment scrawled at the bottom of the page: "is this wretched Yankee in his proper senses? a sneer a[t] the King of England & Sir W. Scott!!!"[34]

The qualities of simple forthrightness and manly independence that Cooper valued in Englishmen – and Americans – should, he felt, be made manifest by language that would reinforce these traits. Cooper inveighed against the infatuation of Americans for turgid and pretentious expressions – a tendency that seemed (in 1838) to be gaining ground. "One of the most certain evidences of a man of high breeding," he observed, is his simplicity of speech; a simplicity that is equally removed from vulgarity and exaggeration. He calls a spade, a "spade." His enunciation, while clear, deliberate and dignified, is totally without strut, showing his familiarity with the world, and, in some degree, reflecting the qualities of his mind, which is polished without being addicted to sentimentalism, or any other bloated feeling. He never calls his wife, "his lady," but "his wife," and he is not afraid of lessening the dignity of the human race, by styling the most elevated and refined of his fellow creatures, "men and women." He does not say, in speaking of a dance, that "the attire of the ladies was exceedingly elegant and peculiarly becoming at the late assembly," but that "the women were well dressed at the last ball;" nor is he apt to remark, "that the Rev. M. G—— gave us an elegant and searching discourse the past sabbath," but, that "the parson preached a good sermon last sunday."[35]

This is a passage that might have been written by Mark Twain; how can we account for the fact that it was, instead, written by his victim – the same writer who, a decade earlier (in *The Last of the Mohicans*), said of a nursing foal that it "exacted the maternal contribution"? Cooper practiced what he preached about simple and direct expression in his social criticisms; in his fiction, however, he tended toward the pretentious and inflated style which he himself condemned.[36] This is a sound observation; but it is also true that Cooper could practice what he preached – that he was fully capable, in his fiction as well as in other writings, of that vivid and straightforward style which he advocated so forcefully in *The American Democrat*.

Joseph Conrad's tribute to Cooper points toward the sources of the strength and weakness: he speaks of Cooper's faulty method and genuine art, of "the leisurely manner of his time," of his "knowledge of simple hearts" and large sympathy, of his genuine humor, of certain passages in which "he reaches, very simply, the heights of inspired vision." Conrad reminds us that Cooper "wrote before the great American language was born, and he wrote as well as any novelist of his time."[37] Mark Twain's essays on Cooper (written about the same time as Conrad's tribute) hilariously and mercilessly dissect a style that wildly vacillates between the grandiose and the colloquial. Something further remains to be said about Twain's devastating attacks – and about Cooper's strugglings toward a Twainian Americanness.

Two voices

The two voices of Fenimore Cooper – the one artificial and
derivative, the second natural and colloquial – reveal a great
deal about the birth of the American language and the rise of
the American novel. The fusion and confusion of both these
voices in one character named Natty Bumppo irritated Mark
Twain no end and he had a high old time ridiculing Cooper's
laughable inconsistencies. The rules governing literary art,
says Twain, require that "when a personage talks like an
illustrated, gilt-edged, tree-calf, hand-tooled, seven-dollar
Friendship's Offering in the beginning of a paragraph, he shall
not talk like a negro minstrel in the end." This rule, alas, "is
flung down and danced upon in the *Deerslayer* tale" – a work in
which Natty utters "the showiest kind of book talk sometimes,
and at other times the basest of base dialects." In a second
essay, Twain quotes an elaborately wordy and cloudy passage
from *The Last of the Mohicans* and then translates it into plain
talk one-third of its former length.[38]

It is unnecessary to dwell on the prolixity and inconsistency
of Cooper's style. But it may be useful here to quote two
lengthy passages, both descriptions of an elaborate meal. The
first is from Cooper's *The Pioneers* (1823):

Before Elizabeth, was placed an enormous roasted turkey, and
before Richard, one boiled. In the centre of the table, stood a pair
of heavy silver castors, surrounded by four dishes; one a fricassee,
that consisted of gray squirrels; another of fish fried; a third of
fish boiled; the last was a venison steak. Between these dishes and
the turkeys, stood, on one side, a prodigious chine of roasted bear's
meat, and on the other a boiled leg of delicious mutton. Interspersed
among this load of meats, was every species of vegetables that the
season and country afforded. The four corners were garnished with
plates of cake. On one was piled certain curiously twisted and
complicated figures, called "nutcakes." On another were heaps of a
black-looking substance, which, receiving its hue from molasses,
was properly termed "sweet-cake;" a wonderful favourite in the
coterie of Remarkable. A third was filled, to use the language of
the housekeeper, with "cards of gingerbread;" and the last held a
"plum-cake," so called from the number of large raisins that were
showing their black heads, in a substance of a wonderfully similar
colour. At each corner of the table, stood saucers, filled with a thick

fluid, of somewhat equivocal colour and consistence, variegated with small dark lumps of a substance that resembled nothing but itself, which Remarkable termed her "sweet-meats." At the side of each plate, which was placed bottom upwards, with its knife and fork most accurately crossed above it, stood another, of smaller size, containing a motley-looking pie, composed of triangular slices of apple, mince, pumpkin, craneberry, and *custard*, so arranged as to form an entire whole. Decanters of brandy, rum, gin and wine, with sundry pitchers of cider, beer, and one hissing vessel of "flip," were put wherever an opening would admit of their introduction. Notwithstanding the size of the tables, there was scarcely a spot where the rich damask could be seen, so crowded were the dishes, and their associated bottles, plates and saucers. The object seemed to be profusion, and it was obtained entirely at the expense of order and elegance.[39]

The second is a passage, written in 1897–8, from Mark Twain's *Autobiography*:

In the summer the table was set in the middle of that shady and breezy floor, and the sumptuous meals – well, it makes me cry to think of them. Fried chicken, roast pig; wild and tame turkeys, ducks, and geese; venison just killed; squirrels, rabbits, pheasants, partridges, prairie-chickens; biscuits, hot batter cakes, hot buckwheat cakes, hot "wheat bread," hot, rolls, hot corn pone; fresh corn boiled on the ear, succotash, butter-beans, stringbeans, tomatoes, peas, Irish potatoes, sweet potatoes; buttermilk, sweet milk, "clabber"; watermelons, muskmelons, cantaloupes – all fresh from the garden; apple pie, peach pie, pumpkin pie, apple dumplings, peach cobbler – I can't remember the rest.[40]

Cooper's account, though lengthy and full of detail, is by no means guilty of the ambiguous "surplusage" that Twain found in the passages he ridiculed (from *The Last of the Mohicans*). The elaborateness of Cooper's description serves two purposes: to re-create a facet of a world that has disappeared; and to contrast the elegance and civilized sumptuousness of Judge Temple's banquet (or, at least, Remarkable Pettibone's version of these) with the wilderness that surrounds this frontier settlement. Cooper's leisurely style serves these purposes well. Its ponderous and self-conscious touches (Remarkable's colloquialisms are carefully set apart from the narrator's language by quotation marks; the narrator's total recall may seem both affectionate and excessive) are counterbalanced by

functional sentences and concrete diction – by an overall vividness that is impressive. Not to be overlooked in this characteristic passage are Cooper's humorous strokes; the high-flown
diction used to describe Remarkable's "sweet-meats" ("equivocal"; "variegated") is effectively contrasted with some plain
(and slyly playful) talk about "small dark lumps of a substance
that resembled nothing but itself." The Twain passage has a
narrator humorously involved with his subject ("it makes me
cry to think of them") and, like Cooper, engages in a detailed
and loving re-creation of vanished glories. In place of Cooper's
elaborate sequence of periodic sentences, Twain provides a
lengthy catalog of delectable items – and finally the stinger: "I
can't remember the rest." (Both Cooper and Twain effectively
crowd their sentences to depict their crowded tables.) But
Twain, ninety-five years after Cooper wrote his passage, is still
self-conscioulsy enclosing colloquial phrases in quotation
marks ("wheat bread," "clabber"). Richard Bridgman has noted
that when writers "first began to introduce questionable
diction into their prose, they quarantined it with quotation
marks."; John Neal was still formally setting off his colloquial
expressions "as late as 1869."[41] And Mark Twain as late as 1897.

It is all too true, as Twain claimed, that "Cooper's word-
sense was singularly dull" – but it could, on occasion, be
singularly keen. A British reviewer of *The Pioneers* found
especially praiseworthy Cooper's realistic rendering of a
gallery of sharply-drawn, widely diversified characters: "In
Mr. Cooper's descriptions we are at once presented with
characters and habits so probable, and so like the modes into
which such society as that of America would most probably fall,
that their authenticity is believed at once, and their singular
originality is in the highest degree amusing."[42] Noteworthy
among Cooper's representative men is Benjamin Penguillan
(Ben Pump), "a dapper Cockney" who had landed, "before the
sound of Bow bells is fairly out of his ears, within the roar of
the cataract of Niagara."[43] One of the comic high points in the
novel is a lengthy exchange between the old sailor and Remarkable Pettibone – enlivened by "a supply of stimulants, that
would have served to keep the warmth in [Ben Pump's] system,
without the aid of the enormous fire he had been building."[44]
As the evening wears on, and the level of the bottle descends,

Ben enrages Remarkable by suggesting that she has not made herself clear to Elizabeth Temple: "Perhaps she didn't understand you, woman; you are none of the best linguister; and then Miss Lizzy has been exercising the King's English under a great Lon'on lady, and, for that matter, can talk the language almost as well as myself, or any native born British subject." To this, the indignant Remarkable replies proudly that she "was born and raised in Essex county; and I've always heer'n say, that the Bay State was provarbal for pronounsation." (Here Ben and Remarkable sound remarkably like Mark Twain's Jim Baker, who testifies that "I've never heard a jay use bad grammar but very seldom, and when they do, they are as ashamed as a human, they shut right down and leave.")[45]

Predictably, critics who valued refinement and gentility were shocked by Cooper's coarse realism. The New England poet and critic James G. Percival wrote to a friend (in April 1823) in terms remarkably similar to those used a half-century later to express outrage about *Adventures of Huckleberry Finn*: "I ask nothing of a people who will lavish their patronage on such a vulgar book as 'The Pioneers.'" In a later letter Percival suggested that the novel "might do to amuse the select society of a barber's shop or a porter-house" but "'tis wondrous pitiful for the country that not only suffers it but encourages it." These excerpts from Percival's letters are quoted in Thomas Lounsbury's *James Fenimore Cooper* (1882); Mark Twain passed over these and similar passages to draw on Lounsbury's praise of Cooper's artistry for the first of the epigraphs introducing his "Fenimore Cooper's Literary Offenses."[46]

That Cooper was fully aware of and amused by fastidious critics like Percival is made clear by his interpolated comment at the close of the Ben Pump episode that I have been citing. As Benjamin finally falls back into his chair in a drunken stupor, the narrator pokes fun at his refined critics by incorporating a genteel figure into the same sentence in which he is reporting Ben's not-so-genteel epithets: "Before, however, he was quite locked, to use the language that would suit the Dellacruscan humour of certain refined critics of the present day, 'in the arms of Morpheus,' he spoke aloud, observing due pauses between his epithets, the impressive terms of 'monkey,' 'parrot,' 'pic-nic,' 'tar-pot,' and 'linguisters.'"[47]

I have dwelled on the Ben Pump–Remarkable Pettibone episode and its language because they reveal a side of Cooper that was not visible to Twain – a Twainian side. That side is most clearly displayed in a gallery of characters whose simple–shrewd attitudes are pungently conveyed in a colorful, colloquial idiom. Harvey Birch, Tom Coffin, Captain Truck, Miles Wallingford, Ned Myers, Aristabulus Bragg, Steadfast Dodge – and a host of others – point toward rather than away from Mark Twain.

Notable among these memorable characters is an English seaman, Ben Pump, as he was usually called, a comic figure with serious dimensions. It is Ben Pump who offers his savings in a vain attempt to save Natty from jail – and it is Ben who voluntarily shares Natty's ignominy in the stocks. This cockney seaman displays some of the sturdy manliness Cooper found and admired in the British aristocrat Lord Grey. Cooper's sense of being an American, and an American novelist, was bound up with a conception of "manliness and mental independence" that enabled him not only to defend America against British misrepresentation but to value British honesty and courage over American pretension and venality.

Cooper's novels are seriously flawed by his uncertain vacillation between watered-down imitations of British models and authentically American expression. Mark Twain has documented Cooper's shortcomings with entertaining gusto, but it may be that Francis Parkman was just as close to (or far from) the mark when he wrote (in 1852) that "of all American writers, Cooper is the most original, the most thoroughly national."[48] The truth is somewhere in between.

4

Yankee invasion: John Neal's campaign

A Byronic Yankee in Baltimore

In February of 1822, the Philadelphia publishers Carey and Lea received an extraordinary letter from an American writer named John Neal, a Yankee from the District of Maine now residing in Baltimore. In it, Neal proclaimed that his novels (*Logan, Randolph, Errata, Seventy-Six*) were "materially *American*" and would represent a formidable challenge to Sir Walter Scott: "I am impatient . . . and therefore I would have you come down upon them (the publick) clap after clap, before they can get their breath. They are startled at the celerity of the Scotch novelist – Let us appal them – if we can."[1] After several delays occasioned by the firm's concern over the incoherence and indecency of Neal's novel, Carey and Lea published *Logan* – but begged off any further involvement. Their concern seemed justified when *Logan* was greeted, in some quarters, by ridicule and abuse. One British critic suggested that its style "is like the raving of a bedlamite" and its "incidents are such as fill a sick man's dream." The reviewer identified the author of *Logan* among those American writers who fail because of a misguided determination not to imitate English models.[2] Neal was, in fact, a highly original American writer whose *Logan* and other wild romances were to have a profound impact on, among others, an impressionable undergraduate (and budding author) at Bowdoin College named Nathaniel Hawthorne.

A native of Portland in the District of Maine ("a Quaker broken loose," one British reviewer called him), John Neal had settled in Baltimore to study and practice law. In 1816, he launched his literary career as a member of the Delphian Club and contributor to its journal, *The Portico*, which announced in its first number that both political and cultural dependence on foreign governments and minds were degrading and disgrace-

ful – the result of "indolence" and "stupidity."[3] In keeping
with their militant advocacy of an American literary revolution,
the Delphians had adopted Lord Byron as their literary patron
saint; Neal's first contribution to *The Portico* was a 150-page
commentary on Byron and his poetry, written at white heat in
four days and published in five installments. The Delphians
were, on the whole, a genteel and conservative group responsive to neoclassical models and ideals (as the name of their club
and magazine indicates) as well as to new romantic voices. "We
can never," proclaimed one of its editors concerning some
Latin verse of dubious propriety, "consent to admit into the
pages of the *Portico* in any other language what may not be
interpreted in our own, without raising a blush on the cheek of
modesty."[4] Neal's Byronism was somewhat too daring for his
fellow Delphians; he was, in turn, increasingly impatient with
them and precipitously resigned from the club in January of 1820.

Logan "is not a nice story," wrote Alexander Cowie; he
observed that "sensuality, colossal hatred, delirium, rape,
insanity, murder" are, among other ingredients, "the stuff out
of which Neal weaves a Gothic tapestry never quite paralleled
by Charles Brockden Brown or Poe."[5] For his wild romance of
the pre-Revolutionary frontier, Neal drew heavily on both
Brown and Byron – but also on a rhapsodic style and vision
distinctively his own.

Neal claimed that *Logan* was written as "an experiment" and
hoped to control its "rambling incoherency, passion, and
extravagance" in his next novel.[6] Contributing to his new
resolution was his electrifying encounter with Cooper's *The
Spy*. This was the work that opened up the glorious possibilities
of a truly American novel drawing on the American struggle
for existence as its subject. But Cooper's novel, Neal later
claimed, merely served as a catalyst to transform his own recent
contributions to Paul Allen's *History of the American Revolution*
into a novel: "I had got charged to the muzzle with the doings
of our Revolutionary fathers . . . and wanted only the hint, or
touch, that Cooper gave in passing, to go off like a Leyden jar,
and empty myself at once of all the hoarded enthusiasm I had
been bottling up, for three or four years."[7] Cooper's success
encouraged Neal, in October 1822, to turn to the suddenly
famous author of *The Spy*; he sent Cooper copies of *Logan* and

the manuscript of a novel later titled *Randolph*. No record of a response from Cooper has survived; it may be that it was Cooper's neglect or seeming rebuff that contributed to Neal's later hostility – and to his determination to eclipse the soaring reputation of the "American Scott."[8]

Many English readers had found *The Spy*, as did one reviewer, distinctively American – "Yankee to the back bone." It satisfied their intense interest in America while, at the same time, promoting virtue and religion in a "light and agreeable" style.[9] Neal's *Seventy-Six* was stronger stuff and aroused a stronger response – on occasion, a curious mixture of repugnance and grudging praise.

Neal's narrator in *Seventy-Six* is an old man, Jonathan Oadley, whose first-hand record of Revolutionary times, purportedly written for his descendants, was not elegant or polished; his style, he says, will always be the *"talk on paper"* of "an uneducated, plain soldier."[10] Neal displays, in *Seventy-Six* considerable control in manipulating historical events to enlarge and intensify his love story – and all is told with a colloquial realism that represents a new advance in the American novel. It is a tribute to that realism that one British reviewer mistook Neal's narrator for the actual author; the critic for the *Monthly Review Enlarged* proceeds from strong disapproval of the "anti-monarchial" sentiments to grudging praise for this vivid account of a war depicted by someone who must have been there:

[*Seventy-Six*] relates to the unfortunate contest between this country and the American colonies which raged in the year *seventeen hundred and seventy-six*. We know not that any good purpose can be answered by recalling the events of that lamentable warfare, vividly and painfully as they are here depicted to the eye, by one who certainly must have been an actor in them; and whose sentiments are so violently anti-Anglican, and anti-monarchial, that they by no means soften the effect produced by his delineations.

Still the interest excited by this tale, and the command over our feelings which the writer exerts, are very far from trifling and ordinary. His energies are somewhat rough, indeed, but they are powerful; like much of his vast continent, not cultivated but fertile, not polished but naturally impressive; his battle pieces plunge us into the midst of them; and his hero is "every inch" a hero . . .

The language of this narrative is often inelegant and peculiar.[11]

The "inelegant and peculiar" language of *Seventy-Six* aroused an otherwise admiring American reviewer to rebuke Neal for his mistaken belief that oaths and "irreligious exclamations" necessarily belong to the vocabulary of soldiers.[12] The reviewer may have had in mind such lively and uninhibited talk as this: "I wheeled, made a dead set, at the son-of-a-bitch in my rear, unhorsed him, and actually broke through the line."[13] Such authenticity points toward – and beyond – Twain, as does also this first attempt, in a serious novel, to reproduce the rhythms and nuances of Yankee vernacular (the speaker, a minor character named Hanson, is a frontiersman turned soldier):

"Well – (the yankees, and Hanson was a yankee, had the practice of prefacing almost every remark, and every question, and every answer, then, as now, with a *well*, or a *why*) – after he got well, they let him go out on parol; and, one night some of 'em run off; and, he might a'gone – but he would'nt – out 'pon honour, he said – so he would'nt – never mind 'em – they braced him up – served him all the same as the rest – now look out, said he – I'm clear o' my word, now – keep me if you can – so, not a week after, we escaped – see here – (showing his wrist –) I had a bayonet through, there – and here, and here – the balls whistled like hail; they sent hundreds arter us, through the bushes – but we got clear –!"[14]

The opening aside concerning Hanson's speech mannerisms seems to betray the kind of self-consciousness toward colloquialism that, according to Richard Bridgman, "dissociated the writer from intimacy with it."[15] But there is also, in this re-creation of Hanson's live talk, a loving involvement with its vitality and power – an exuberant dimension rarely evident in Cooper. And there is, in Neal, a pervasive resolution (not always successful) to avoid bookish talk at all times. His recognition that live talk is the truest vehicle for the deepest emotion (and not merely a showpiece for humor) is most clearly revealed in this passage from another novel, *Randolph*, written at about the same time:

Call up a mother, who has just lost her infant – bid her tell the story – look at her – study her. There is no wearying preparation. She repeats the same thing, over and over again, a hundred times. – There is no poetry; no play of the imagination, in what she says. There is not even the simplest observance of rule – her sentences are short – broken – exclamatory – familiar – colloquial – vulgar, it may be, and ungrammatical. But your tears follow – and your heart heaves to it.[16]

It was, of course, a commonplace of the English romantics to look to the humble and low for lofty truths. But the self-educated John Neal (whose formal schooling had ended when he was twelve) seemed to have been the first American writer to make spontaneity and unpretentiousness central tenets of authorship. This did not rule out heightened language; Neal was all too frequently guilty of the shrillest bombast. But at their best, his heightened passages are (like this one, taken from a climactic moment in *Logan*) biblical evocations of man and cosmos in cadenced periods that anticipate Whitman:

The whole world sleeping below me, like the beings of another planet. The stars hovering around me and over me; the heavens turning round about us, over our heads and under our feet; and we, standing as in the centre of the universe, maintaining our sublime and solitary sway, over the fish of the sea, and the beast of the field, and the fowl of the air . . . when all our united force, all our wisdom, and all our policy, cannot stay or impede the smallest of yonder lights in its journeying.[17]

The year 1823 was a stormy one in Neal's life and a turning-point in his literary career. Two more novels rapidly followed *Seventy-Six*: *Randolph*, which loosely yoked critical essays on American orators and writers with a lurid Gothic plot; and *Errata*, which did the same for events in his early life in Portland and the villages of Maine. A satiric commentary in *Randolph* on the professional incompetence and dubious ethics of a well-known Baltimore lawyer and statesman, William Pinkney, resulted in a challenge to a duel from Pinkney's son. (The elder Pinkney died while the book was in press and Neal refused to delete the offending matter.) After refusing the challenge, Neal was posted as a coward in the streets of Baltimore. Even worse, a scandal arising from Neal's romantic entanglement with the fourteen-year-old sister-in-law of his closest friend, John Pierpont, had led to a rupture of their friendship – a situation not helped when Neal incorporated his version of the affair into *Randolph* and an editorial postscript appended to his autobiographical novel *Errata*.[18] *Errata* especially outraged Portland because of its corrosive treatment of several prominent citizens. Writing from Portland, Neal's mother tearfully urged him to give up his sinful ways and writings: "I must beg thee never to send us any books or reviews, it dont give us any pleasure, but the reverse." And she implored him not to answer her because "thy letters contain nothing to render us happy; thy life will be in danger 6 months hence thousands of times have I said, thy end would be in a duel, or shot privately, or stabbed unawares."[19]

But it is doubtful that it was fear of bodily harm that precipitated Neal's decision, in December 1823, to leave Baltimore for England. He was bored with his languishing law practice and disgusted "with the whole tribe of lawyers in America, from the highest to the lowest."[20] He had broken with his closest friend and was hard pressed by personal problems. And he was vastly excited by the fact that *Logan* and *Seventy-Six* had been reprinted and reviewed in London – that it might be within his grasp to match and eclipse the literary success of Irving and Cooper. In December of that fateful year, Neal was dining with Henry Robinson, an Englishman then residing in Baltimore. Long years later, Neal recalled that dinner and its fateful aftermath:

The conversation turned, I know not how, upon American literature, and he, being full of admiration for the "Edinburgh" and "Quarterly," asked, in the language of the day, "Who reads an American book?" I know not what I said in reply; but I know how I felt, and that, finally, I told him, "more in sorrow than in anger," that I would answer that question from over sea; that I would leave my office, my library, and my law-business, and take passage in the first vessel I could find – we had no regular packets then – and see what might be done, with a fair field, and no favor, by an American writer. Irving had succeeded; and, though I was wholly unlike Irving, why shouldn't I? Cooper was well received; and I had a notion, that, without crossing his path, or poaching upon his manor I might do something, so American, as to secure the attention of Englishmen.[21]

On December 15, Neal set sail for Liverpool from Baltimore; he landed on British soil on January 8 1824. The invasion was on.

"Carter Holmes" and the House of Blackwood

Neal's first months in London were deeply discouraging. He could find no publisher interested in reprinting *Randolph*; and the British periodicals, though filled with critiques of America and American writers written by Britons, were reluctant to give space to an American writer. Neal hit on a wild scheme thoroughly characteristic of the man – one far-fetched and desperate enough to succeed beyond his greatest expectation.

In Baltimore he had read, with great interest, *Blackwood's Edinburgh Magazine*, a lively and hard-hitting journal founded in 1817 to compete with the *Edinburgh Review*. Adopting "Carter Holmes" as a pseudonym of a purported Englishman well acquainted with the United States, Neal wrote to *Blackwood's*, asking for employment as a contributor; and along with his first letter, Neal enclosed an article, "Sketches of the Five American Presidents." Editor and proprietor William Blackwood responded enthusiastically; he accepted Neal's article, enclosed a draft for five guineas, and invited "Carter Holmes" for more contributions.[22]

During the next two years, Neal was a frequent contributor and was treated with extraordinary deference. His "Summary View of America" is the leading article of the December 1824 issue and has an introductory note by John Wilson ("Christopher North") proclaiming that this longest review in the history of *Blackwood's* (thirty-six double-column pages) "contains more facts, more new reasonings, more new speculations of and concerning the United States of America, than have yet appeared in any ten books . . . upon that subject."[23]

Among Neal's most striking contributions – and of particular importance in the history of Anglo-American literary relations – was his "American Writers," an explosive series of commentaries, alphabetically arranged, on 120 American authors living and dead (with most space given to John Neal). The opening installment set the tone by announcing that, with very few exceptions, "there is no American writer who would not pass as readily as an English writer." British disdain for American writers had given way, in recent times, for an equally erroneous exaggerated praise. The anonymous Neal–"Holmes," posing as an Englishman, concluded with brief commentaries

on a dozen writers at the top of the alphabet. His dismissal of
William Cullen Bryant is characteristic: "He wants fire – he
wants the very rashness of a poet." In later installments, Neal
gave Cooper short shrift, in half a column, as an imitator of
Scott; and he praised Irving for *Knickerbocker's History* ("bold"
and "altogether original") – far superior to the popular *Sketch
Book*, a mixture of "bold poetry" and "squeamish, puling, lady-
like sentimentality."[24]

In a later *Blackwood's* essay–review, Neal hit out at Cooper
with even greater vigor, picturing him as a timid Aladdin who
scampered away in fright after accidentally opening up (in *The
Spy*) "the great unvisited store-house of North-American
riches." And he suggested that Cooper's representation of
American speech and manners reflects a similar timidity:

The people of his book, with two or three exceptions, talk too well;
too much alike, wherever he wishes to make them appear well bred.
He is afraid of his dignity, perhaps; afraid, if he put bad grammar
into the mouths of people, who, as everybody knows, talk nothing
else, in real life, that he himself may be charged with bad grammar.
We are sorry for this. It is a great error but one which we hope to
see done away with on every side, before long – everywhere – by
everybody. Truth, whatever people may say, truth is not vulgarity;
nor is untruth refinement.[25]

Earlier in his critique, Neal had cried out for "a real North
American story . . . a brave, hearty, original book, brimful of
descriptive truth – of historical and familiar truth; crowded
with real American character; alive with American peculiarities
. . . in imitation of nobody, however great."[26] In October of
1824, Neal forwarded the manuscript of such a novel ("altogether American – scenery – incidents – characters"). Shortly
before the novel was published, Blackwood came to London
and Neal sent a hasty note to Somerset House on Dorset Square
signed, for the first time, with his "true name." On June 26,
1825, Blackwood called on Neal's Warwick Street lodgings to
conclude their financial arrangements, and that evening Neal
dined with the publisher and another *Blackwood's* stalwart,
William Maginn, at an eating-house in the Strand. Neal found
Blackwood "frank and fearless; without being either boastful or
aggressive." It was their first and last meeting, the high point –
and the beginning of the end – of a remarkable association.[27]

A week later, *Brother Jonathan, or the New Englanders* made its appearance in Edinburgh and London – in three handsomely printed and bound volumes totaling more than 1300 pages. This second of Neal's novels of the Revolutionary war depicts with enormous vigor and virtuosity a single year in the life of "our hero," young Walter Harwood, an enraptured innocent, atremble with animal vitality and dangerously susceptible to women – "an overgrown lout of a boy, brought up in the Back Woods of America, – with a stoop in his shoulders, a swing in his gait, hob-nailed shoes upon his feet, a smock frock upon his back, a nasal twang in his speech, and almost every phrase he utters regular Yankee!"[28] D. M. Moir, an editorial consultant to Blackwood who had read the novel in manuscript, paid tribute to its power ("of a kind that is unhackneyed and original"), but also charged it with two fatal flaws: its sprawling and prolix "metaphysical ingenuity" and exaggeration; and its pervasive indecency.[29]

Moir's (and Blackwood's) fears about the novel found confirmation in the opinions of a reviewer for the *British Critic* who expressed regret that a writer capable of such superb descriptions of New England wrestling matches and quilting frolics should "wilfully devote three huge close-printed volumes to the adventures of profligates, misanthropes, liars, and louts, for such are the serious personages of 'Brother Jonathan.'"[30] But other British critics found much to praise in it, one going so far as to suggest that it was worthy of Scott:

The work displays a vigour and pathos which are only to be found in novels of the first rank. In Brother Jonathan, there are scenes which the "Great Unknown" might be proud to acknowledge; and the whole construction and management of the story is such as no person but an author possessing powers of the first order could have executed.[31]

An "imaginary" review–article purporting to be written by "F. J." (Francis Jeffrey) for the *Edinburgh Review* (but apparently the production of P. G. Patmore) characterizes *Brother Jonathan* as "the most extraordinary work of its kind which this age of extraordinary works has put forth" – at the same time ridiculing "the extraordinary and headlong rapidity of style, as well as the insane incoherence of matter, which prevail throughout these volumes."[32]

Surveying the state of American literature in 1829, William Hazlitt found fault with Cooper for excessive particularity and minuteness of detail ("He is not so much the master of his materials as their drudge"); in contrast, the author of *Brother Jonathan* went to the opposite extreme, recounting "the over-turning of a travelling stage-waggon with as much impetuosity, turbulence, and exaggerated enthusiasm, as if it were the fall of a Phaeton."[33] (An examination of this episode in Neal's novel – involving as it does a wild journey ending at the edge of a precipice, enlivened by a keg of dynamite, a fire and a madden-ingly casual driver – suggests an anticipation of Melville's most intense serio-comic flights in *Moby-Dick*; Hazlitt might well have dismissed "Stubb kills a Whale" in similar terms.) Hazlitt was reacting negatively to the mythologizing and serio-comic tendencies in American fiction that were to find their fullest expression in Melville – and, in this century, in Faulkner and Bellow.

Other British critics saw something distinctively American and praiseworthy in the exaggerations that Hazlitt deplored. *Brother Jonathan*, says a commentator in the *Edinburgh Literary Journal*, is "full of vigour and originality," and abounds in "descriptions of scenery, and illustrations of the natural passions of the human heart and soul, worthy of that prodigious continent, whose hills are mountains and whose mountains are immeasurable."[34]

Despite the high praise that *Brother Jonathan* elicited from some critics, the novel was a financial failure and Neal's association with Blackwood began to cool. To enhance the sale of his novel and to make *Blackwood's* more popular in America, Neal had earlier proposed that the magazine should feature a series of North American tales, written by himself. Neal submitted a preface to the projected series and one long story, "New-England Witchcraft" – later expanded into the novel *Rachel Dyer*. Blackwood found the story "very striking and powerful," but delayed publication for a protracted time after accepting and setting it in type. In February 1826, this delay (and other disagreements) precipitated an explosive and terminal quarrel between the Scottish editor and Yankee author.[35]

Neal turned to other journals, most notably, the *London*

Magazine. He contributed there a racy autobiographical sketch, "Yankee Notions," and a savage review of *The Last of the Mohicans* that opened with a comment on the deteriorating quality of both Cooper and Scott: "The family failing . . . is as conspicuous in the American, as in the parent tree – the produce has grown worse and worse each year; it is now dry and jejune, and trashy."[36]

During the last year of his stay in London, Neal lived at Queen-Square Place, in the residence of the eminent Jeremy Bentham. Neal had become interested in Bentham's writings while studying law in Baltimore and, after he met the great man in November 1825, was pleased to accept Bentham's invitation to join his household. On Bentham's suggestion, Neal submitted an essay "United States" to *The Westminster Review*, a journal dedicated to Utilitarian principles. When the article appeared, Neal was outraged that the editor, John Bowring, had inserted a passage that completely misrepresented his views:

Violent exaggeration [says Bowring in the sentence he added] is the character of American literature at the present day, and, compared with the chaster and more rational style of our best writers, the style of the North American authors is usually the rant and unmeaning vehemence of a strolling Thespian, when placed beside the calm, appropriate and expressive delivery of an accomplished actor.

This was hitting hard not merely at American literature in general but at the author of *Brother Jonathan* in particular. To have such sentiments interpolated without consultation after the author had already corrected the proofs would have stirred up a less volatile temperament than Neal's. Four decades after the event, Neal's recollection is still pungent:

Bear in mind that I had gone over to England to take up the gage of battle, offered by the arrogant and supercilious writers of England; to answer the "Edinburgh Review," face to face, where it ventured to say, "that eloquence and the power of fine writing were denied by nature to the American race . . ."

And yet, such being my errand, or mission, if you will, this meddling, gossiping [*sic*], sly, and treacherous man, had the audacity to put words into my mouth, not only in flat contradiction to what I said, but in direct confirmation of what his unprincipled countrymen had said of us! How could he do this, and "hope to be forgiven"?[37]

Neal was understandably exercised; he was already being attacked at home as a traitor to the cause of American letters because of his *Blackwood's* "American Writers" series. Bowring's editorial "improvement" contributed to the hostility that greeted him on his return home in 1827. But Neal's reputation aside, Bowring's interpolation was a revealing indication of the *Westminster's* attitude toward American literature during the 1820s – an attitude productive of explosive results when an uncompromising Yankee like Neal contributed to its pages.

According to Neal, he consented to overlook this outrage in response to Bentham's urging. The strained relations between Neal and Bowring, however, eventually led to the American's departure from Queen-Square Place in April of 1827. (In his version of the affair, Bowring declared that "the rough republican frequently annoyed Bentham by his abruptness and incaution" and that "[Neal's] mind and manners had not been trained to that gentle and courteous bearing which so peculiarly distinguished Bentham, and to whose absence he could not reconcile himself"; Bowring does not mention his editorial "improvement" of Neal's article and the storm it aroused.)[38]

During his stay in Bentham's household, Neal worked on a translation of Bentham's *Traités de législation* and assisted the Utilitarian cause in a variety of other ways. The indefatigable Yankee also completed, at Queen-Square Place, most of a novel titled *Authorship, A Tale. By a New Englander Over-Sea*. A wild and witty account of the romantic adventures in England of an American author (who calls himself "Carter Holmes"), its early chapters poke fun at British foibles and landmarks in ways that anticipate the irreverent satire of *Innocents Abroad*. Neal's account of a pilgrimage to England's most sacred shrine, however, is much more irreverent than Mark Twain's generally respectful and reverential description of the place:

I saw no sceptered shadows gliding hither and thither among the pillars and tombs; no crowned nor headless apparitions parading slowly in the "dim religious light" . . . I saw too a crowd of people, with their hands in their pockets, running about after a guide, all bare-headed and most of them with lips blue and teeth chattering – perhaps with awe – perhaps with cold. I saw . . . a group of waxen

images – wax heroes and kings fairly set up for show in the habili-
ments of the toy-shop among the sepulchres and solitudes of
Westminster-Abbey! Who would not have come over the waters
for a peep at such a spectacle in such a place? and who would not,
if such a thing were told of the barbarians of the South-Sea, or of the
Dutch, who would not speak of it as altogether characteristic of
their barbarous condition, or deplorable want of taste?[39]

The financial failure of *Brother Jonathan* and Blackwood's
rejection of his grand scheme for a series of North American
tales were mortal blows to Neal's campaign for a literary fame
that would equal or surpass that of Irving and Cooper. But he
did claim another kind of victory for his three-year British
invasion:

When it is remembered, that, up to this period, May, 1824, no
American had ever found his way into any of these periodicals, and
that American affairs were dealt with in short, insolent paragraphs,
full of . . . downright misrepresentation, as if they were dealing with
Fejee islanders, or Timbuctoos . . . it must be admitted, I think,
that my plan was both well-conceived, and well-carried out.[40]

Neal's boast was no empty one, for he was indeed the first
American to break into the British periodical press. His critical
perspectives on what was needed for an authentic American
literature as he conveyed them in *Blackwood's* and other periodicals were a significant contribution; equally significant – or
even more so – were *Brother Jonathan* and "New England Witchcraft," works that point unmistakably toward Melville and
Hawthorne.

Return to Portland: Poe and other discoveries

Neal arranged his itinerary from England to America so that it
would include a one-month visit to France; he arrived in New
York from Le Havre in June 1827. A return to Baltimore was
out of the question and he began arrangements to set up a law
practice in New York. But the hostile reception he received in
his native Portland on a visit to his mother persuaded him to
change his plans. He faced down his enemies and settled in his
native town. For the next fifty years – until his death in 1876 –
Neal practiced law, engaged in business, participated in civic
affairs and campaigned vigorously for women's rights.

Neal's campaign for American literary independence and career as a writer took a fresh start in Portland with the inauguration of *The Yankee*; the publication of three remarkable novels – *Rachel Dyer* (1828), *Authorship* (1830), *The Down-Easters* (1833) – and a series of powerful tales. In addition, Neal produced a vast quantity of critical writings that display the "moral energy" he persistently advocated.

Is it nothing [he asked during an 1830 address at Waterville-College], that our whole body of literature, is the literature, not of a Republic but of a Monarchy; not of our people but of another people; that our authors want courage to think for themselves, or to do anything indeed but copy others; that of the millions and millions of books to be found in every part of our country, there is hardly one to be met with, which does not either directly or indirectly, uphold opinions, customs, usages, and social practices, entirely opposed in their nature and effect to the spirit of our institutions?

He warned against the pervasive intolerance against dissenting views and reminded his audience that America was subject to the same historical forces that had reduced to rubble the great nations of the past.[41] At the heart of Neal's critical and political writings is a basic distrust of institutions and a continuing plea for self-examination and self-reliance.

It was in the pages of *The Yankee*, in 1829, that Neal published a brief notice concerning "E. A. P. of Baltimore" that was to have far-reaching consequences for young Poe. Poe never forgot the critic who gave him "the first jog in my literary career" (as he put it in a letter of 1840 to Neal). But it was more than a sense of personal gratitude that led Poe to dedicate "Tamerlane" to his mentor; to rank John Neal "first, or at all events second, among our men of indisputable *genius*"; to predict that Neal's "philosophical and self-dependent spirit . . . will even yet lead him . . . to do something for the literature of the country which the country 'will not willingly,' and cannot possibly, 'let die.'" Another American writer who acknowledged Neal's compelling influence was Nathaniel Hawthorne. Shortly before the publication of *Twice-Told Tales*, Jonathan Cilley wrote to his old Bowdoin College classmate: "What sort of book have you written, Hath? I hope and pray it is nothing like the damned ranting stuff of John Neal, which you, while at Brunswick, relished so highly." Hawthorne, in 1845, referred to "that wild fellow, John Neal, who almost turned my brain with his romances." A dimension of Neal's genius that drew both Poe and Hawthorne to his writings was a Gothicism tinged with romantic irony. G. R. Thompson has observed that in Poe's ironic mode "a tragic response to the perversities of fortune and to the treacheries of one's own mind is contrasted by a near-comic perception of man's condition in the universe."[42]

In one of his rare ventures into literary criticism, Hawthorne found wanting William Gilmore Simms' view of the way history may serve the purposes of the literary artist.[43] Simms' brilliant paragraphs "bring out, as by a skilfully applied varnish, all the lights and shades that lie upon the surface of our history; but yet, we cannot help feeling that the real treasures of his subject have escaped the author's notice." The themes emphasized by Simms, observed Hawthorne, are "cast in the same worn out mould that has been in use these thirty years, and which it is time to break up and fling away." What is needed, what is lacking in Simms, is an original and creative approach to American history – a "magic touch that should cause new intellectual and moral shapes to spring up in the reader's mind, peopling with varied life what had hitherto been a barren waste." Shortly after, Hawthorne applied his "magic touch" to transform the dusty annals of old Boston into "the truth of the human heart" in *The Scarlet Letter*. Two decades earlier "Carter Holmes," reviewing a historical romance in *Blackwood's*, complained that it was "full of good sense, which we have no sort of patience with; surcharged with historical truth, which nobody cares for; crowded with sober stuff, the insupportable accuracy of which were enough to damp the poetical ardour of a whole nation."[44]

In his "Unpublished Preface" (offered to Blackwood as an introduction to his series of North American stories and first published as part of his Preface to the *Blackwood's* witchcraft story that became *Rachel Dyer*), Neal called Washington Irving an American Addison and Cooper an American Scott. He would show his countrymen "that there are abundant and hidden sources of fertility in their own beautiful brave earth, waiting only to be broken up; and barren places . . . teeming below with bright soil." He would plunge, whatever the result, "to the very bottom of the human heart."[45] The result, *Rachel Dyer*, is an impressive forerunner of *The Scarlet Letter* and a possible source of the witchcraft elements in *The House of the Seven Gables* ("Ye shall drink blood and breathe blood, you and yours, for the work of this day!" cries out Sarah Good to her accusers from the gallows; the old wizard Maule informs the onlookers at his execution, pointing his finger at Colonel Pyncheon, that "God will give him blood to drink").

Neal's novel foreshadows (perhaps influences) Hawthorne's fictional treatments of witchcraft in other, more important, ways. In 1847, Hawthorne dismissed as unconvincing Whittier's attempts "to converse with [New England] ghosts and witches" because "Mr. Whittier never fails to express his incredulity either before or after the narrative, and often in the midst of it." Hawthorne suggests that "If he cannot believe his ghost-story while he is telling it, he had better leave the task to somebody else."[46] Whittier had admired the "magnificent poetry" of the opening section of *Rachel Dyer*, but was unable to absorb its magic into his own treatments of the subject. Neal's magic draws effortlessly on an upbringing steeped in supernatural lore: young Neal heard, for example, his mother's vivid account of a disembodied hand ("a long, slender hand like thy father's") that made its appearance at the fireplace shortly before the sudden death of his father. "I knew it was thy father's hand the moment I saw it; and I believed it was meant for a warning," Rachel Neal told her son many years later. Knowing her "calm cool judgment in all the business of life," John Neal was deeply impressed by these and other family reminiscences of "second-sight and apparitions."[47] The tragic drama of Salem is powerfully animated in Neal's novel by a point of view sympathetic to a belief in witchcraft and other manifestations of the invisible world.

At the same time, by centering his drama on the minister George Burroughs, chief victim of the witchcraft trials, Neal would present "a history of the human heart" truer than the historical facts on which his novel is based. Burrough's vain and heroic struggle against Puritan legalism would generate, Neal claimed, "a far more healthful excitement than we feel while reading either [Cooper's] or Walter Scott's stories – that excitement which is attendant on a search after *rational* truth."[48]

Just as Hawthorne would later "mingle the Marvelous" with "the truth of the human heart," Neal sought to dramatize a rational struggle against human error in a world that accepts without question a belief in witchcraft.

Rachel Dyer represents an experiment in colloquialism unprecedented in American fiction and clearly signalling the coming of Melville, Whitman and Twain. "Our best writers are English writers, not American writers," complains Neal in the "Unpublished Preface" to *Rachel Dyer*:

> Not so much as one true Yankee is to be found in any of our native books: hardly so much as one true Yankee phrase. Not so much as one true Indian, though you could hardly take up a story on either side of the water now, without finding a red-man . . . that uniformly talks the best English the author is capable of – more than half the time out-Ossianing Ossian . . .
>
> For my own part . . . I never shall write what is now worshipped under the name of *classical* English. It is no natural language – it never was – it never will be spoken alive on this earth: and therefore, ought never to be written. We have dead languages enough now; but the deadest language I ever met with or heard of, was that in use among the writers of Queen Anne's day.[49]

Neal's adventurous colloquialism in *Rachel Dyer* results in an authenticity of dialect that foreshadows Mark Twain. Thus, the down-east youngster Robert Eveleth tells of his encounter with George Burroughs in language rarely encountered in the romances of Neal's day:

> an' so he stopped me an' axed me where the plague I was runnin to; an' so I up an' tells him all I know about the knife, an' so, an' so, an' so, that air feller, what dooze he do, but he jounces me up on that air plaguy crupper and fetches me back here full split, you see, and rides over everything, and makes everybody get out o' the way, an' *will* make me tell the story whether or no.[50]

This feeling for live talk is no mere embellishment or virtuoso display, but an adjunct of Neal's concern for the living truth in the terrible drama he has re-enacted.

Virtually ignored in its own time (in part because Neal insisted on publishing the novel in remote Portland instead of New York or Boston), *Rachel Dyer* might well convey with greater urgency a century and a half after its first publication the reasons why William Blackwood found the original tale "very striking and powerful." The same holds true for the most notable of the stories that came out of Neal's grand plan for a series of North American stories, a plan that made only fitful progress after his break with Blackwood. Published between 1828 and 1843, *Rachel Dyer*, "Otter-Bag," "David Whicher," "The Squatter," "Idiosyncrasies," deserve to be remembered and read as anticipations of Hawthorne, Melville and Faulkner and, more important, as significant additions to the American literary heritage – as illuminating and corrosive explorations of early America, of the American frontier, of the American soul.[51]

Poe was virtually the only critic during Neal's lifetime who recognized Neal's importance as a storyteller – though he perennially complained about the Nealian proclivity toward sprawl. "In the higher requisites of composition," Poe wrote in 1847, "John Neal's magazine stories excel – I mean in vigor of thought, picturesque combination of incident, and so forth – but they ramble too much, and invariably break down just before coming to an end."[52] Poe's complaint about Neal's tendency to ramble has justification, but Neal's best stories exhibit greater poignancy and horror than the younger man's more polished productions. When Poe died, Neal called attention to a dimension of his art largely unrecognized during Poe's lifetime: his penetrating insight into "the elements of darkness."[53] It was an important dimension of his own story-telling. In an age dominated by sentimentality and timid conventionality, Neal cried out for those "faithful representations of native character" that would reveal "what we are most anxious to conceal . . . [about] our own peculiarities and our own faults."[54]

5

Poe's England and the divided self

How to Write a Blackwood Article

It has been widely known for half a century and more that Poe was intensely involved with the British magazines of his day – foremost among them, *Blackwood's*.[1] In this involvement, Poe was not alone: "For one reader of *Blackwood's Magazine* in the old country [wrote R. Shelton Mackenzie], there cannot be less than fifty in the new."[2] The widespread appeal of *Blackwood's* in America can, in large part, be attributed to its vivacity and boldness. "I hardly know any work except Maga [as *Blackwood's* was called]," wrote William Blackwood to John Neal on the completion of Neal's "American Writers" series, "where you could have felt yourself so much at ease in most fearlessly saying what you thought right of men and things. Washington Irving once told me he considered my Maga as a daringly original work. It was too much for his delicate nerves."[3] *Blackwood's* greatest importance to Poe, however, was not its boldness but the models it provided, both in its criticisms and stories (or "articles" as tales were then designated), for his own critical views and tales; using almost identical language, both *Blackwood's* and Poe emphasized the horrible and terrible as the proper sphere for the writer of fiction.[4] Thus, J. G. Lockhart says, in his *Blackwood's* review of E. T. A. Hoffmann's *The Devil's Elexir*, that "the *horrible* is quite as legitimate a field of poetry and romance, as either the pathetic and ludicrous." Other *Blackwood's* critics make a strong plea for terror that arises from some real experience; fairy tales in England "do not touch the soul" and "the German terrible" did not have a natural resting-place in the British temperament. In a similar vein, Sir Walter Scott (writing in another British journal) suggested that Hoffmann's fantastic extravagance is far less effective than those Scottish tales which convey more terror by

offering the possibility of natural explanations for the strange
events they recount. These views were well known to Poe and
point directly to his famous pronouncement, in his preface to
Tales of the Grotesque and Arabesque: "If in any of my productions
terror has been the thesis, I maintain that terror is not of Germany, but of the soul."[5] Equally important to Poe's critical
theory and literary practice were what has been called "*Blackwood's* doctrine of the short poem, adopted from Schlegel"
– a doctrine that incorporated concepts of "unity" or "totality
of effect"; a *Blackwood's* writer argued that the successful
literary artist requires a "cool, cautious, artificial mood of mind,
akin to that of the mathematician or the algebraist."[6]

The "*Blackwood's* pattern" was characterized by a fusion of
erudite learning and blatant sensationalism – a fusion facilitated
by emphasizing personality and bitter critical controversy, a
hoaxing spirit and a spate of morbid pseudo-scientific fiction.
Between 1821 and 1837, *Blackwood's* featured such tales as "The
Man in the Bell," "The Buried Alive," "The Night Walker,"
"The Metempsychosis," "The Murderer's Last Night," "The
Iron Shroud" and "The Involuntary Experimentalist." Other
Blackwood's stories (e.g., "The Man with the Nose," "The
Barber of Gottingen") poke fun at fashionable literary trends
or philosophic ideas. These *Blackwood's* tales of sensation and
burlesque found frequent expression in Poe's fiction, early and
late.[7]

Poe's famous letter to Thomas W. White defending the "far
too horrible" subject of "Berenice" clarifies his view of such
fiction and his indebtedness to *Blackwood's* and other British
journals. His story, Poe says, is similar in nature to many tales
currently appearing in the celebrated magazines of the day. Of
what does this "nature" consist? "In the ludicrous heightened
into the grotesque: the fearful coloured into the horrible: the
witty exaggerated into the burlesque: the singular wrought into
the strange and mystical." Poe points to "such articles" in the
London Magazine and *Blackwood's* ("M. S. found in a Madhouse"
and the "Man in the Bell"), and reminds White that "the first
men in [England] have not thought writings of this nature unworthy of their talents, and I have good reason to believe that
some very high names valued themselves *principally* upon this
species of literature." Poe then adds an important sentence: "To

be sure originality is an essential in these things – great attention must be paid to style, and much labour spent in their composition, or they will degenerate into the tu[r]gid or the absurd."[8]

Poe's own originality may be illustrated by a brief look at the way in which he transformed a typical *Blackwood's* mediocrity, M. William Mudford's "The Iron Shroud" (1830), into the powerful and profound "The Pit and the Pendulum" (1842). The *Blackwood's* tale opens with a description of a medieval castle where "the young, the brave, the proud" Vivenzio languishes in a dungeon prison ("Even the intrepid soul of Vivenzio shrunk with dismay as he entered this abode, and heard the ponderous doors triple-locked by the silent ruffians who conducted him to it").[9] He is in an iron cage, and much of the tale consists of his protracted expressions of horror and agony over his discovery, early on, that his cell is gradually contracting and must inevitably crush him. A few lines of several double-column pages must suffice to convey Vivenzio's plight and Mudford's style:

"Yes!" he exclaimed looking wildly round his dungeon, and shuddering as he spoke – "Yes! it must be so! I see it! – I feel the maddening truth like scorching flames upon my brain! Eternal God! – support me! it must be so! – Yes, yes, that is to be my fate! Yon roof will descend! – these walls will hem me round – and slowly, slowly, crush me in their iron arms!

Eight long columns later, Vivenzio's life (and the story) close with this sentence: "He was horribly crushed by the ponderous roof and collapsing sides – and the flattened bier was his *Iron shroud*."

Drawing on Mudford's basic situation, and combining it with the plight of "The Man in the Bell" (another *Blackwood's* tale), Poe created a small, original, permanent masterpiece. The opening sentence of "The Pit and the Pendulum" puts us into the middle of the story – and makes us know and feel what the narrator is experiencing: "I was sick – sick unto death with that long agony; and when they at length unbound me, and I was permitted to sit, I felt that my senses were leaving me (v, 67)."[10] In place of the unvarying crescendo of Vivenzio's tormented outcries, Poe's narrator speculates and feels in widely varying ways. There are meditations on the nature of consciousness and

unconsciousness, death and immortality, memory and forget-
fulness, "the state of seeming nothingness" and madness ("the
madness of a memory which busies itself among forbidden
things"). There is a pendulum as well as a pit – but more
important than this diversification of the hero's ordeal is the
complexity of the hero's mind. In the midst of his suffering –
because of his suffering – he is able to think his way out of one
danger with a stroke of ingenuity worthy of Dupin; under the
razor-edge of the descending pendulum, he experiences the
"calmness of despair" and recovers his power to reason; "For
the first time during many hours – or perhaps days – I *thought*"
(v, 581). Compounding the horror and hopelessness of the
narrator–prisoner's plight have been the rats – "wild, bold,
ravenous; their red eyes glaring upon me as if they waited but
for motionlessness on my part to make me their prey." With
desperate ingenuity, the narrator makes use of the loathsome
rats to free his bonds just as the deadly pendulum begins to cut
into his chest. "For the moment, at least, *I was free.*" He is free,
has saved himself for the next ordeal – the fiery-hot, contracting
walls of the pit (v, 82–5). As the walls close in, he understands
that all the fortuitous elements and all the ingenuity that have
kept him alive to this moment have, ironically, served only to
intensify his agony by preserving him for further torment. The
ultimate irony is the rescue – a totally unexpected event and one
having no visible connection to the narrator's strugglings and
travail. The ultimate horror is hinted at early in the story when
the narrator, lying at the bottom of the pit into which he has
been cast, dares not open his eyes: "It was not that I feared to
look upon things horrible, but that I grew aghast lest there
should be *nothing* to see" (v, 71).[11] Here (as also in *The Narrative
of Arthur Gordon Pym, Eureka* and other works) Poe anticipates
the apocalyptic nihilism of Ishmael's meditations on the
whiteness of the whale: "Is it that by its indefiniteness it
shadows forth the heartless voids and immensities of the
universe, and thus stabs us from behind with the thought of
annihilation. . . ?"[12]

"The Pit and the Pendulum" and other masterful tales of
terror drew on *Blackwood's* and other British magazines. At the
same time, Poe was fully aware of the absurdity and mediocrity
of many of his models; his emphasis on the need for originality

and literary craftsmanship was made abundantly clear in his letter to Thomas W. White – and in the vast superiority of his own efforts in the *Blackwood's* vein. In a sense, "The Pit and the Pendulum" is a devastating critique of "The Iron Shroud" (and of *Blackwood's*); it compellingly demonstrates the vast gulf between a mediocre model and an artistic triumph. Despite the modest tone he adopted concerning "Berenice" in his letter to White, Poe was fully aware of that gulf and, on occasion, poked fun openly at the mechanical and slipshod way in which a *Blackwood's* tale was typically put together.

In "How to write a Blackwood Article" (1838), Poe's satiric target is Mr Blackwood and his advice on how to put together a successful contribution. After citing several models for emulation (among them, "The Man in a Bell"), Mr Blackwood informs his visitor (Signora Psyche Zenobia, secretary to a society of literary aspirants) that "Sensations are the great thing after all. Should you ever be drowned or hung be sure and make a note of your sensations – they will be worth to you ten guineas a sheet." A variety of possible misadventures are recounted, far-fetched (tumbling out of a balloon) or familiar (being run over by an omnibus). Having selected the predicament, the would-be *Blackwood's* contributor should then choose an appropriate tone or manner of narration. There are – among those suggested by Mr Blackwood – the tones "didactic," "enthusiastic," "natural," "laconic," "elevated," "metaphysical," "transcendental" and "heterogeneous." If the "tone elevated" is adopted, "the words must be all in a whirl, like a humming-top, and make a noise very similar, which answers remarkably well instead of meaning." This style is most highly recommended to the writer "in too great a hurry to think" (II, 269–76). In Poe's companion piece, "A Predicament" (1838), Signora Psyche Zenobia looks out of a church steeple for a better view of Edinburgh; the aperture from which she thrusts her head is in the dial-plate of a gigantic clock. She is so transfixed by the heavenly scenery that half an hour goes by in its contemplation. When she is ready to pull in her head, the minute-hand of the clock has descended too close to the hour-hand; she is now literally transfixed. There follows a second-by-second account of her sensations as the minute-hand slowly cuts into her neck until, "at twenty-five minutes past five in the

afternoon precisely," Signora Zenobia's head is severed from
her body; Zenobia "sees" her head roll down the steeple and
into the middle of the street below (II, 283–93).

Poe's attacks on and lampoons of *Blackwood's* fiction seem to
some critics the manifestation of a basic ambivalence or
inconsistency – since he also praised this fiction on occasion.[13]
But Poe was quite consistent and straightforward in his approach to *Blackwood's*. In his 1835 letter to White, Poe praised
these sensation tales, but also expressed concern about the ease
with which they could degenerate into the "turgid" and
"absurd"; in his Hawthorne review of 1842, Poe mentioned
the "many fine examples in the early numbers of Blackwood,"
but concluded his paragraph with a proviso similar to his
cautionary advice of 1835: "The true critic will but demand
that the design intended be accomplished, to the fullest extent,
by the means most advantageously applicable" (XI, 109). Such a
demand by the true critic might indeed reveal that, along with
the "many fine examples" in *Blackwood's*, were many mediocre
examples – sensation tales produced in a mechanical and
imitative way. Such tales could and should be lampooned, not
only because they were ludicrously bad but because they
impugned the reputation of the entire genre – including (and
especially) Poe's own.

Having said this, it is also necessary to add that such parodies
of *Blackwood's* as "A Predicament" have serious dimensions.
The decapitation of Zenobia and its aftermath is a triumph of
Poe's imagination over the reader's assumptions.[14] Indeed, the
surreal world of Zenobia in "A Predicament" is a mirror image
(wildly distorted) of the nightmare world of the hero in "The
Pit and the Pendulum."[15] The connection between these vastly
different tales is clarified by Poe's ironic mode that characteristically presents a double perception of man's condition in the
universe – one that is simultaneously tragic and absurd.[16]

In this vision Poe was not alone. Like Poe's, the tales of
Hawthorne and Melville range from burlesque and self-parody
to the serious; and the serious frequently verges on the absurd.
The irrepressibly contagious laughter of the villagers in which
young Robin joins at the terrible conclusion of Hawthorne's
"My Kinsman, Major Molineux" is linked to the terrible
laughter of Fortunato in "The Cask of Amontillado"; the

amused half-smile of the narrator–victim in "The Pit and the Pendulum" as he reflects on his plight during a lull in the proceedings is akin to Ishmael's half-comic meditation on making a will after his first pursuit of a whale (*Moby-Dick*, ch. 49). In "The Pit and the Pendulum," "William Wilson" and other of his most successful tales, Poe demonstrated how to write a Blackwood article in ways undreamed of in *Blackwood's Magazine*.

In a misty-looking village of England

Among the great writers of his generation, Poe alone lived a portion of his childhood in England.[17] From the summer of 1815 to the summer of 1820, Poe lived in England with the Allans while his foster-father pursued his business ventures with a lack of success that finally made it necessary for him to return to America with his family. Between the years of six and eleven, young Poe went to several schools; his most extended attendance, from July 1818 to May 1820, was at the Manor House School, a classical academy at Stoke Newington, near London. "Edgar is growing wonderfully and enjoys a good reputation as both able and willing to receive instruction," wrote John Allan to his uncle about his nine-year-old foster-son on September 28, 1818. These were impressionable years for a growing boy, especially for so sensitive and observant a boy as Edgar Poe. Arthur Hobson Quinn suggests that Poe's British experience was fortunate in helping "to remove the provinciality which is the inevitable handicap of those whose vision has been limited to their native land." But it also had other, more direct, consequences for his literary career. Although it was not published until 1839, "William Wilson" has, according to Quinn, a convincing reality in its depiction of Poe's schooldays that must stem "from impressions made so deeply in his childhood that they lay ever ready for his call." Poe's narrator reports that "My earliest recollections of a school-life, are connected with a large, rambling, Elizabethan house, in a misty-looking village of England, where were a vast number of gigantic and gnarled trees, and where all the houses were excessively ancient" (III, 300–1). Poe's school-master at the Manor House School in Stoke Newington was the

Reverend Mr John Bransby; William Wilson's schoolmaster is "the Reverend Dr. Bransby." Poe's childhood experience did indeed leave a deep impression and contributed significantly to "William Wilson."

In an opening sentence that anticipates the opening sentence of *Moby-Dick*, Poe's narrator begins: "Let me call myself, for the present, William Wilson." His real name would be too vile to mention to his readers. He will not recount all his wickednesses but, as death approaches, seek for understanding and sympathy by telling how – through one event – he "passed, with the stride of a giant, into more than the enormities of an Elah-Gabulus." Others had been tempted to wickedness before, but no man was heretofore *thus* tempted – no man heretofore *thus* fell. Was he not therefore unique in the suffering that he had experienced? "Have I not indeed been living in a dream? Am I not now dying a victim to the horror and the mystery of the wildest of all sublunary visions?" (III, 299–300).

The "one event" that led to William Wilson's great leap forward into wickedness – and to his dying confession – is the fatal stabbing by Wilson of his double. The story ends as Wilson confronts his dying antagonist, but finds instead what seems to be a large mirror ("where none had been perceptible before") and sees his own image, dabbled in blood and dying, advance to say ("and I could have fancied that I myself was speaking"): "In me didst thou exist – and, in my death, see by this image, which is thine own, how utterly thou hast murdered thyself" (III, 323–5).

William Wilson's encounters with his double are regarded by some critics as hallucinatory; we are to understand that in killing his counterpart, Wilson has destroyed his own conscience. This is how the story ends – but by looking again at the beginning, one critic suggests, we see a Wilson who has recovered his sanity and his conscience.[18] But by looking again at the beginning we find an elaborate and complex plea for sympathy that calls for our closer attention. The dying Wilson pleads, in the opening paragraphs of his narrative, for a belief among his fellow men that "I have been, in some measure, the slave of circumstances beyond human control. I would wish them to seek out for me, in the details I am about to give, some little oasis of *fatality* amid a wilderness of error." Wilson explains his undisciplined childhood by the inability of his parents ("Weak-minded, and beset with constitutional infirmities akin to my own") to control his "evil propensities" (III, 299–300). It may be that William Wilson has not recovered his "sanity" or "conscience" – and that we must explore and expand the boundaries of these terms in order to assess Poe's achievement in this tale.

After citing the Russian critic Merezhkovsky's observations on Dostoevsky's genius for laying bare the criminal impulses of the human heart, Thomas Mann offers his own explanation of the novelist's distinctive power: it resides, says Mann, in the fact that

we are only apparently dealing with objective and quasi-medical scrutiny and diagnosis – it is in reality psychological lyricism in the widest sense of the word, admission and horrible confession, pitiless revelation of the criminal depths of the author's own conscience – and this accounts for the terrible moral force, the religious frightfulness of Dostoevsky's knowledge of the soul.

Dostoevsky's early story, "The Double" (1846), Mann observes, "did not surpass Edgar Allan Poe's *William Wilson*, where the same arch-romantic motif is treated in a morally profounder manner, resolving the clinical in the poetic."[19]

The arch-romantic motiff is that of the Doppelgänger; it is a revelation of Poe's moral profundity and poetic power to examine this motif in the two main sources of "William Wilson" and to see the ways in which Poe makes use of it for his own purposes.

The first important source is E. T. A. Hoffmann's tale, *Elexiere des Teufels* (*The Devil's Elexir*), published in English translation by William Blackwood in 1824 – and reviewed by J. G. Lockhart in *Blackwood's Magazine* shortly thereafter. "William Wilson" derives from *The Devil's Elexir* in several ways; but there is a significant inversion in Poe's adaptation of Hoffmann's Doppelgänger relationship: in *The Devil's Elexir* Medardus's double, Viktorin, represents evil, while William Wilson's double is an influence for the good.[20]

Poe's inversion of Hoffmann was spurred by his encounter with a second source, Washington Irving's brief but provocative account of "An Unwritten Drama of Lord Byron" –

published in *The Gift* for 1836. It recounts the strange fate of
the Spanish nobleman Alfonso, whose passions, "from early and
unrestrained indulgence, have become impetuous and un-
governable." He finds himself stalked by a mysterious stranger,
"masked and muffled up so as to conceal both countenance and
figure." This shadow – Alfonso's "second self" – follows our
hero about everywhere, thwarting all his schemes and spoiling
all his intrigues. Tormented into gloomy despair and jealousy,
Alfonso finally stabs his tormentor. As the double falls, he
exclaims, "Are you satisfied!" and Alfonso discovers to his
horror that beneath the mask and mantle is "his own image –
the spectre of himself." He dies, and Irving adds this explanation: "The spectre is an allegorical being, the personification
of conscience, or of the passions." After telling of Byron's
unconsummated plan for this story, based on an old Spanish
play, Irving closes with this sentence: "The foregoing sketch
of the plot may hereafter suggest a rich theme to a poet or
dramatist of the Byron school."[21]

"I see that *The Gift* is out," Poe wrote to a friend on September 11, 1835; his story "M.S. Found in a Bottle" appeared a
hundred pages away from "An Unwritten Drama of Lord
Byron" and we know, from Poe's own testimony, that he read
and found a rich theme for "William Wilson" in Irving's
essay.[22] "There is no greater mistake," wrote Poe in 1836, "than
the supposition that a true originality is a mere matter of
impulse or inspiration. To originate is carefully, patiently, and
understandingly to combine" (xiv, 37). Drawing on Hoffmann, Byron–Irving, and on his own deepest experience, Poe
created a tale that (in Melville's words about Hawthorne and
Shakespeare) probes "at the very axis of reality," that "speaks
the sane madness of vital truth."[23]

The description of William Wilson's school in the opening
pages of the story stand out as one of the most vivid and
impressive passages in all of Poe's writings. There are no end
to the windings of this "palace of enchantment" with its
bewildering multiplicity of rooms and lateral branches so
"innumerable – inconceivable – and so returning in upon themselves, that our most exact ideas in regard to the whole mansion
were not very far different from those with which we pondered
upon infinity" (III, 303). It seems to be an unknowable house –

one that stretches the narrator's powers of observation to a state of tension and uncertainty.

The unknowable schoolhouse is presided over by an unknowable schoolmaster, the Reverend Dr Bransby, who also serves as the pastor of the village church:

> With how deep a spirit of wonder and perplexity was I wont to regard him from our remote pew in the gallery, as, with step solemn and slow, he ascended the pulpit! This reverend man, with countenance so demurely benign, with robes so glossy and so clerically flowing, with wig so minutely powdered, so rigid and so vast – could this be he who, of late, with sour visage, and in snuffy habiliments, administered, ferule in hand, the Draconian laws of the academy? Oh, gigantic paradox, too utterly monstrous for solution! (III, 302)

In Hoffmann's tale much space is given to the gradual growth of evil in Medardus, first in his exposure to sexual temptation and second in the acceleration of the process when he drinks the forbidden elexir. Medardus' downfall is reversed when the seeming murder of his double proves to be only an illusion. Irving's brief sketch supplies only the barest outline of a sensualist's frustrations as he is thwarted again and again by a mysterious masked man who turns out to be his double. Poe's tale, in contrast, focuses on a misty-looking village of England, a schoolhouse, a schoolmaster – and on a sensitive boy's intense, bewildered involvement with this world. William Wilson is different, stands apart, becomes ascendant over all his schoolmates in "the ardor, the enthusiasm, and the imperiousness of my disposition" – until another scholar, his namesake, challenges that ascendancy. Only William Wilson is aware of the secret, subtle influence of the second William Wilson and his singular whisper (*"the very echo of my own"*).

The schoolhouse and the schoolmaster are unknowable to William Wilson – and the strange double makes inroads into William Wilson's consciousness that make him increasingly restive. He flees, redoubles his folly and viciousness, is confronted by his double and flees again – until a final confrontation and the destruction of his tormentor (and himself).

To say (as several critics have suggested) that William Wilson hallucinates or projects his double is a beginning point, not an explanation of the story and its power. It is the same with the

obvious fact that the story is autobiographical. Not only does
Poe give us a real English village and a real school (somewhat
transformed) and an actual schoolmaster (somewhat transformed, but with a real name) – but he supplies William Wilson
with his (Poe's) own birth date. And not only does Poe give
William Wilson – and his namesake – his (Poe's) birth date but,
in three separate printings, he varies the birth years (1809, 1811,
1813) in a pattern consistent with the versions he was supplying
to editors gathering information for brief biographical
sketches.[24]

Poe's extraordinary description of his English school may
provide a clue to the special meaning that "William Wilson"
had for its creator. That special meaning reinforces rather than
interferes with Poe's artistry in "William Wilson." The "misty-
looking village" faithfully mirrors the Stoke Newington of
1818; the Reverend Dr Bransby and his school are modified to
serve the purposes of the tale; the climactic scene depicting
Wilson's downfall while gambling at Oxford is transplanted
from Poe's experiences at the University of Virginia. But it is a
commonplace that the creative imagination draws on actual
experience selectively and with embellishments. William
Wilson's changing birth years, on the other hand, stand apart
in a special and extraordinary way as talismanic touches that
serve as secret signs of the special relationship between the
artist and his creation, between Poe and William Wilson.

Such signs appear elsewhere in Poe's fiction, but never elsewhere with the intensity revealed in "William Wilson." "This
is the book's motto (the secret one)," Melville wrote to Hawthorne as *Moby-Dick* was nearing completion; and, as Ishmael
meditates on the eternal mystery of the whale's spout, he notes
that "down to this blessed minute (fifteen and a quarter minutes
past one o'clock p.m. of this sixteenth day of December, AD
1850), it is still a mystery."[25] Melville's secret motto and public
display of a private moment shed light on Poe's private display
in "William Wilson." Melville's excitement in reaching out to
Hawthorne, in reaching out, through Ishmael, to his reader, is
clarified by Baudelaire's comment on Poe: "For him, imagination is . . . an almost divine faculty which perceives immediately and without philosophical methods the inner and
secret relations of things, the correspondences and the ana-

logies."[26] By giving William Wilson his birth date (January 19) and varying his birth years (1809, 1811, 1813) in successive printings to make them correspond with varying biographical accounts, Poe provides himself with the secret signs of his own overpowering perceptions "into the inner and secret relations of things."

These talismanic touches make sense when "William Wilson" is read as more than a story about a weak and wicked youth who destroys himself by destroying his conscience, or as a clinical study of hallucination formation in a schizoid personality; they make sense when the story is read as an imaginative flight of the highest order, as a mythic fable in which the impossible quest is not for the Grail or white whale but for an authentic self. What enlarges William Wilson as a character is his poetic gift, his ability to transform the forces that surrounded him as a boy (his school, his schoolmaster, his classmates, his village) and his inner turmoil into forceful, poetic drama. After a preliminary reference to the rambling schoolhouse, the misty-looking village, the gigantic trees, the ancient houses, William Wilson sums up the peace and exultation stirred by the memory of that place:

At this moment, in fancy, I feel the refreshing chilliness of its deeply-shadowed avenues, inhale the fragrance of its thousand shrubberies, and thrill anew with undefinable delight, at the deep hollow note of the church-bell, breaking, each hour, with sullen and sudden roar, upon the stillness of the dusky atmosphere in which the fretted Gothic steeple lay imbedded and asleep. (III, 301)

These exultation-breeding memories are marred by ominous portents ("the first ambiguous monitions of the destiny which afterwards so fully overshadowed me"). The extensive grounds of the schoolhouse are surrounded by "a high and solid brick wall, topped with a bed of mortar and broken glass" – a "prison-like rampart" that serves to reinforce the prison-like routine imposed on the students. (In the first printing of the tale, it was an "enormously high" wall; Poe's deletion of intensifying adverbs in the final version here and in numerous other instances attests to his recognition of the fact that restraint is more forceful.)[27] The "gigantic paradox" of two Dr Bransbys – one in the pulpit with a countenance "demurely benign," the second, with a "sour visage," administering corporal punishment – is, to the boy, "too utterly monstrous for solution!" Beyond the prison-like wall "frowned a more ponderous gate. It was rivetted and studded with iron bolts, and surmounted with jagged spikes." The schoolroom, Wilson recalls, "was the largest in the house – I could not help thinking of the world." Dr Bransby's sanctum in this vast room is a small square enclosure with a massive door; the schoolboys would sooner undergo death by torture than open this door in the absence of the schoolmaster.

It is in this double world – simultaneously "spirit-soothing" and terrifying – that William Wilson (in "the ardor, the enthusiasm, and the imperiousness of my disposition") sets himself apart from and above all his schoolmates. In this he succeeds, until the second William Wilson successfully challenges his ascendancy – and eventually causes the narrator to flee forever from the old school. (The second William Wilson, the narrator later learns, leaves Dr Bransby's academy on the same day.) The pattern is repeated at Eton; and still another crucial encounter takes place at Oxford.

W. H. Auden has singled out a particularly noteworthy sentence from this section of the story; William Wilson is describing his wasteful and vicious life at Oxford: "Let it suffice, that among spendthrifts I out-Heroded Herod, and that, giving name to a multitude of novel follies, I added no brief appendix to the long catalogue of vices then usual in the most dissolute university of Europe" (III, 315–16). Auden says of this sentence that it is "terrible, vague, verbose" but dramatically "right" in revealing William Wilson "in his real colors, as the fantastic self who hates and refuses contact with reality."[28] Wilson is lurid and unconvincing in cataloging his crimes; he is powerfully eloquent in re-creating the double world of boyhood from which he vainly attempts to escape. Could it be that Wilson (and his crimes) are unconvincing to us because they are unreal to himself? There is very little concrete imagery in Poe's tale outside of the descriptions of the school of Wilson's boyhood.[29]

One of Poe's most misunderstood critical pronouncements is the extraordinary praise he gave, in an 1844 *Marginalia* item, to a little-known, early Dickens tale (from *Sketches by Boz*) titled "The Black Veil." I will say more about Poe's criticism and Dickens' tale in the next section of this chapter but it is useful here to suggest ways in which both illuminate "William Wilson." Poe calls "The Black Veil" "a strangely pathetic and richly imaginative production, replete with the loftiest tragic power." It is, he says, a neglected work – "one of the most forcible things ever written" (xvi, 10–11). This is extraordinary praise for a tale that has scarcely been noticed; a recent full-length study of *Sketches by Boz* relegates it to a footnote, grouping the tale with others dealing with the "wayward son" archetype.[30] Told from the point of view of a young physician, Dickens' story depicts the desperate ("insanely" desperate) attempt of a mother to save her son from death – *after* "her orphan boy" has been hanged for murder.

In 1829, young Poe had written to John Neal in language that may help explain his remarkable praise for this minor Dickens tale:

I am young – not yet twenty – *am* a poet ... I appeal to you as a man that loves the same beauty which I adore ... It cannot ... be said that

> "I left a calling for this idle trade,
> A duty broke – a father disobeyed" –

for I have no father – nor mother.[31]

The desperate mother in "The Black Veil" spoke to his personal condition; the praise Poe bestowed on "The Black Veil" may serve to clarify Poe's depiction of the desperate son in "William Wilson."

William Wilson establishes his vast superiority over his schoolmates in a vain attempt to prove to himself that he exists; he convinces them but he cannot convince himself. He can convince himself of his own authenticity only by creating a second self who will test him – and destroy him; William Wilson's double is his imp of the perverse. But unlike other Poe tales in this vein, this one is a "strangely pathetic and richly imaginative production, replete with the loftiest tragic power" because of the consummate artistry with which Poe makes use of his sources and his English childhood to create a portrait of existential despair that speaks to us all.

Sketches by Boz: visits with Boz

Poe praised Dickens' "The Black Veil" and other short psychological case-studies because these resembled his own similar pieces. The dark tales incorporated into the *Pickwick Papers* suggest that, if not for its bright and pervasive humor, the gloom might have spread and made Dickens a fellow explorer with Poe of the haunted and tormented regions of the mind.[32] The affinities between Dickens and Poe are clarified by a closer examination of "The Black Veil" and several other *Sketches by Boz*; and of "A Madman's MS." (in *Pickwick*, chapter 11) – all greatly admired by Poe.

The young physician in "The Black Veil" is our observer from whose point of view all the events take place – though he is not (as in Dickens' "A Madman's MS." and many Poe tales) the narrator. A singularly tall woman dressed in mourning, her face shrouded by a thick black veil, makes her unexpected approach to his office with an urgent, ambiguous request. Her voice is low and deep and she breaks down several times as she pleads with the young doctor to give medical assistance to someone close to her who desperately needs it. When the physician offers immediate assistance, she refuses. She insists that he must call at nine o'clock the following morning at her lodgings. When asked whether she could offer the patient treatment through the night if he provided her with instructions, the woman weeps bitterly and tells him it is impossible.

The remainder of the story portrays the mounting fear and suspicion of the physician as he travels through a desolate and dangerous-looking neighborhood in search of the mysterious woman and the patient. He finds her house and, after strange delays and significant sounds (an approaching carriage, a body being carried to a room above), the woman with the black veil suddenly appears and silently motions him to follow her. "The singular height of her form, coupled with the circumstance of her not speaking, caused the idea to pass across his brain, for an instant, that it might be a man disguised in woman's attire."[33] Almost immediately, his suspicions are dispelled by her convulsive weeping; she leads him to the patient: he finds a man who is unmistakably dead. She pleads wildly with the doctor to revive the corpse – and he then discovers the marks of the rope on the young man's throat. It is the veiled woman's son, executed that very morning.

An important dimension of the story is the way in which appearances alternately arouse the young physician's compassion for the suffering woman and suspicion that she may be an agent in some dark scheme to entrap him. (In this, the physician's mental state resembles that of Captain Delano in Melville's "Benito Cereno.") The concluding paragraph of Dickens' tale depicts the redemptive influence of the young physician's continuing ministrations on behalf of the bereaved, demented mother. Just before she dies, a "transient gleam" of sanity returns and she utters a prayer for his welfare. "That prayer flew to Heaven, and was heard" – but amid all the honors and rewards that the physician received over many years, "he can have no reminiscence more gratifying to his heart than that connected with the Black Veil." (Here Dickens is closer to Hawthorne than to Poe.)

"The Black Veil" elicited the highest praise from Poe in 1844 ("one of the most forcible things ever written"), long years after he had first read and written about it; in one of his earliest criticisms, an 1836 review of *Sketches by Boz*, Poe had singled out this tale as "distinct in character from all the rest – an act of stirring tragedy, and evincing lofty powers in the writer." Dickens' humor was also praised and quoted in this early review ("The Dancing Academy" and "A Passage in the Life of Watkins Tottle" are given special mention), but there seems evident a lack of enthusiasm ("Broad humor"; "a vivid sketch of Cockney low life") in Poe's response to this important aspect of Dickens' art. Again, it is another of Dickens' early but masterful studies in pathos, "The Pawnbroker's Shop," that elicts Poe's most intense admiration. In this sketch, Dickens depicts, with great verisimilitude, first the shop and shopkeeper and then a ludicrous and pathetic succession of customers, closing with a poignant scene involving "a young delicate girl of about twenty" and a young prostitute of about the same age. The poignancy and pathos of "The Pawnbroker's Shop" would seem to set it apart from Poe – but he is enthusiastic about its unity of effect:

In the sketch of the Englishman [Dickens' tale is being compared to a similar but miscellaneous account in W. L. Stone's *Ups and*

Downs of a Distressed Gentleman] we have no anecdotes at all – the *Pawnbroker's Shop* engages and enchains our attention – we are enveloped in its atmosphere of wretchedness and extortion – we pause at every sentence, not to dwell upon the sentence, but to obtain a fuller view of the gradually perfecting picture – . . . and when our eyes are taken from the canvass, we remember the personages of the sketch not at all as independent existences, but as essentials of the one subject we have witnessed – as a part and portion of the *Pawnbroker's Shop*.

Poe concludes with the observation that comparing the efforts of W. L. Stone to Dickens' would be like comparing "the scratchings of a schoolboy with a slate pencil on a slate . . . to the groupings of Buonarotti" (ix, 45–8).

Several months after reviewing *Sketches by Boz*, Poe prefaced a notice of the *Pickwick Papers* with a reference to his "high opinion of the comic power, and of the rich imaginative conception of Mr. Dickens – an opinion which the 'Pickwick Club' has fully sustained" (ix, 205). Poe's brief review, in the *Southern Literary Messenger* of November 1836, is given over almost entirely to a lengthy excerpt from one of the dark tales in *Pickwick* – "a vigorous sketch, entitled 'A Madman's MS.'"

"A Madman's MS." is an important source for Poe's "Ligeia," (1838).[34] Both tales convey a madman's compulsive-obsessive thoughts dwelling on the murder of a wife – openly in Dickens, much more subtly in Poe. The madman in *Pickwick* almost literally frightens his wife to death; Poe's narrator, obsessed by the dark Ligeia, poisons the fair Rowena. B. F. Fisher suggests that: "Contemporaneous readers would have found in 'Ligeia,' as in 'A Madman's MS.,' another of the *Blackwood's* sort of terror tales"; Poe's tale, however, represents in its subtle shadings "a sophisticated outdistancing of his model."

In his review of *The Old Curiosity Shop* and *Master Humphrey's Clock*, Poe comments on the two misleading title pages and the fact that what is presented is a single, loosely-constructed, poorly-penned work. Among the preliminary tales Poe has high praise for the "Confession Found in a Prison in the Time of Charles the Second" as "a paper of remarkable power" and original conception (x, 142–8). Dickens' "Confession" is indeed a penetrating study in madness and murder – especially horrible

since the victim is an innocent child. Told by the murderer on
the eve of his execution, it deals with the obsessive violence
that builds in the narrator under what seems the knowing and
accusing eye of the boy–victim, his nephew and foster-son.
This powerful sketch is transformed by Poe into a small
masterpiece, "The Tell-Tale Heart" (1843). In Poe's version the
accusing eye of the boy becomes an old man's eye, "the eye of a
vulture – a pale blue eye, with a film over it." In Dickens' tale,
the murderer places his chair over the grave of his victim –
until bloodhounds melodramatically bound in to nose out and
howl their discovery; in "The Tell-Tale Heart" the pressure
builds in the narrator until he can stand it no longer – until he
must point to where his victim is hidden and reveal himself to
the unsuspecting investigators.[35] Poe's high praise for "Confession Found in a Prison" is restrained by comparison to the
admiration he conveys (in the rest of his review) for Dickens'
achievement in *The Old Curiosity Shop*. He finds numerous
imperfections in the book – but he also finds a "chaste, vigorous,
and glorious *imagination* . . . which alone would suffice to
compensate for a world more of error than Mr. Dickens ever
committed." Poe highly valued originality and found in *The Old
Curiosity Shop* "more *originality* in every point, but in character
especially, than in any single work within our knowledge."
Exaggeration is an essential feature in the representation of
truth, and he defends Dickens against the charge that his
characters are caricatures. A defect in many of Dickens'
characters, however, is that he has allowed "the overflowing
kindness of his own bosom to mislead him in a very important
point of art, when he endows so many of his *dramatis personae*
with a warmth of feeling so very rare in reality." Poe found the
death of little Nell handled in such a way as to make it "excessively painful," but the "concluding scenes are so drawn that
human language, urged by human thought, could go no farther
in the excitement of human feelings." A passage from Poe's
review, comparing Dickens' art with that of Edward Bulwer
establishes Poe (in May 1841) as Dickens' most perceptive
American critic and champion:

The Art of Mr. Dickens, although elaborate and great, seems only
a happy modification of nature. In this respect he differs remarkably
from the author of "Night and Morning." The latter, by excessive

care and patient reflection, aided by much rhetorical knowledge and general information, has arrived at the capability of producing books which might be mistaken by ninety-nine readers out of a hundred for the genuine inspiration of genius. The former, by the promptings of the truest genius itself, has been brought to compose, and evidently without effort, works which have effected a long-sought consummation, which have rendered him the idol of the people, while defying and enchanting the critics. Mr. Bulwer, through art, has almost created a genius. Mr. Dickens, through genius, has perfected a standard from which Art itself will derive its essence, its rules. (x, 149–55)

In half a dozen years, half a dozen books – *Sketches by Boz, Pickwick Papers, Oliver Twist, Nicholas Nickleby, The Old Curiosity Shop* and *Barnaby Rudge* – had conquered both England and America. "I am still haunted by visions of America, night and day," Dickens wrote to John Forster on September 13, 1841; on the following day, he informed another friend: "Washington Irving writes me that if I went, it would be such a triumph from one end of the States to the other, as was never known in any Nation."[36]

Dickens' 1842 visit to America was indeed a triumphal one – with some ominous rumblings. When Dickens' tour reached Philadelphia, Poe sought out the British lion for two extended interviews.[37] Poe had paved the way by asking for a meeting – and enclosing his reviews of *Old Curiosity Shop* and *Barnaby Rudge*; and he had also sent the two volumes of his *Tales of the Grotesque and Arabesque* (1840). Poe's letter has not survived but Dickens' response, dated March 6 from the United States Hotel in Philadelphia, was friendly and encouraging.

During their meetings, the two writers discussed many topics – including the need for an international copyright law and the state of American letters. In the course of one of their discussions, it seems that Poe read Emerson's "The Humble Bee" to Dickens. And a later letter sent from London by the British writer makes it clear that Poe asked Dickens' help in placing his book of tales with an English publisher. Several months after his return to London, Dickens wrote to Poe expressing regret about his inability to interest a publisher in Poe's tales. "And the only consolation I can give you," Dickens added, "is that I do not believe any collection of detached pieces by an unknown writer, even though he were an Englishman, would be at all likely to find a publisher in this metropolis just now."

That Dickens' vain attempt to find a British publisher for Poe was not a perfunctory gesture is made clear by a letter he wrote to an Irish friend in 1862 indicating that he has never succeeded in persuading a publisher to bring out a book on his recommendation. To the best of his recollection, "the last trial I made in this wise, was in behalf of Mr. Edgar Poe, then only known in the United States." His effort has failed and he did not try again; at least ten years passed before Poe's tales were published in England "by another bookseller."[38] Dickens' genuine feeling for Poe is also attested to by the fact that, in 1868, during Dickens' second visit to America, the British writer sent $1,000 to Mrs Maria Clemm, Poe's mother-in-law, to ease her impoverished circumstances.[39]

There was a painful aftermath for Poe in his association with Dickens – but it is one that sheds valuable light on the American writer's critical integrity and his unswerving belief in Dickens' genius. In the *Foreign Quarterly Review* of January 1844 appeared a lengthy anonymous review–essay on American poetry that Poe was convinced *must* have been written by Dickens. "It has been denied that Dickens wrote it – but, to me, the article affords so strong internal evidence of his hand that I would as soon think of doubting my existence," wrote Poe to Lowell on March 30, 1844. Most troublesome to Poe was Dickens' accusation that his poems were a "metrical imitation" of Tennyson. In the same letter, Poe mentions the great need for an American journal to advance, as its central aims, "Independence, Truth, Originality"; an insistence on originality was a recurrent note in his critical writings and to have Dickens (as he believed the author to be) accuse him of imitation must have been especially aggravating. Two months later, in response to Lowell's suggestion that the author was not Dickens but a friend of his named Forster, Poe repeated his conviction that Dickens had been "either author, or dictator," of the troublesome review. "Nearly every thing in the critique, I heard from him [Dickens] or suggested to him, personally. The poem of Emerson I read to him," Poe informed Lowell.

The extensive quotation in the offending review–essay from Emerson's "The Humble Bee" (almost half of the 63-line poem) – the only Emerson poem mentioned by title or quoted (among the five included in the Griswold anthology under review) – makes Poe's certainty about the authorship of the piece understandable, especially so if it was the only Emerson poem he (Poe) read to Dickens in Philadelphia; and there were, apparently, other internal evidences that Poe did not specify. But Dickens was not the author of the review after all; Lowell was right in attributing it to John Forster, Dickens' intimate friend and confidant. Forster had seen Dickens off on his departure for America from Liverpool and wept with joy on his return. It is possible that Forster's view of Poe as an imitator of Tennyson was shared by Dickens; and, though he was scarcely the "dictator" of the piece (as Poe suspected), Dickens may well (as Lowell suggested) have "given him [Forster] hints" for the article.[40]

It is a measure of Poe's critical integrity that – whatever disappointment he may have felt in the man for his part in a public disparagement of Poe's originality as a poet – he continued to give the highest praise to Dickens' literary artistry. In December of 1844 – at the end of the same year in which the *Foreign Quarterly* essay appeared and Poe expressed his strong belief that Dickens was its author or "dictator" – Poe took occasion once again to compare Bulwer and Dickens. As he had done in 1841, Poe praised Dickens' superior genius in emphatic and unmistakable language:

Dickens is a man of higher *genius* than Bulwer. The latter is thoughtful, industrious, patient, pains-taking, educated, analytic, artistical (using the three last epithets with much mental reserve); and therefore will write the better book upon the whole – but the former rises, at times, to an unpremeditated elevation altogether beyond the flight, and even beyond the appreciation of his contemporary. Dickens, with care and culture, *might* have produced "The Last of the Barons," but nothing short of mortal Voltaism could have spirited Bulwer into the conception of the concluding passages of the "Curiosity Shop." (XVI, 61)

Poe's consistently high assessments of Dickens' artistry before and after his meetings with Dickens in Philadelphia open up new approaches to a better understanding of Poe and Poe's fiction. His own darker view of mankind and man's condition led him to see a defect in what he believed to be Dickens' excessively rosy view of "the overflowing kindness" that prevails among men. But the great enthusiasm that Poe displayed for Dickens' poignant scenes and characters suggests that his own corrosive explorations of self-destructiveness may be significantly linked to Dickens' world and art – and may be better understood in the light of that connection.

In the American Grain

According to Vernon Louis Parrington, "the problem of Poe, fascinating as it is, lies quite outside the main current of American thought, and it may be left with the psychologist and belletrist with whom it belongs."[41] As a result, Parrington gives to Poe little over two pages in his massive *Main Currents of American Thought* (1926–30). Parrington's view was the prevailing one prior to World War II; it was strongly reinforced by F. O. Mathiessen's decision to omit Poe from his pantheon of great American writers (in his brilliant and influential *American Renaissance* [1941]) because, according to Matthiessen, Poe was hostile to democracy and wrote tales lacking the moral depth of Hawthorne and Melville.[42] But there were other voices and other views.

In 1923, William Carlos Williams described Poe's topics as "Typically American – accurately, even inevitably set in his time." Two years later, Williams published his eighth book – the first for which he was able to find a commercial publisher. His purpose in writing and arranging the twenty essays on American history that he titled *In the American Grain* was, he recalls in his *Autobiography*, "to try to find out for myself what the land of my more or less accidental birth might signify."[43] Linda Welshimer Wagner has argued persuasively that the *Grain* essays were not, as is commonly believed, a response to D. H. Lawrence's studies in American literature; on the contrary, they are a refutation of the despair conveyed by T. S. Eliot's dramatic questions in *The Waste Land*. In a series of prose-poetic essays, Williams presents vignettes of early explorers and their approaches to America; episodes dramatizing the conflicts between "loving men and hating Pilgrims"; sketches of historical figures (Washington, Hamilton, Franklin,

Lincoln); and historical topics (on historiography, on the advent of the slaves). In all these essays, Williams substitutes for "history" or "fact" a "masterful synthesis of the spirit of America" in which there is both "brutal desolation" and a promise of a "flowering." Daniel Boone is presented as a vital force, "a great voluptuary" working "against the niggardliness of the damning puritanical tradition." Franklin's "small, hard" wisdom is contrasted unfavorably with the spirited pride and self-effacement of John Paul Jones.

In the original plan for *In the American Grain*, the next-to-last essay (on Sam Houston) closes with Williams' pronouncement that "we must go back to the beginning; it must all be done over; everything that is must be destroyed." He planned to conclude his book with an essay on Edgar Allan Poe – but yielded to his publisher's insistence that he close with something about Lincoln (an eloquent, one-page tribute). "Raleigh, Columbus, Boone, Jones, Lincoln – Williams [says Wagner] sees them all in this perspective: chosen, in spite of themselves, yet repressed, even murdered, by the very men they care for." In Williams' view, Poe belongs alongside these heroic figures.

Poe is the only writer in Williams' book – the one who speaks directly for his own beliefs as "a new De Soto," as one who "gives the sense for the first time in America, that literature is *serious*, not a matter of courtesy but of truth."[44] According to Williams, Poe is *the* representative American writer – more American than Fenimore Cooper in his avoidance of the easy, attractive subjects (e.g. Indians and forests), in his fashioning a style that sprang from "the local conditions, not of trees and mountains, but of the 'soul' . . . " Williams pictures Poe as a monomaniacal, literary Ahab whose fury is directed against the unoriginal, "the copied, the slavish, the FALSE literature about him." In no sense, insists Williams, is Poe "the bizarre, isolate writer"; on the contrary, "there is a sense of him *surrounded* by his time, tearing at it, ever with more rancor, but always at battle, taking hold."

Williams' view of Poe as a truly American writer – as one deeply engaged in the literary controversies of his time – has been amply documented in recent decades by the researches of Perry Miller, Sidney P. Moss, Robert D. Jacobs and Michael Allen – among others. There is a need, however, to clarify Poe's place in the movement that many of the writers of his time believed to be of central importance: the campaign for a national literature. Poe has been variously pictured as aristocratically hostile or opportunistically "flexible." He was, in fact, basically consistent and his vision of an authentic and independent American literature helps us better understand his contribution to that literature.

Poe's 1845 commentary on "the necessity of maintaining a proper *nationality* in American Letters" deserves our special attention because it reveals an important side of Poe that has largely been overlooked or misunderstood.[45] After dismissing as political rather than literary the idea that an American should stick to "American" themes (an idea developed at length in "Exordium"), Poe warms to his task of calling for a "nationality which defends our own literature, sustains our own men of letters, upholds our own dignity, and depends upon our own resources." There follows an impassioned attack on American subserviency to British critical opinion:

Is it too much to say that, with us, the opinion of Washington Irving – of Prescott – of Bryant – is a mere nullity in comparison with that of any anonymous sub-sub-editor of The Spectator, The Athenaeum or the "London Punch"? It is *not* saying too much, to say this. It is a solemn – an absolutely awful fact. Every publisher in the country will admit it to be a fact. There is not a more disgusting spectacle under the sun than our subserviency to British criticism. It is disgusting, first, because it is truckling, servile, pusillanimous – secondly, because of its gross irrationality. We *know* the British to bear us little but ill-will; we know that in the few instances in which our writers have been treated with common decency in England, these writers have either openly paid homage to English institutions, or have had lurking at the bottom of their hearts a secret principle at war with Democracy: – we *know* all this, and yet, day after day, submit our necks to the degrading yoke of the crudest opinion that emanates from the fatherland. Now if we *must* have nationality, let it be a nationality that will throw off this yoke.

Poe continues with a devastating assault on John Wilson ("Christopher North") of *Blackwood's*, "the man whose simple *dictum* (to our shame be it spoken) has the power to make or to mar any American reputation!"

These sentiments are rarely so passionately expressed elsewhere but they are not inconsistent with other critical pronouncements, early and late. One of Poe's earliest reviews (of
Robert Montgomery Bird's novel, *Calavar*) opens with Sydney
Smith's old taunt – "Who reads an American book?" – and
proceeds with the suggestion that if Sir Walter Scott were still
living he would have to admit that *Calavar* "was vastly superior
to some five or six of the last litter of his own great genius."[46]
Toward the end of his life, Poe's high praise for John Neal was
couched in terms that make clear his (Poe's) concern for our
emerging national literature; he expresses the hope that Neal
will "even yet . . . do something for the literature of the
country which the country 'will not willingly,' and cannot
possibly, 'let die'" (xvi, 46).

Almost equally revealing was Poe's association with another
ardent literary nationalist, James Kirke Paulding. In a letter to
the publisher of the *Southern Literary Messenger* written during
Poe's editorship, Paulding declared that: "Your Publication is
decidedly superior to any Periodical in the United States and
Mr. Poe is decidedly the best of all our going writers."[47]
Paulding served as a friendly intermediary in a vain attempt to
have Poe's first collection of tales brought out by Harper and
Brothers. On this occasion, the elder statesman of the American
literary revolution conveyed some advice (through T. W.
White) to young Poe:

I hope Mr. Poe will pardon me if the interest I feel in his success
should prompt me to take this occasion to suggest to him to apply
his fine humour, and his extensive acquirements, to more familiar
subjects of satire; to the faults and foibles of our own people, their
peculiarities of habits and manners, and above all to the ridiculous
affectations and extravagancies of the fashionable English Literature of the day which we copy with such admirable success and
servility. His quiz on Willis, and the Burlesque of "Blackwood,"
were not only capital, but what is more, were understood by all.
For Satire to be relished, it is necessary that it should be leveled at
something with which readers are familiar.

In a postscript, Paulding applauded the "talent, originality, and
independence" of the most recent number (February 1836) of
the *Southern Literary Messenger* and singled out Poe's review of
Paul Ulric for special praise.[48]

Morris Matson's novel had been castigated by Poe as "despicable in every respect," as typical of "the works which daily bring discredit on our national literature. We have no right to complain of being laughed at abroad when so villainous a compound . . . of incongruous folly, plagiarism, immorality, inanity, and bombast, can command at any moment both a puff and a publisher" (VII, 205). Poe's blast at this long-forgotten writer and novel is revealing in separating Poe from those literary nationalists who were uncritically and indiscriminately trumpeting the praise of inferior American works solely because they were *American*. For such an insistence on critical standards, Poe earned Paulding's praise and reflected the point of view of his mentor, John Neal, who had announced in the opening installment of his series on "American Writers" (in *Blackwood's Magazine* of September 1824) that "if we would not over-cuddle the young American writers; kill them with kindness; turn their heads with our trumpeting, or produce a fatal revulsion in the popular mind, let us never make a prodigious fuss about any American book, which if it were English, would produce little or no sensation."[49]

A closer look at Paulding's praise of Poe, however, suggests the ways in which Poe stood apart from this elder statesman of American letters who admired and tried to help him. In his friendly advice to Poe, Paulding had urged "more familiar subjects of satire." Earlier in his letter, he had conveyed (with apparent approval) the complaint of Harper and Brothers that Poe's tales suffered from "a degree of obscurity . . . which will prevent ordinary readers from comprehending their drift"; and he transmitted the Harpers' assurances that if Mr Poe "will lower himself a little to the ordinary comprehension of the generality of readers . . . they will make such arrangements with him as will be liberal and satisfactory."[50] Paulding saw neither contradiction nor irony in his asking Poe to lower his sights to gain a publisher while, at the same time, praising Poe's critical blast at a bad book able to "command at any moment a puff or a publisher."

Poe understood his dilemma very well and continued to the end of his life in his own self-destructive and indestructible way. A reviewer of his *Tales* in the London *Critic* sensed something peculiarly American in Poe's method: "He has learnt from the dwellers in the American woods a marked acuteness, which he has dealed out again to his readers in the Tales before us." To the details of horrors and cruelties in the stories, however, the reviewer objects for there are already enough of these in the newspapers and "they form no part of the glories of literature."[51] Another British critic, Martin Tupper, praised Poe's "microscopic power of analysis" in much the same terms (Poe is compared to a Blackfoot or Ojibway on the trail) – and also deplored his "specification of [horrible] instances," such as those presented in "The Black Cat," as "impossible and revolting."[52] It remained for a *Blackwood's* reviewer, William Henry Smith, to sum up the mingled feelings of admiration and distaste that greeted Poe's tales on both sides of the Atlantic. "Commonplace is the last epithet that can be applied to them," Smith observes – and proceeds to call the tales "strange – powerful – more strange than pleasing, and powerful productions without rising to the rank of genius."[53] "The Man of the Crowd," Poe's extraordinary Doppelgänger story set in London, is singled out for lengthy summary; but the reviewer substitutes for any critical insights into the sources of its power some observations on its inaccuracy about London topography ("We are led to notice it chiefly from a feeling of surprise, that one so partial to detail should not have more frequently profited from the help which a common guide-book, with its map, might have given him") and its implausibility concerning the "pedestrian powers" of the old man who wanders the streets and the convalescent narrator who vigilantly stalks his trail.

In the decades following Poe's death, a few voices – most notably Baudelaire and Dostoevsky – took the measure of Poe's greatness. In this century, William Carlos Williams has led the way in reassessing Poe and restoring him to his native land; the concluding sentence of Richard Wilbur's brilliant lecture, "The House of Poe," may help to explain the continuing vitality of "his prose allegories of psychic conflict" in our time: "Poe's mind may have been a strange one; yet all minds are alike in their general structure; therefore we can understand him, and I think that he will have something to say to us as long as there is civil war in the palaces of men's minds."[54]

6

Hawthorne and Our Old Home

A dark time:
an overture to "Blackwood's": a new beginning

The last days of July 1849 were the bitterest in Nathaniel Hawthorne's life. He wrote copiously in his journal, perhaps to relieve an otherwise intolerable strain. For the most part, Hawthorne's notebooks served "as an artist's sketchbook and not as a diary of private emotion."[1] But the entries of those long summer days and troubled nights are among the most personal expressions of feeling that Hawthorne ever committed to paper.

His mother was dying and the end was near. On Sunday, July 29 ("A beautiful fresh summer morning"), Hawthorne began a long account filled with detailed descriptions of little Una and Julian at play – their bright liveliness contrasting with the grim drama being enacted in his mother's room. At five o'clock in the afternoon, he went to the dying woman and was shocked by her altered appearance. He loved his mother, but there had been, "ever since my boyhood, a sort of coldness of intercourse between us, such as is apt to come between persons of strong feelings, if they are not managed rightly." She recognized him, murmured a few indistinct words – and he found the tears welling up, "till, for a few moments I shook with sobs. For a long time, I knelt there, holding her hand; and surely it is the darkest hour I ever lived" (VII, 423–9).[2] Out of the bitter spectacle of his mother's suffering and death came the handclasp and tears that reunited them in her closing hours and released in him a new faith in eternal life. Out of that long summer came the strength and determination "to work as if the devil were in me, if it were only to put my enemies to the blush."[3]

Added to the grief of that terrible summer was the distress and humiliation occasioned by his political enemies, the Whigs of Salem – who saw to it not only that he was turned out of his post as Surveyor but that he was kept out by accusations of fraud and corruption. (Hawthorne got his revenge in the introductory Custom House chapter of *The Scarlet Letter* and in the slyly contemptuous Preface to the second edition, dated March 30, 1850; two weeks later Hawthorne "bid farewell forever to this abominable city" of Salem.)[4]

Hawthorne had secured the surveyorship of the Custom House in considerable part through the intervention of his lifelong and closest friend Horatio Bridge. A decade earlier, Bridge had made possible the publication of *Twice-Told Tales* by a financial subsidy (kept secret from Hawthorne). At the height of the furor – just four days after Hawthorne received his notice of dismissal – Bridge wrote to John Jay seeking employment for the author as a contributor to *Blackwood's Magazine*. Jay, a New York lawyer, had been engaged to protect the journal from the piratical practices of a New York publisher. References to Jay's engagement had appeared in *Blackwood's* for January 1848; and both Bridge and Hawthorne must have also read (in the same number which featured an extended commentary on Poe, Hawthorne and other American writers) an impassioned diatribe on "American Copyright" and the sad plight of American authorship ("it is safe to say, that under present circumstances there will be no more Irvings and Coopers").[5]

Blackwood's loomed largest among the numerous British periodicals Hawthorne read assiduously during his formative years as a writer: during the year 1827 alone he borrowed from the Salem Athenaeum all the early volumes of *Maga* – the same volumes that Poe studied so attentively.[6] It is likely that he read John Neal's "American Writers" series in *Blackwood's*, for those articles appeared in the volumes he borrowed; the same ironic tone and exuberant irreverence that drew Neal to *Blackwood's* help to explain its appeal to the quieter, more reserved Hawthorne – and also clarify the great fascination that Neal's writings had for young Hawthorne. And it contributes to our better understanding of the admiration expressed by Poe (also an admirer of Neal) for the tales of Hawthorne.

"His was a divided mind," wrote Randall Stewart about Hawthorne's lifelong reactions to England.[7] Born only two

decades after the close of the Revolutionary War, Hawthorne
was eleven years old at the time of Jackson's great victory over
the British at New Orleans. Forty years later, observing some
American flags captured during that same war and on display
in the chapel of Chelsea Hospital, Hawthorne was comforted by
the fact that they were tattered and almost unidentifiable ("the
moths do us a good office with these dishonored flags").[8]
Hawthorne's patriotism, observes Stewart, "was bound up
inextricably with a traditional and deep-seated feeling of enmity
toward England."[9] These feelings were accompanied by others
in direct conflict; a brief sentence in the opening chapter of *Our
Old Home* forcefully conveys Hawthorne's divided mind and
heart: "After all these bloody wars and vindictive animosities,
we have still an unspeakable yearning toward England" (v, 18).
An integral part of that yearning was the profound admiration
he felt for the great English writers – for Shakespeare, Scott,
Burns, Pope, Defoe, Goldsmith, Addison, Johnson, among
others. "How proud you would feel to see my work praised by
the reviewers as equal to the proudest productions of the
Scribbling Sons of John Bull," the seventeen-year-old Hawthorne had written to his mother in the spring of 1821;[10] in
June of 1849, the 45-year-old Hawthorne retained a goodly
measure of that feeling.

Hawthorne's involvement with *Blackwood's* was a manifestation of his divided mind at a turning-point in his literary
career. Horatio Bridge must have sensed the conflict in his
friend before making his approach; the shabby way in which
Hawthorne had been dismissed from his Custom House post
must have intensified the writer's disillusion with American
philistinism and corruption – with his native country and his
native town. All this Bridge must have known when he wrote
to John Jay, American representative of *Blackwood's*, on behalf
of the author of *Twice-Told Tales* and *Mosses from an Old Manse*.

Nothing ever came of Bridge's attempt to interest *Blackwood's*
in Hawthorne as a contributor. But, though the surviving
record is scanty, it is possible to reconstruct what happened
with considerable confidence. Jay's reply to Bridge has not
survived, but he summarized its contents in the covering letter
he wrote to Robert Blackwood when he forwarded Bridge's
communication to the publisher.

I wrote to Mr. Bridge [Jay informed Blackwood] . . . that he had better advise Hawthorne to send you one or two articles written expressly for Maga from which you could judge better than from his books how you would like him as a correspondent as I greatly doubted whether you would consent to engage him in advance as a permanent contributor.[11]

This is, at best, a lukewarm invitation to a great American author – one consistent with the lukewarm praise given half a year earlier to *Mosses from an Old Manse* by a *Blackwood's* reviewer. We do not know whether Bridge transmitted Jay's unenthusiastic proposal to Hawthorne. He may have done so, for it offered at least a prospect of financial relief to his beleaguered friend. This small encounter with *Blackwood's* takes on importance because it may well have added impetus to Hawthorne's production, in the fall and winter of 1849–50, of an American classic entitled *The Scarlet Letter* – to be followed in short order by *The House of the Seven Gables* and *The Blithedale Romance*. It was a new beginning.

These three great works represented the kind of unfolding that Melville, while nearing the completion of *Moby-Dick*, described to Hawthorne with passionate eloquence: "But I feel that I am now come to the inmost leaf of the bulb, and that shortly the flower must fall to the mould."[12] For Hawthorne, such a flowering involved a long period of extraordinary storytelling – and a sudden great unfolding after the fateful summer of 1849. A great revelatory work, *The Blithedale Romance*, was Hawthorne's inmost leaf.

The Master Genius of American literature: toward "Blithedale"

At Bowdoin College, in the fall of 1824, young Hawthorne and his classmate Longfellow came under the spell of a new professor of mental and moral philosophy (also a poet), Thomas C. Upham. One of Longfellow's favorite books, acquired a year before he entered Bowdoin, was Upham's *American Sketches* (1819), a collection of poems on native scenes and historical subjects. In his preface, Upham suggested that stories about the first settlers, the frontier villages and the Indians, provided "enchanting topics" to the tale-writer and poet; and in another part of the preface he had added his voice to those yearning for a national literature: "If then other countries almost universally cultivate in a greater or less degree the arts of song, and contrive to encircle with a sort of local enchantment their mountains, waters, and windshaken woods . . . shall not our native country listen to a single 'witchnote' in the commemoration of its glories?"[13]

Upham's vision of a great new national literature was, of course, very much in the air and his views were a reflection of, as much as a possible influence on, the fervent nationalism of Longfellow's graduation address, "Native Writers"; in it he expressed rejoicing "in the hope and sublimity in our national literature, for no people are richer than we are in the treasures of nature."[14] Hawthorne's advocacy of a native literature was less strident and more deeply rooted. Shortly after his graduation from Bowdoin he completed a group of stories titled "Seven Tales of my Native Land." His sister Elizabeth read them in manuscript and found them "very striking"; but after submitting his collection in vain to the booksellers (and being told "that no American publisher will meddle with an American work"), Hawthorne burned his manuscripts.[15]

But despite these profound discouragements, he had chosen his vocation. The ironic tone and mode of "A Select Party" (1844) does not disguise the sense of mission and underlying earnestness of this extended portrait of a young man (who bears a resemblance to the young Hawthorne in more ways than one) – the "Master Genius" of our emerging American literature:

But now appeared a stranger, whom the host had no sooner recognized, than, with an abundance of courtesy unlavished on any other, he hastened down the whole length of the saloon, in order to pay him emphatic honor. Yet he was a young man in poor attire, with no insignia of rank or acknowledged eminence, nor anything to distinguish him among the crowd except a high, white forehead, beneath which a pair of deep-set eyes were glowing with warm light. It was such a light as never illuminates the earth, save when a great heart burns as the household fire of a grand intellect. And who was he? Who, but the Master Genius, for whom our country is looking anxiously into the mist of time, as destined to fulfil the great mission of creating an American literature, hewing it, as it were, out of the unwrought granite of our intellectual quarries. From him, whether moulded in the form of an epic poem, or assuming a guise altogether new, as the spirit itself may determine, we are to receive our first great original work, which shall do all that remains to be achieved for our glory among the nations. How this child of a mighty destiny had been discovered by the Man of Fancy, it is of little consequence to mention. Suffice it, that he dwells as yet unhonored among men, unrecognized by those who have known him from his cradle; – the noble countenance, which should be distinguished by a halo diffused around it, passes daily amid the throng of people, toiling and troubling themselves about the trifles of a moment – and none pay reverence to the worker of immortality. Nor does it matter much to him, in his triumph over all the ages, though a generation or two of his own times shall do themselves the wrong to disregard him. (x, 65–6)

True, the Master Genius receives his recognition from no one but the Man of Fancy during an entertainment at one of his castles in the air. But Hawthorne's awareness of the importance of American literature and of his own destined contribution to it of something "altogether new" – "our first great original work . . . for our glory among the nations" – is clearly evident despite the ironical touches that pervade the piece.

The ninety tales and sketches that Hawthorne produced before his sudden shift from tale-writing to the writing of *The Scarlet Letter* and other romances was, of course, a significant part of that contribution. In examining Hawthorne's conception of himself as a champion of America and American literature, it is useful to look closely at "My Kinsman, Major Molineux" (1832), a tale that is unique in the Hawthorne canon – and is also richly representative of Hawthorne's essential genius.

"My Kinsman, Major Molineux" (xi, 208–31) explores the bewildered heart and mind of a youth during a nightmarish initiation into the ways of the world – a monstrously cruel world. Young Robin, a country boy, has come to a New England town to seek the help of a relative, Major Molineux, an official loyal to the Crown during the troubled years just before the Revolution. One of his many strange, dreamlike encounters during his search is with a stranger with a painted face ("One side of the face blazed of an intense red, while the other was black as midnight") who tells Robin to: "Watch here an hour, and Major Molineux will pass by." Robin seats himself upon the steps of the church door for a long wait full of disturbing reveries. The sounds of a jubilant procession grow louder, windows open as inquiring neighbors peer out, and the sleepy street fills with a great stream of people led by a single horseman, the mysterious stranger with the painted face. Then the confused youth senses that he is more than just a spectator to these ominous proceedings: " 'The double-faced fellow has his eye upon me,' muttered Robin"; the leader halts the procession and the shouts and laughter die away: "Right before Robin's eyes was an uncovered cart . . . and there, in tar-and-feather dignity, sat his kinsman, Major Molineux!" He sits there, a proud man overwhelmed by the agony of his physical and spiritual humiliation ("But perhaps the bitterest pang of all was when his eyes met those of Robin"). A wave of laughter builds among the townspeople at the spectacle – and Robin finds himself involuntarily laughing with the others ("every man emptied his lungs, but Robin's shout was the loudest there").

A clearer understanding of the emotional intensity of "My Kinsman, Major Molineux" might well begin with Hawthorne's comment about the people of Salem in a letter to Horatio Bridge shortly after the publication of "The Custom House" and *The Scarlet Letter:*

I feel an infinite contempt for them – and probably have expressed more of it than I intended – for my preliminary chapter has caused the greatest uproar that has happened here since witch-times. If I escape from town without being tarred and feathered, I shall consider it good luck. I wish they would tar and feather me; it would be such an entirely novel kind of distinction for a literary man. And from such judges as my fellow-citizens, I should look upon it as a higher honor than a laurel crown.[16]

What Hawthorne experienced in Salem in 1849 was not unlike the fate he created for Major Molineux two decades earlier. Noteworthy in the tale is the sketchiness (less than a page) with which Hawthorne renders the animosity between the American colonists and the representatives of British rule. The emphasis is on Robin as naive witness of a terrible crime to which he becomes an accomplice. The decapitated ex-Surveyor and narrator of "The Custom House" is no young Robin: he describes his bureaucratic prison, its denizens and his own execution with amused detachment. But beneath the ironic stance is a deep feeling of outrage at the crime to which he (Hawthorne) has been subjected by the citizens of Salem – a feeling he clearly conveys in his letter to Bridge.

"My Kinsman, Major Molineux" was disinterred and given a place of honor as the final tale in Hawthorne's last collection of tales during the last months of the extraordinary three-year period in which he produced, in rapid succession between 1849 and 1852, his three great romances. In the fall of 1849, Hawthorne – liberated by the ordeal of his final break with his native town and his final separation from his mother – was free to write his ironic introductory chapter, "The Custom House" – as he called it, "an entrance-hall to the magnificent edifice which I throw open to my guests." The magnificent edifice itself, *The Scarlet Letter*, was completed with a rapidity that Sophia Hawthorne (in a letter to her mother) described as frightening. On Sunday, February 3, 1850, Hawthorne finished the book. That evening he read the concluding portion of it to Sophia. "It broke her heart," the author–husband informed his friend Bridge, "and it sent her to bed with a grievous headache, which I look upon as a triumphant success."[17]

But much more revealing than Sophia's intense response to her husband's reading was Hawthorne's own – a recollection recorded years later for reasons that are equally revealing. In 1855, in England, Hawthorne was moved by a comment about Thackeray to describe in his journal the way his reading from *The Scarlet Letter* to Sophia had stirred his own emotions. At a London dinner party, a friend of Thackeray reported that the last number of *The Newcomes* was "so touching that nobody can read it aloud without breaking down." With a characteristic ironical thrust, Hawthorne despatched Thackeray's susceptible friend: "I read all the numbers of the Newcomes to my wife, but happened not to have an opportunity to read this last, and was glad of it – knowing that my eyes would fill and my voice quiver." Then Hawthorne adds a comment about Thackeray's response to his own emotional scenes ("I cannot but wonder at his coolness in respect to his own pathos") – a humorous reference to a reading given by Thackeray in a cider cellar. But he is serious as he describes his own feelings:

When I read the last scene of the Scarlet Letter to my wife, just after writing it – tried to read it, rather, for my voice swelled and heaved as if I were being tossed up and down on an ocean, as it subsides after a storm. But I was in a very nervous state, then, having gone through a great diversity and severity of emotion, for many months past. I think I have never overcome my own adamant in any other instance.[18]

Hawthorne had erased from his memory the only other recorded instance of a loss of emotional control, one that took place during a time of "great diversity and severity of emotion" – at his dying mother's bedside.

That ardent and perceptive British admirer of Hawthorne, Anthony Trollope – whose realistic novels Hawthorne greatly envied and admired – paid tribute to *The Scarlet Letter* for probing so deeply and unsparingly "these black deeps of the human heart."[19] Trollope saw more clearly than most critics, American or British, an aspect of Hawthorne's art that is central: its searching irony. He did not use the term explicitly but clearly had it in mind when he described the relationship that is established between the narrator-persona and Hester: " . . . the author deals with her in a spirit of assumed hardness, almost as though he assented to the judgement and the manner in which it was carried out." And – though E. P. Whipple (among others), took note of "pathos and power . . . relieved by touches of that beautiful and peculiar humor"[20] – it was Trollope alone among Hawthorne's contemporaries who could confidently (and accurately) declare that "there is never a page written by Hawthorne not tinged by satire." And Trollope was also keenly responsive to "a vein of drollery" that runs through the somber narrative ("He is always laughing at something with his weird, mocking spirit").

Hawthorne's masterful irony reinforces the overwhelming impact of the dying Dimmesdale's public acknowledgment of Hester and Pearl. He had finally found, at the very end, the strength to act and speak in accordance with the truth. But after his death, there are "highly respectable witnesses" who believe the minister entirely innocent of the sins to which he had confessed, who regard his dying acts and words as a pious parable "to impress on his admirers the mighty and mournful lesson, that, in view of Infinite Purity, we are sinners all alike"

(1, 259). Dimmesdale's dying attempt to be true to himself, to his lover and child, to his congregation has, in a measure, failed – and this is, of course, supremely ironic. But Kierkegaard's observation that "the more irony is present, so much the more freely and poetically does the poet hover above his composition"[21] helps to explain why the minister's behavior illuminates rather than beclouds our understanding of Hawthorne's intention and achievement. "I love all men who *dive*," wrote Melville about Emerson and "the whole corps of thought-divers, that have been diving & coming up again with bloodshot eyes since the world began."[22] In *The Scarlet Letter* and the two romances that followed in rapid succession Hawthorne was both a "thought-diver" and a diver into his own soul.

In *The House of the Seven Gables* Hawthorne moved away from the past to the present – a present haunted by the past. In his treatment of the past in *The Scarlet Letter*, he had broken and flung away the old worn-out mold of historical novels and applied the "magic touch" to throng "with varied life what had been a barren waste."[23] Now, for the first time since his youthful novel *Fanshawe*, Hawthorne turned to his own time and to his own native town for a book-length narrative that he himself considered to be superior to *The Scarlet Letter* and "more characteristic" of his mind.[24] Trollope saw in *The House of the Seven Gables* an author "pouring out his scorn on the padded respectables of his New England world."[25] What made Hawthorne regard *The House* as closer to his own heart and mind, however, is not its shrewd satire but the fact that it represents, on a larger scale and with greater complexity than in the tales, a fresh attempt "to open an intercourse with the world." "I have made a captive of myself," wrote Hawthorne to Longfellow in 1838, "and put me into a dungeon, and now I cannot find the key to let myself out, – and if the door were open, I should be almost afraid to come out."[26] The price Hawthorne paid for his searching vision into the truths of the human heart was the sense of being an observer rather than a participant in the world of everyday experience. Clifford at the arched window observing the procession of life, unable to enter it ("For, what other dungeon is so dark as one's own heart! What jailor so inexorable as one's self!") is so vividly realized because Hawthorne knew and understood him very well. Clifford's weaknesses – even his self-centered inconsiderateness toward his loving sister – are both ludicrous and endearing because the underlying truth of the matter is always made clear to us: he has been a prison inmate for many years and, now that he is "free," is still a captive of himself.

Melville, in a passionately revelatory letter written during the closing stages of the writing of *Moby-Dick*, informed Hawthorne that he dated his life from his twenty-fifth year; if not for his more reserved nature, Hawthorne could have – less than a year later – conveyed similar sentiments to Melville (or, as a more likely confidant, to Bridge). "My Kinsman, Major Molineux" can be dated, roughly, from his twenty-fifth year; on May 2, 1852, the manuscript of *The Blithedale Romance* – Hawthorne's inmost leaf – was finished.

Though he found it possible to bestow some praise on *The House of the Seven Gables*, Trollope found it greatly inferior to *The Scarlet Letter*. And he apparently thought even less of *The Blithedale Romance*, for he passed over that novel completely in his 1879 tribute to Hawthorne's genius. But, according to another British commentator, Henry F. Chorley (in an *Athenaeum* review[27] that appeared shortly after *Blithedale*'s London publication), "Mr. Hawthorne's third tale . . . puts the seal on the reputation of its author as the highest, deepest, and finest imaginative writer whom America has yet produced." Chorley praises the author for capturing the spirit of reform in New England and translating these doctrinal concerns into human terms. Coverdale, Hollingsworth, Zenobia and Priscilla are "exceptional personages" but convey important truths about "human characteristics and feelings" that are "pregnant with universal emotion as well as with deep special meaning."

It is not accidental that Hawthorne uses a first-person point of view in *The Blithedale Romance* – a narrative device employed in many of his essayistic sketches but never in his tales and never in any other novel. It is a narrative method ideally suited to Hawthorne's purposes in conveying with the utmost subtlety and power the dark truth that Coverdale is even more desperate than the desperate and tragic Zenobia. "You tell me that you have met with troubles and changes," wrote Hawthorne to Longfellow in the same letter in which he describes himself as a self-made captive. "I know not what these may have been, but

I can assure you that trouble is the next best thing to enjoyment, and that there is no fate in this world so horrible as to have no share in either its joys and sorrows."[28] Hawthorne understood this well, and understood Coverdale's horrible fate; and he understood that Coverdale's final confession ("I – I myself – was in love – with – Priscilla!") is an ironic comment on Coverdale's inability to love and to live.

Chorley was not alone among the British critics in finding *The Blithedale Romance* the best of Hawthorne's novels. A reviewer for the *New Monthly Magazine* (London) called it "the highest and best of Mr. Hawthorne's works"; and *The Critic* praised Hawthorne's gift in *Blithedale* for laying bare "the most delicate anatomy of the human heart" and riveting "our attention, even while he pains us by the process, upon the links in the chain of thought and feeling that lie hidden in the innermost cells of the human breast, unseen by all without, and but half recognized, perhaps, by their possessor."[29] In contrast, E. P. Whipple was almost alone among American critics in praising *Blithedale* during Hawthorne's lifetime. Whipple described the novel as "the most perfect in execution of any of Hawthorne's works, and as a work of art, hardly equaled by anything else which the country has produced."[30]

Hawthorne felt deeply about this book and Whipple's high praise must have been a great encouragement; that very few other American critics found it possible to praise *Blithedale* and that only the British critics matched Whipple in their insight and enthusiasm were facts that must have contributed to Hawthorne's decision, when he was offered a consulship, to leave America for an extended stay in England. *Blithedale*, he informed Bridge in October of 1852, "has brought me – besides its American circulation – a thousand dollars from England; whence, likewise, have come many favorable notices." And in the next sentence he conveys to his closest friend his gratification for this British recognition: "Just at this time I rather think your friend stands foremost there as an American fiction-monger."[31]

Whipple praised Hawthorne for the skill and accuracy with which he recorded, in *Blithedale*: "The peculiarities of New England life at the present day"; and the British critic Chorley described *Blithedale* as "eminently an American book." "Hawthorne appalls, entices," wrote Emily Dickinson – an American poet akin to the novelist in her explorations of the truths of the heart and of the mysteries of existence.[32] By 1852, with the publication of *Blithedale*, Hawthorne was indeed the "Master Genius of American Literature."

"In a day or two I intend to commence a new romance," he announced to Bridge in the same letter in which he conveyed his pleasure over the British reception of *Blithedale*. This may be the same projected work Hawthorne wrote about in a letter to Ticknor and in his journal a few years later – a romance centering on the idea of an American's pilgrimage to his ancestral English home. His own pilgrimage began on July 6, 1853, when the Hawthornes sailed from Boston on the screw steamer *Niagara* and docked in Liverpool ten days later.[33]

Ancestral Footsteps

The Liverpool consulship absorbed most of Hawthorne's creative energies; always a conscientious civil servant, he was unable to do more in a literary way than record in his journal copious details concerning his impressions of England. In May 1855 his projected romance was still very much in his mind: "It is good," he wrote to Longfellow, "for the moral nature of an American to live in England among a more simple and natural people than ourselves. Ale is an excellent moral nutriment; so is English mutton; and perhaps the effect of both will be visible in my next Romance." ("They precisely suit my taste [Hawthorne declared about Trollope's novels in 1860]; solid and substantial, written on the strength of beef and through the inspiration of ale)."[34] For four years and more Hawthorne observed the sights and sounds of England as an avid sightseer and as an author gathering materials for his English romance. It was not until he had resigned his consulship and settled with his family in Italy that he could begin to write what was hardly more than a working outline.[35] The final result was no single completed work but four interrelated fragments (unpublished and in varying stages of incompleteness when he died): *The Ancestral Footstep, Doctor Grimshawe's Secret, Septimius Felton* and *The Dolliver Romance*. Despite their fragmentariness, these unfinished works contain passages, as Newton Arvin has observed, which bear comparison with some of Hawthorne's best writing; indeed, these four books deserve to be ranked, in Arvin's view, with such unfinished masterpieces as *The Faerie Queen*, *The Mystery of Edwin Drood*, James' uncompleted novels and much of Kafka.[36] Arvin's praise may be excessive, but the brooding power of these flawed fragments may be explained by the depth of feeling that Hawthorne invested in them.

"Of all things," wrote Hawthorne from England to his friend Fields shortly after his arrival there, "I should like to find a gravestone in one of these old churchyards with my own name upon it, although, for myself, I should wish to be buried in America."[37] In his journal, he conveyed his sense of returning to his native homeland: "My ancestor left England in 1635. I return in 1853. I sometimes feel as if I myself had been absent these two hundred and eighteen years."[38] When he visited the villages and countryside of England he almost always "had a singular sense of having been there before" (v, 63). In a Leamington churchyard, Hawthorne – overwhelmed by a sensation of *déjà vu* – speculated on rational explanations, but also on the possibility that "the image of them [English rural churches], impressed into the minds of my long-ago forefathers, was so deep that I have inherited it."[39] In *The Ancestral Footstep*, the central character Middleton, an American on a pilgrimage to England, feels "as if he were the original emigrant who, long resident on a foreign shore, had now returned, with a heart brimful of tenderness, to revisit the scenes of his youth, and renew his tender relations with those who shared his own blood." In *Doctor Grimshawe's Secret*, an American's visit to Braithwaite Hall, the residence of his English ancestors, "seemed to him like a coming home after an absence of centuries."[40]

Hawthorne was strongly attracted to the beauties of the English landscape and the grandeur of its architectural monuments. "To my uninstructed vision," Hawthorne wrote of Lichfield Cathedral, "it seemed the object best worth gazing at in the whole world . . . [It] showed me how earthly I was, but yet whispered deeply of immortality" (v, 124–5). He visited with enthusiasm the places of literary association; his purpose in journeying to Lichfield was "partly to see its beautiful cathedral, and still more . . . because it was the birthplace of Dr.

Johnson" (v, 121). He rejoiced in the landmarks associated
with Shakespeare, Scott, Burns, Leigh Hunt, Wordsworth; and
he took special pleasure in "the London of the writers of [the]
Queen Anne age – whatever Pope, the [S]pectator, De Foe, and
down as late as Johnson and Goldsmith have mentioned."[41]

It was for Shakespeare that his deepest emotions were
reserved. In Boston, on March 5, 1820, young Hawthorne saw
Edmund Kean in *King Lear* and wrote his mother that he would
have cried if he had been in a place where he could cry; "It was
enough to have drawn tears from a millstone," he told her.[42]
The journal entry written on the day he wept for his dying
mother – the most anguished and revealing he ever wrote –
includes, in its reference to "the dusty midst" of existence, an
echo of Macbeth's bitter meditation on "dusty death" (v. v.
23).[43] Hawthorne's notebooks are sprinkled with echoes of
Shakespeare and one of the most joyous entries – a description,
in 1843, of a sunny fall day that concludes with a happy comment about his pregnant Sophia and the imminent birth of his
first child ("I see my little wife rounding apace, and anticipate
the greatest blessing that is yet to come" [viii, 393]) – directly
recalls a passage in *A Winter's Tale*: "Hark ye; / The queen
your mother rounds apace: we shall / Present our services to a
fine new prince / One of these days . . . " (ii. i. 15–16).[44] (Una,
the child that was born to Sophia, was watched by Hawthorne
through a crevice in the curtain ["so full of spirit and life, that
she was life itself"] as he sat alongside his dying mother six
years later.) It was fitting, almost inevitable, that Hawthorne's
storyteller in "The Devil in Manuscript," a thinly-disguised
self-portrait, should be called Oberon.

And it was almost inevitable that Hawthorne should have
been drawn to Delia Bacon, an American in England searching
monomaniacally for ultimate truths and ancestral footsteps in
the works (and burial place) of William Shakespeare. Delia
Bacon had been encouraged by Emerson to cross the ocean and
search out, in England, confirmation of the revelations she had
gleaned from an intensive study of the plays – revelations that
for the first time provided the world with the key to the
authorship of these profound philosophical dramas: it was to
be found not in Shakespeare, the "Old Player," but in the great
mind of Francis Bacon, with the help of other brilliant thinkers

of that era. In England she sought help from Emerson's friend Carlyle, who was soon writing to a British friend that "Emerson has sent me from Yankee-land a female enthusiast for Shakespeare . . . of good manners, tho' with the most amazing Yankee drawl; and on the whole, shrewd, veracious, notwithstanding this in[con]ceivable hypothesis of hers."[45] When, after three years, all efforts to find a publisher for her book had failed, she appealed to Hawthorne as a compatriot and government official; her letter of May 8, 1856, admitted to the American consul at Liverpool that

This is not *Consular* business exactly, I suppose . . . But I think when President Pierce appointed one so eminent as yourself in the world of letters, to represent him in this country, he deserved the return which he will have if through your aid this discovery should be secured to the country to which it properly belongs instead of being appropriated here – or instead of being lost rather as it is more likely to be, unless someone will help me.

She was in great need, she added, of "some literary counsel, and such as no Englishman of letters is able to give me."[46] Hawthorne did not fail her.

When Delia Bacon's *The Philosophy of the Plays of Shakspere Unfolded* was published in London in the spring of 1857, its title page announced in large type that the book had "A Preface by Nathaniel Hawthorne, Author of 'The Scarlet Letter,' Etc."[47] Predictably, the British periodicals ridiculed Delia Bacon – and Hawthorne even more so because he could lend his name and distinguished reputation to such nonsense. The concluding sentence in *The Saturday Review* (London) is typical: "The lady, who is perfectly sincere, has deceived herself, by lonely study and constant iteration of one idea, into this strange article of belief; but how Mr. Hawthorne has come to be deceived into it passes our comprehension."[48]

The critic for *The Saturday Review* and other British commentators failed to take into account Hawthorne's sympathetic identification with a kindred spirit – one who in the passionate pursuit of truth transformed the error into which she had blindly fallen into a kind of truth. In *Our Old Home*, Hawthorne reflected on this "remarkable woman," whose

labor, while she lived, was of a nature and purpose outwardly irreverent to the name of Shakespeare, yet, by its actual tendency, entitling her to the distinction of being that one of all his worshippers who sought, though she knew it not, to place the richest and stateliest diadem upon his brow . . . Her faith in her own ideas was so genuine that, erroneous as they were, it transmuted them to gold, or, at all events, interfused a large proportion of that precious and indestructible substance among the waste materials from which it can readily be sifted. (v, 104)

But Delia Bacon's quest struck a sympathetic chord in Hawthorne for reasons never explicitly stated in his preface to her book on Shakespeare or in his tribute in *Our Old Home*. Vivian C. Hopkins has noted strong similarities between Delia Bacon and Hawthorne's American quester in England, Redclyffe, in *Dr. Grimshawe's Secret*: "Delia's possession of a 'secret' that would throw sudden illumination on Shakespeare's plays, her journey to England to fulfill her quest, were close parallels to Redclyffe's search for a material inheritance." Delia Bacon, Hopkins observes, was drawn to Shakespeare's grave as Redclyffe was drawn to Braithwaite Hall, by "a strange, deep, sad, brooding interest, which possesses me, and draws me to it, and will not let me go."[49]

There is another dimension in the Hawthorne–Bacon relationship. On his pilgrimage to Stratford-upon-Avon (a year before his first meeting with Delia Bacon), Hawthorne was able to form a vivid idea of Shakespeare as a living and breathing person – and to learn at first hand "some of the grimy actualities of his life" (v, 100). In Hawthorne's view, it was perhaps, a grave disservice to the imperishable poet to pry into "his perishing earthliness." Shakespeare had lived in Hawthorne's imagination in a palatial abode, "receiving his guest, indeed, in a castle in the air, until we unwisely insist on meeting him among the sordid lanes and alleys of the lower earth" (v, 96). Leaving the church and Shakespeare's burial place, Hawthorne sat alongside the Avon and reflected on the fact that he knew of no American river so tame or small or sluggish (". . . it loiters past Stratford Church as if it had been considering which way to flow, ever since Shakespeare used to paddle in it").[50] Delia Bacon's monomaniacal vision shed a magical aura over the trivial and sordid reminders of Shakespeare's mortality: in a hollow space, in the under-surface of Shakespeare's gravestone would be found the evidences of Bacon's authorship and the key to a new philosophy (v, 107). However mistaken, it was a vision that transformed colorless actuality in a manner and for a purpose that must have been irresistible to the American romancer.

Hawthorne saw his duty clear: Delia Bacon was an American woman in England pursuing her dream, besieged by poverty and an assortment of real and imaginary demons; when she turned to him, he tried gallantly and vainly to help her. Hawthorne paid out eleven hundred dollars of his own money to subsidize the publication of a book patently doomed to ridicule and financial failure. Numerous attempts to assist her were unavailing and, when Hawthorne left for the Continent in January 1858, Delia Bacon had been placed in a private mental sanatorium near Stratford; she died in an American sanatorium the following year.[51]

In *Our Old Home*, published four years after Delia Bacon's death, Hawthorne conveys his outrage at "the brutal vituperations of the English press" directed at her book on Shakespeare – and at the American journalists who republished these ridiculing accounts, "thus pelting their poor countrywoman with stolen mud, without even waiting to know whether the ignominy was deserved." Hawthorne expresses admiration and pity for his dead countrywoman with the eloquence of deep feeling:

What matters it though she called him [Shakespeare] by some other name? He had wrought a greater miracle on her than on all the world besides. This bewildered enthusiast had recognized a depth in the man whom she decried, which scholars, critics, and learned societies, devoted to the elucidation of his unrivalled scenes had never imagined to exist there. She had paid him the loftiest honor that all of renown have been able to accumulate upon his memory. (v, 115, 116)

Hawthorne's own tributary wreath does honor to Delia Bacon and to Shakespeare – and to himself.

Hawthorne's involvement with Delia Bacon and its bitter aftermath intensified his feelings of disenchantment with England. For a long time, his fervor and deep admiration for the landscapes and institutions of "Our Old Home" had been accompanied by increasing impatience with what he felt to be English abrasiveness and hostility toward America. Trollope reported that Hawthorne "once withered me with a scorn which was anything but mystic or melancholy because I expressed a patriotic preference for English peas."[52] Like other visiting Americans, the author was angered by the "condescension" in the English people he met. At a dinner party, his hostess reported with amusement the way in which George Bancroft (then United States minister to Great Britain) had misused the English language while telling somebody about the effect of London's climate on his wife's health. "She is now very delicate," Bancroft is quoted as saying, "whereas, when we lived in New York, she was one of the most *indelicate* women in the city!" To this anecdote told by Mrs Ainsworth – in the same great house where he learned the legend of "The Bloody Footstep" (an important source of *The Ancestral Footstep*) – Hawthorne responded with vigorous contempt in his journal:

And Mrs. Ainsworth had the face to tell this foolish story for truth, and as indicating the mistakes into which Americans are liable to fall, in the use of the English language. In other instances, I have heard stories equally ridiculous about our diplomatic people, whom the English seemed determined to make butts of, reason or none.[53]

Of greater importance than Hawthorne's resentment about British superciliousness and misrepresentation were his expressions of democratic humanism in response to what he believed to be an unjust and declining aristocratic system. "If you would understand me," says the young American Redclyffe (in *Doctor Grimshawe's Secret*) to his English host, "I would tell you of the shame I felt when first, on setting foot in this country, I heard a man speaking of his birth as giving him privileges; saw him looking down on laboring men, as of an inferior race." And Redclyffe conveys his feeling that these and other aristocratic institutions and customs are destined for destruction and will be replaced by patterns that resemble American republicanism.[54] In *The Ancestral Footstep*, a young Englishwoman advises Middleton that, now that he has gratified his "natural yearning" by seeing the birthplace of his forefathers, he can do nothing better than return to America. "I fully believe," she says, "that it is such a lot as the world has never yet seen, and that the faults, the weaknesses, the errors of your countrymen will vanish away like morning mists before the rising sun."[55]

When Hawthorne resigned his consulate post and made preparations for an extended trip to Italy, he felt a new pride in his sovereign status as an ordinary American citizen The religion, the art, the antiquity of Italy left a deep imprint and moved him to create a romance – the last he was able to complete – in which that ancient land (Hawthorne observes in the Preface to *The Marble Faun*) provided him with "a sort of poetic or fairy precinct, where actualities would not be so terribly insisted upon, as they are, and must needs be in America" (IV, 3). These strictures are followed by his catalog of missing items in America ("no shadow, no antiquity, no mystery, no picturesque and gloomy wrong, nor anything but a common-place prosperity") that make the lot of an American romance writer especially difficult.

Italy may have supplied all these missing items to the author of *The Marble Faun*, but Henry Chorley, the British critic who had praised *The Blithedale Romance* as Hawthorne's greatest achievement, expressed disappointment in *Transformation* (as it was titled in England) because the secrets surrounding Miriam and Donatello "are all left too vaporously involved in suggestion to satisfy any one whose blood has turned back at the admirable, clear and forcible last scenes of 'The Scarlet Letter.'"[56] And Trollope, with all of his almost unstinted admiration for Hawthorne's dreamlike romances, suggested that the readers of *The Marble Faun* required from the author, "some explanation of the causes which have produced the romantic details to which they have given their attention, and will be inclined to say that it should have been the author's business to give an explanation neither tedious nor unsatisfactory."[57] Trollope's complaint was written and published after Hawthorne's death, but in response to Chorley's and other pronouncements – and to questions about whether Donatello actually had furry ears – Hawthorne wrote a playful, uninformative Postscript defending his right to give his story and characters "some laws and proprieties of their own [that] should be implicitly and insensibly acknowledged" (IV, 463). To his friend Motley, Hawthorne's answer to these British complaints was more direct: "These beer-sodden beefeaters do not know how to read a Romance."[58]

One need not side with the British detractors of *The Marble*

Faun, however, to sympathize with a modern assessment that finds the moral drama revolving about Miriam and Donatello too abstract and remote to take seriously.[59] At the close of the novel, Hilda comes down from her tower to become Kenyon's bride and the narrator reflects on their decision to return to America:

And, now that life had so much human promise in it, they resolved to go back to their own land; because the years, after all, have a kind of emptiness, when we spend too many of them on a foreign shore. We defer the reality of life, in such cases, until a future moment, when we shall again breathe our native air; but, by-and-by, there are no future moments; or, if we do return, we find that the native air has lost its invigorating quality, and that life has shifted its reality to the spot where we have deemed ourselves only temporary residents. Thus, between two countries, we have none at all, or only that little space of either, in which we finally lay down our discontented bones. It is wise, therefore, to come back betimes – or never. (IV, 461)

But we have been too little involved with Hilda and Kenyon to feel the force of this pronouncement for them. (Its significance for Hawthorne himself is much more evident.) Kenyon is indeed a distant cousin (or faint echo) of Miles Coverdale in *The Blithedale Romance*. Like Coverdale, Kenyon is largely a passive observer in the grim drama being enacted among these American expatriate artists. But Kenyon's "speculative interest" in these proceedings has none of the ironic complexity and passionate intensity of Coverdale's involvements at Blithedale.[60]

Hawthorne conceived the idea for *The Marble Faun* in Italy and completed rough drafts of his novel in Florence and Rome. But it was not until the Hawthornes returned to England in the latter part of 1859 that he was able to finish the book. The "Italian atmosphere," he wrote, was "not favorable to the close toil of composition, although it is a very good air to dream in."[61] And before long the English atmosphere also became uncongenial and he was beset by longings for his home. "Americans are liable to get out of sorts with their native land by being long away from it," he told a friend; and in April of 1860, he informed Ticknor, as the time for his return approached, that "All my homesickness has fallen on me at once, and even Julian is scarcely more impatient than myself." A twelve-day voyage on the *Europa* brought the Hawthornes back to Boston on June 28, 1860.[62]

At home in Concord, Hawthorne busied himself with his never-to-be-completed romances about an American in England and an elixir of life. In September 1863, Hawthorne's English Notebooks – abridged and revised into a series of sketches – appeared under the title *Our Old Home*. Among the many descriptions, affectionate and offensive, that caught the attention of British reviewers, one seemed unforgivably outrageous. After citing the reputation of English women for retaining their beauty late in life, Hawthorne offered a disclaimer in the form of his account of "an English lady of fifty" ("She has an awful ponderosity of frame . . . massive with solid beef and streaky tallow; so that . . . you inevitably think of her as made up of steaks and sirloins" [v, 48]). The critic for *Blackwood's Magazine* was especially incensed over a writer who seemed from his fiction "a gentle and genial man" but instead startled and shocked with his "perpetual carping" and "virulence."[63] Hawthorne took these British criticisms lightly ("their self-conceit can accept nothing short of indiscriminate adulation"), conceding that "It is not a good nor a weighty book, nor does it deserve any great amount either of praise or censure."[64]

More painful were American attacks on the dedication of *Our Old Home* to Franklin Pierce, a lifelong friend whom Hawthorne refused to desert in the midst of a bloody war that aroused fierce animosities against the Democratic ex-President. *Harper's Weekly* denounced Hawthorne's "tone of doubt and indifference" toward the Civil War, comparing its "monstrous" attitude to that of a "most charming companion who should prove to have no objection to infanticide."[65]

In the winter of 1863 Hawthorne was seriously ill. According to Edward Hutchins Davidson, the acrimonious notices of *Our Old Home* spurred him to begin a second romance of immortality, later published as a fragment, *The Dolliver Romance*. He was never able to complete this or any other novel in America after his return. He died on May 19, 1864. During the funeral service in Concord, the manuscript of the first chapter of *The Dolliver Romance* "lay on the coffin throughout the service and remained there" while his friends walked alongside it to the Sleepy Hollow Cemetery.[66] But the tales and the three great romances, all written before his journey across the sea, are his imperishable legacy to his native land and to the world.

In late November of 1856, Herman Melville – en route to the Holy Land on a trip to improve his health – had visited Hawthorne at the Liverpool Consulate, "looking much as he used to do (a little paler, and perhaps a little sadder)." He stayed with the Hawthornes for several days at Southport and, as the two Americans walked among the sand hills, Melville began to raise old and unanswerable religious questions. "It is strange," wrote Hawthorne in his journal, "how he persists – and has persisted ever since I knew him, and probably long before – in wandering to-and-fro over these deserts, as dismal and monotonous as the sand hills amid which we were sitting."[67] In a sense, Hawthorne himself was involved in some dismal and monotonous wandering in his attempts, in England, to shape a romance about an American on a pilgrimage to England. Before setting eyes on England – and, from his earliest youth, with a profound sense of its influence and challenge in his life as an artist – the "Master Genius of American Literature" had responded to England and completed his most vital work.

7

Crosscurrents:
Melville's England and America

Two voyages

On the evening of November 4, 1849, the young and celebrated American author Herman Melville made an entry in his journal while sitting in his stateroom aboard the packet-ship *Southhampton* in the English channel off Dover: "This time tomorrow I shall be on land, & press English earth after the lapse of ten years – then a sailor, now H. M. author of 'Pedee 'Hullabaloo' & 'Pog-Dog.'"[1] Ten years earlier, during the summer of 1839, the nineteen-year-old Herman had shipped as a "boy" aboard the packet-ship *St Lawrence* bound for Liverpool. In the semi-autobiographical novel *Redburn*, Melville's hero finds the dingy warehouses of Liverpool discouragingly similar to the warehouses of New York; indeed, "Liverpool, away from the docks, was very much such a place as New York. There were the same sort of streets pretty much; the same rows of houses with stone steps; the same kind of sidewalks and curbs; and the same elbowing, heartless-looking crowd as ever" (v, 260).[2] But there were sights to be seen in Liverpool unlike any in New York or any other American city. Young Redburn witnesses squalor and wretchedness that make him keenly aware of the fact that he is in another country: "Poverty, poverty, poverty, in almost endless vistas; and want and woe staggered arm in arm along these miserable streets" (v, 259). William H. Gilman has observed that some of the satiric attacks on Western civilization in the books that preceded *Redburn* – from *Typee* on – can be explained in part by the profound impact on the young sailor of Liverpool's terrible slums.[3] The impoverished Melville was in no position to see some of the pleasanter sights of the city – or of the England that lay beyond the docks and slums of Liverpool. "I often thought," says Redburn, "of London's being only seven or eight hours' travel by railroad from where I was; and that *there* surely, must be a world of wonders waiting my eyes" (v, 261). Melville, the novelist, provides young Redburn with a London adventure, but it is unlikely that the young sailor ever came closer to that great place than Redburn did while strolling in the countryside outside Liverpool along the London road ("Who that dwells in America," explains the hero, "has not heard of the bright fields and green hedges of England, and longed to behold them?" [v, 269]). Such a ramble into the country, if Melville was actually able to take one during the summer of 1839, did not provide sufficient diversion to counteract his disappointment with Liverpool – and his growing homesickness. "[Herman] says he would give all the sights of Liverpool to see a corner of home," Melville's mother wrote to his brother Allan on September 25.[4] At the time she wrote, her sailor son was on his way home and only a few days away from New York Harbor. On the last day of September, Melville witnessed a sight from the deck of the *St Lawrence* that is eloquently described by young Redburn – the ships thronging the East River and "the stately old Hudson" – with an accompanying rhapsodic flight that conveyed his deepest feelings about returning to his native land after a long journey away from it: "Oh! he who has never been afar, let him go once from home, to know what home is. For as you draw nigh to your old native river, he seems to pour through you with all his tides, and in your enthusiasm, you swear to build altars like milestones, along both his sacred banks" (v, 387).

Fifteen months later, on December 31, 1840, young Melville signed on as a deckhand to the whaling vessel *Acushnet* for what proved to be the first leg of a fateful series of voyages and adventures. Accompanied by a shipmate, he jumped ship and lived among cannibals in the Marquesas. He joined a mutiny on another ship and was jailed in Tahiti. He escaped to become a beachcomber and, later, a harpooneer on another whaling vessel. On October 3, 1844, five years after his return from England, ordinary seaman Herman Melville was discharged in Boston harbor from the navy frigate *United States*. Out of these wide-ranging experiences came a series of exotic and satiric romances that marked the emergence of a great new

American writer: *Typee, Omoo, Mardi; Redburn*; and it was with
the proof sheets of *White Jacket* that author Herman Melville
landed at Dover in November 1849.

The young author reached London on Tuesday, November
6, found a cheap room on the Strand ("a guinea & a half per
week") and, later, visited Drury Lane where he found his novel
Redburn on sale for a guinea – and the current *Blackwood's
Magazine* featuring what proved to be the longest review the
novel was to receive (fourteen double-column pages). It was
also one of the harshest. The reviewer (Frederick Hardman)
was glad that "much of the obscurity and nonsense" in *Mardi*
was not present in *Redburn*, but found much to ridicule in
Melville's characterization of the young sailor hero, "a sharp
enough lad on shore" who "seems converted, by the first sniff
of salt water, into as arrant a simpleton as ever made mirth in
a cockpit." The terrible events witnessed by young Redburn
in Liverpool – the gradual death by starvation in a public
street of a mother and her three children – are dismissed by
the *Blackwood's* reviewer as "more than improbable" and
"utterly absurd." Melville should have kept to shipboard
events; his treatment of Redburn's London adventure was
"utter rubbish." Hardman concludes with some advice to
"Mr Herman Melville" who will undoubtedly see this review.
Adverse criticisms of the author's failings were offered "in the
hope of inducing him to amend them." Hardman had earlier
praised Melville's good qualities as a writer for: "It always
gives us pleasure to speak favourably of a book by an American
author, when we conscientiously can do so." Three reasons
were offered for doing so: though cousins, Americans were
"in some sort strangers" and it was only courteous to praise
strangers; American writers with talent needed encouragement and "the words of Maga have much weight" in America;
an increase in the number of good American books would
hasten the adoption of an international copyright law that
would make it unnecessary for American writers to publish
their books abroad in order to protect the financial benefits
that were their rightful due. To all this Melville responded in
his journal with "wonder . . . that the old Tory should waste
so many pages upon a thing which I, the author, know to be
trash, & wrote . . . to buy some tobacco with."[5]

Melville's self-deprecatory remarks reflect his precarious status as a serious writer in an age that had little use for his most serious efforts; he was still smarting from the financial failure and disastrous critical reception of *Mardi*. (Two years later, he unburdened himself about his dilemma to Hawthorne: "What I feel most moved to write, that is banned, – it will not pay. Yet, altogether, write the *other* way I cannot. So the product is a final hash, and all my books are botches.")[6] But another British reviewer of *Redburn* anticipated some of the most perceptive critical insights of this century by suggesting that the book centers on "the details of the process by which" the hero was "disenchanted of his pleasant delusions concerning life at sea" and "in the natural development of the feelings of the boy throughout the startling ordeal of his first voyage."[7] Redburn's response to the starving family in Launcelott's-Hey and the monstrous crowd of beggars that throng the Liverpool docks ("this picture of all that is dishonorable to civilization and humanity" [v, 2391]) directly parallels the desperate starvation of an Irish family in England depicted by Carlyle in the opening chapter of *Past and Present* ("A human Mother and Father had said to themselves, What shall we do to escape starvation?"). Melville's democratic humanism is pervasive, not only in the Liverpool episodes but during the voyage home, when Redburn eloquently defends the right of impoverished Irish immigrants to find a home in America – a right bitterly opposed by many American nativists: ". . . if they can get here they have God's right to come; though they bring all Ireland and her miseries with them" (v, 378).

During his 1849 visit to London, Melville was pleased to receive a note for a hundred pounds from publisher Bentley that was due him on account of *Redburn*. "Hurrah & three cheers!" he was finally able to enter in his journal on Saturday evening, December 15, when – after several delays and complications – he concluded an arrangement with Bentley for a two-hundred-pound advance in payment for the British publication rights of *White Jacket*.[8]

Three days later, Melville wandered among the old bookstores on Great Queen Street and Lincoln's Inn and unearthed ("for 3 & 6 pence") a 1766 map of London ("I want to use it in case I serve up the Revolutionary narrative of the beggar").

Before leaving for England, Melville had acquired a slender
volume, *The Life and Remarkable Adventures of Israel R. Potter*
(1824), an autobiographical account of a veteran of the American Revolution "exiled" for fifty years of hardship and poverty
in London. For Melville, a second important purpose in
visiting London – in addition to finding a British publisher for
White Jacket – was gathering material for a novel based on
Israel Potter's experiences.[9] Other London impressions gathered during this same visit provided materials for three extraordinary Anglo-American sketches: "The Two Temples,"
"Poor Man's Pudding and Rich Man's Crumbs," "The Paradise of Bachelors and The Tartarus of Maids." But these
sketches – like *Israel Potter* – were to germinate for several
years before being written.

When Melville disembarked from the *Independence* on February 1 1850, the story of an American exile in England and
Paris was uppermost in his mind. But the unexpected financial
success of *Redburn* and the favorable notices of *White Jacket*
seem to have contributed to a change in his writing plans.
Soon after his return, there followed on the next Cunard
steamer copies of the London *Athenaeum* containing Henry F.
Chorley's enthusiastic praise of Melville as a writer of sea
fiction – praise that may have contributed to his decision to
write a novel based in part on his own whaling experience.[10]
Pierre ("a rural bowl of milk") rapidly followed *Moby-Dick*.
When *Israel Potter* and the Anglo-American sketches eventually appeared in 1854–5 ("The Two Temples" was rejected as
too daring and was not published until 1924), they revealed
new dimensions of Melville's genius – dimensions that have
not yet been fully measured.

Two Temples: Anglo-American landscapes of
heaven and hell

In April 1854, Melville submitted the first of his Anglo-
American diptychs, "The Two Temples," to *Putnam's Monthly
Magazine*. The first part of the sketch depicts the vain attempt
of a shabbily dressed man to enter a fashionable New York
church; the second tells about the happy experience of the

same man when – as a penniless stranger in London a short
time later – he receives a friendly welcome among the poor
people in the topmost gallery of a theatre. When he is prevented from entering the church service ("had I . . . tickled the
fat-paunched, beadle-faced man's palm with a bank-note, . . .
I would have had a fine seat in this marble-buttressed, stained-
glass, spick-and-span new temple"), the narrator finds a stair-
case to the bell tower. Through a tiny window high above the
congregation, he is able – after a fashion – to hear a sermon to
the text, often repeated: "Ye are the salt of the earth." Because
it is a spectacle seen from afar and he is more a witness than a
participant, the narrator's special vantage point seems to
"[enhance] the theatric wonder of the populous spectacle of
this sumptuous sanctuary." "Better perish 'mid myriad sharks
in mid Atlantic than die a penniless stranger in Babylonian
London," observes the narrator a few weeks later, now a
penniless American abroad. It would be best for a lonely
stranger in a great bewildering city to find "a genial humane
assembly of my kind" as one may encounter "at its best and
highest' . . . in the unified multitude of a devout congregation."
But it is a Saturday night and he finds instead refuge and good
cheer in a theater featuring the celebrated Macready. A kindly
working-man understands his penniless plight and offers him
a ticket. He accepts ("if it be gloriously right to do a charitable
deed, can it be ingloriously wrong to receive its benefit?")
and mounts the innumerable stairs to the gallery (reminded
"of my ascent of the Gothic tower on the ocean's far other
side"). When he finally reaches his seat, it is to a burst of
orchestral music that revives memories of the organ music he
had heard in the fashionable church. For a brief time he
experiences – as he looks down upon the great throng below
and hears the music – a sense of *déjà vu*; it requires an effort
"to remind myself that this time I had no small morocco book
with me, and that this was not the house of prayer." There is
little doubt that this was not the fashionable, inhospitable
temple on the other side of the ocean when a vendor of ale – a
ragged boy who recognizes him as an impoverished Yankee –
cheerfully presents him with a free mug ("'Tis not always
poverty to be poor, mused I; one may fare well without a
penny"). At the close of the evening's entertainment, the

narrator reflects at length about "the First Temple and the Second Temple; and how, at home in my own land, I was thrust out from the one, and, a stranger in a strange land, found sterling charity in the other" (XIII, 173–91). It is not surprising that Melville should dedicate "The Two Temples" to Sheridan Knowles, an English dramatist who, in 1843, renounced the theater for the pulpit and was – during Melville's year in London and the period in which the sketch was written – a living symbol of the two temples.[11] And it is not surprising that "The Two Temples" should be rejected by *Putnam's* as too abrasive to the genteel sensibilities of its "church readers"; editor Briggs regretfully informed Melville that "my editorial experience compels me to be very careful in offending the religious sensibilities of the public, and the moral of the 'Two Temples' would sway against us the whole power of the pulpit."[12]

"Poor Man's Pudding and Rich Man's Crumbs" (XIII, 192–209) is a study of poverty in two cultures: in the American countryside and in the great city of London. The American sketch sets the narrator – who has a genuine sympathy for the terrible poverty and suffering of William and Martha Coulter – against his friend, the poet Blandmour – who is full of pious platitudes designed to explain away the harsh realities that surround them. In London the following summer, the narrator is taken in hand by an overly friendly civic official who shows the American visitor the most important sights of the city – namely, "the noble charities of London." Foremost among these is the Guildhall Charity – an affair that follows the annual grand Guildhall Banquet. A mob of beggars storms the Guildhall for "the broken meats – the cold victuals and crumbs of kings" left over from the preceding night. At the close of "Poor Man's Pudding," the narrator observes that the native American poor never lose their pride – with the result that, though their physical degradation is never as great as that of the European pauper, their mental anguish is greater. He concludes, however, that there is not much to choose between American proud endurance of the unendurable and British obsequiousness (coupled with an unpredictable violence); the central targets on both sides of the Atlantic are those who – like the American poet Blandmour and his British counterpart, the unnamed civic functionary–guide – see suffering and in-justice about them and respond with unfeeling fatuousness.

In the third and most powerful of the Anglo-American diptychs, "The Paradise of Bachelors and The Tartarus of Maids" (XIII, 228–54), Melville links a seemingly harmless and genial sketch depicting an American's convivial evening with nine carefree London bachelors to a nightmarish evocation of a New England paper mill on a bitter January day. The pleasures of the palate and of good company seem lovingly dwelled upon in the London sketch – but the ironic strain is also present and there is a touch of venom in the midst of all the good feeling: "The thing called pain, the bugbear styled trouble – those two legends seemed preposterous to their bachelor imaginations. How could men of . . . capacious philosophical and convivial understandings – how could they suffer themselves to be imposed upon by such monkish fables? Pain! Trouble! As well talk of Catholic miracles. No such thing. – Pass the sherry, sir" (XIII, 237). This sterile disengage-ment from human suffering, from life itself, among the English bachelors underscores the bleak sterility of the American maids employed in the paper mill. The working-girls have been robbed of sexuality, of life itself, by the mill; the vast mach-inery and its workings are a parody and perversion of sexuality and reproduction. (In a room, "stifling with a strange, blood-like, abdominal heat" a sheet of white pulp marked "Cupid" travels through the great paper-making machine until it is snipped off, exactly nine minutes to the second later – "and down dropped an unfolded sheet of perfect foolscap, with my 'Cupid' half faded out of it, and still moist and warm.") Though vastly different, the dark, frozen terrain surrounding the paper mill "strangely brought back to my mind my first sight of dark and grimy Temple Bar"; the factory itself with its adjacent tower used for hoisting boxes recalls to the narrator the Temple Church. Newton Arvin has called the opening London sketch a "Lambesque," essayistic reminiscence of a bachelor dinner – "a mild and rather tame affair" that con-trasts inexplicably with "The Tartarus of Maids," a sketch that "does not so much recall Charles Lamb as foreshadow 'The Penal Colony.'" But the narrator says to himself, on viewing the New England paper mill and its environs: "This is the very counterpart of the Paradise of Bachelors, but snowed upon, and frost-painted to a sepulchre." In this he spoke for Melville who well understood that the jolly English bachelors are hollow men, as empty of true vitality – amidst all their pleasures – as the American maids doomed to a living death in the paper factory.

Another kind of living death is Melville's subject in *Israel Potter*, published serially in *Putnam's* (beginning in July 1854 as "A Fourth of July Story" and concluding in the March 1855 issue). When he was serving as American Consul in Liverpool some time later, Hawthorne was reminded of Melville's "excellent novel or biography of 'Israel Potter'" by an encounter with an American stranded in England who had been trying unsuccessfully to return to his native land for more than a quarter of a century.[13] Potter's exile is more protracted: from 1776, when he was taken prisoner during the Revolutionary War, to the Fourth of July in 1826, when he returns to Boston amidst scenes of patriotic rejoicing. He narrowly escapes being run over by a triumphal car bearing a proud banner proclaiming glory to the heroes who fought at Bunker Hill – where Israel had served half a century before. The tone is light and satiric in its treatment of Israel's naive encounters with Franklin, John Paul Jones and Ethan Allen. The extended and detailed treatment, in the real Israel Potter's autobiography, of poverty in London and of his own varied experiences there are compressed, in Melville's version, into two apocalyptic chapters that draw not on Potter but on Melville's own experiences as recorded in his 1849 journal.

On November 9, two days after Melville's arrival in London, he reflected on how the scenes he was witnessing could be transformed into literature:

While on one of the Bridges, the thought struck me again that a fine thing might be written about a Blue Monday in November London – a city of Dis (Dante's) – clouds of smoke – the damned &c. – coal barges – coaly waters, cast-iron Duke &c. – its marks are left upon you, &c. &c. &c.[14]

When Melville finally came to write chapter 25 of *Israel Potter* ("In the City of Dis"), he echoes and transmutes his journal entry to emphasize the dehumanizing influence of the city:

It was late on a Monday morning, in November – a Blue Monday – a Fifth of November – Guy Fawkes' Day! – very blue, foggy, doleful and gunpowdery, indeed, as shortly will be seen, that Israel found himself wedged in among the greatest everyday crowd which grimy London presents to the curious stranger: that hereditary crowd – gulf-stream of humanity – which, for continuous centuries, has never ceased pouring, like an endless shoal of herring, over London Bridge. (XI, 210)

There follows a description of the polluted Thames and the great flow of muddy traffic over the bridges suggestive of a scene in hell ("as if some squadron of centaurs, on the thither side of Phlegethon . . . was driving tormented humanity, with all of its chattels, across") – and of the London fog and mud in the opening chapter of *Bleak House* (serialized in *Harper's Monthly* in 1852–3). Israel's long years of suffering and privation, summed up in chapter 26 ("Forty-Five Years"), substitute for the real Potter's lengthy autobiographical account a prose poem on poverty. Israel marries, ekes out a starveling's existence, fathers eleven children ("One after the other, ten were buried") – and finally comes home with his surviving son to his native land. He lives out the short time remaining to him in the mountain township of western Massachusetts where he was born. But there is no one there to remember him and the precious landmarks and landscape of his childhood are so transformed as to be unrecognizable.

Hawthorne's observation about the pitiful old American vainly attempting, for decades, to return to his native land and city ("I want to get home to Ninety-second street, Philadelphia") has equal force for Israel Potter. After struggling with his conscience, Hawthorne decided that he could not take the responsibility of sending the old man home after so many years of exile for he would inevitably "find his friends dead . . . and the whole country become more truly a foreign land to him than England was now, and even Ninety-second street . . . made over anew and grown unrecognizable by his old eyes."[15] Hawthorne did not want his homeless American to suffer the fate of Israel Potter.

In his three Anglo-American diptychs and *Israel Potter*, Melville explored aspects of dehumanization, alienation, suffering and failure – variations on themes he was treating in other works in this period; in *Pierre* and "Bartleby," there are scenes of a New York hell that match Melville's vision of London in *Israel Potter* as a "cindery City of Dis." But the presence of the great Atlantic as a mighty barrier between two intimately linked but significantly different cultures (intensifying the suffering of an Israel Potter, providing a refuge far from home for the narrator of "The Two Temples") provided Melville with rich opportunities for dramatizing and exposing the cruelties and hypocrisies prevalent in both cultures.

Two captains: an American Ahab and a British Vere

On June 27, 1850 – several months after his return from England – Melville wrote his British publisher that his new book, "a romance of adventure, founded upon certain wild legends in the Southern Sperm Whale Fisheries," would be ready for publication by late autumn; *Moby-Dick* was, in fact, still not finished a year later when he informed Hawthorne that "The tail is not yet cooked."[16] During the fateful year that intervened between the imminent and actual completion of his masterpiece, Melville had met Hawthorne and read with intense excitement his *Mosses from an Old Manse*. The extraordinary essay that Melville wrote as a result, "Hawthorne and His Mosses," announced to the readers of *The Literary World* his admiration for Hawthorne's genius and, to an even greater extent, conveyed something of the "joy-giving and exultation-breeding"[17] mood that permeates *Moby-Dick* – that moved Melville to expand his romance of the whaling fisheries into a vast wild improvisation fusing epic celebration of whalers and whaling with fiery hunt and dark Shakespearean–Hawthornesque tragedy.

Shakespeare loomed large for Melville, but in his Hawthorne essay there was an insistence on the imminent arrival of a great American writer who would equal or surpass the great bard. For Melville, literature was "the great art of Telling the Truth" – a goal linked to America's political struggle for liberation from artificial British constraint with the help of Jefferson's self-evident "truths."[18] Melville had written to Evert Duyckinck in 1849: ". . . I hold it verity, that even Shakespeare, was not a frank man to the uttermost. And indeed, who in this intolerant Universe is, or can be? But the Declaration of Independence makes a difference."[19] In his essay on Hawthorne, Melville pleads for originality in American writers ("No American writer should write like an Englishman"), and predicts the imminent arrival, on the American scene, "of a great literary genius among us." When Melville speaks in these terms, Michael Davitt Bell observes, "his tone is positively millenarian, imaging the creation of a national literature as the 'coming' of a redeemer, the advent of a divine being from the realm of 'truth' into this world of lies."[20]

Melville's millenarian tone pervades both his Hawthorne essay and the epic whaling romance in the making at the time the essay was written.[21] The verse from Isaiah 27 quoted by Melville in the "Extracts" ("In that day, the Lord with his sore, and great, and strong sword, shall punish Leviathan . . . and he shall slay the dragon that is in the sea") prepares the way for a dedicated quest that recalls the traditional iconography of Christ as a dragon-slayer. To Ahab, the white whale is the incarnation of: "That intangible malignity which has been from the beginning; to whose dominion even the modern Christians ascribe one-half of the worlds . . ."; he has "piled upon the whale's white hump the sum of all the general rage and hate felt by his whole race from Adam down."[22] In his madness, Ahab has transformed the millenarian dream of the churches of New England and America's conception of itself as a redeemer nation into a fiery hunt that makes use of the powers of Satan. Ahab is an American messianic Lear who will strike through the mask and speak the sane madness of vital truth – fully aware of the fact that (despite, or because of, his madness) he is "most malignantly damned in the midst of Paradise!" (p. 147).

During his quest, Ahab encounters the *Samuel Enderby*, of London, and has a gam with its English captain. Captain Boomer has lost an arm during a catastrophic encounter with Moby Dick. There have been additional encounters and to Ahab's question as to whether he could not make an additional attempt the English captain is brief and eminently sensible: "Didn't want to try to: ain't one limb enough?" (p. 367). He has lowered for the white whale once, and that is enough.

There would be great glory and large profit in killing him, but "he's best left alone" – and, glancing at Ahab's ivory leg (the counterpart of his ivory arm), asks the American captain if he does not agree. Ahab agrees but proclaims that "he will still be hunted, for all that." Having determined which way Moby Dick was heading when last seen, Ahab puts an abrupt end to the gam and resumes the hunt.

Four decades later, Melville depicted another unforgettable sea captain, this time an aristocratic Englishman whose full title is resoundingly given as Captain the Honorable Edward Fairfax Vere. In contrast to the hearty simplicity of his plebeian Captain Boomer, "Starry" Vere is a complex and introspective man whose bookish and philosophical manner is curiously intertwined with unquestioned abilities as a sea officer in His Majesty's navy.

Melville dedicates *Billy Budd* to "Jack Chase / Englishman / Wherever that great heart may now be / here on earth or harbored in Paradise"; his dedicatory note further identifies Chase as "Captain of the Main-Top in the year 1843 in the U. S. Frigate *United States*."[23] In *White Jacket* (1850), a novel based on Melville's experiences as an ordinary seaman (and shipmate of Jack Chase) on this same vessel, a chapter is devoted to his English friend and Melville conveys his deep feeling in language almost identical to that used forty years later in the dedicatory note preceding *Billy Budd*: "Wherever you may be now rolling over the blue billows, dear Jack! [exclaimed White Jacket] take my best love along with you; and God bless you, wherever you go!" (VI, 14).

Like Captain Vere, Jack Chase is set apart from his fellow sailors by his gentlemanly ways and familiarity with books. He knows "all the verses of Byron, and all the romances of Scott" and can recite parts of Camoens' *Lusiad* in the original. He would be at ease in the Queen of England's drawing-room and "must have been a by-blow of some British Admiral of the Blue." A warm-hearted and generous-spirited man, Jack is, when ashore, "a stickler for the Rights of Man and the liberties of the world" – though "bowing to naval discipline afloat . . ." (VI, 14, 19).

Starry Vere is also bookish – but his bias is toward factual accounts of men and events and toward writers who, like

Montaigne, "honestly and in the spirit of common sense philosophize upon realities." An aristocrat, he opposes the innovators not only because "their theories were inimical to the privileged classes" but because their views were "at war with the peace of the world and the true welfare of mankind" (pp. 36–7).

Vere's aristocratic humanism contrasts sharply with the democratic credo of the narrator – one which cautiously sees, after the bloody wrongs of the French Revolution and of the Great Mutiny at Nore, an eventual "political advance" for Europeans and "important reforms in the British navy" (p. 98).[24] And it contrasts sharply with the warm humanity and anti-authoritarian egalitarianism of Jack Chase, to whom Melville dedicates his last book. The Jack Chase of *White Jacket* helped defend a democratic revolution on land; on a man-of-war, during "the Great Massacre of Beards," he yields to Captain Claret's arbitrary ruling with the utmost reluctance. When Jack finally surrenders to the inevitable, he first forgives and blesses the ship's barber – who, in turn, after clipping Jack's beard with a sigh, cries aloud: "D'ye hear, fore and aft? This is the beard of our matchless Jack Chase, the noble captain of this frigate's main-top!" It is this action that signals the end of the great Mutiny of the Beards.

The tyrannical American captain of the *Neversink* (Captain Claret) is a stereotype out of Smollett. The individuality of Captain Ahab (with all his Shakespearian declamation and posturing) is pervasively American. He is a monarch of a kind: ". . . a Khan of the plank, and a king of the sea, and a great lord of Leviathans was Ahab" (p. 114). But for Ishmael, "Ahab, my Captain" has nothing to do with "Emperors and Kings" and "all outward majestical trappings." That which is grand in Ahab, "poor old whale hunter" that he is, "must needs be plucked at from the skies, and dived for in the deep, and featured in the unbodied air!" (p. 130). His monomaniacal quest ("That certain sultanism of his brain") has led him to defy the rule of man and God.

For Captain Vere the rule of God manifests itself solely through the king and the laws designed to protect his authority. How can we condemn Billy Budd "to summary and shameful death" when we know and feel him to be "innocent before

God"? asks Vere before the drumhead court. But it is nature's god (the god of the American Declaration of Independence) before whom Billy Budd is innocent. The buttons worn by Captain Vere and his fellow officers, he reminds them, attest to their allegiance not to nature but to the king. The Articles of War and the Mutiny Act, designed to protect the king (as a necessary mediator of God's will in an imperfect world of imperfect men) dictate that Billy Budd must die.

In *Moby-Dick*, the narrator half-mockingly, half-seriously reflects on the circumstances that make it impossible – and undesirable – to complete any of his works ("For small erections may be finished by their first architects; grand, true ones, ever leave the copestone to posterity" [pp. 127–8]). Though constructed on a much smaller scale and presented in a much quieter and more essayistic mode, *Billy Budd* is neither less nor more finished than the whaling epic that preceded it forty years before. Some further revision may have been carried out if he had seen his last novel through the press. But Melville's concluding announcement ("End of Book," followed by a date) is the counterpart of Ishmael's concluding announcement in the "Epilogue" of *Moby-Dick* ("The drama's done. Why then here does any one step forth? – Because one did survive the wreck" [p. 470]). When "End of Book" was written at the close of *Billy Budd*, the narrator is informing us that the drama of Captain Vere and Billy is done "and I only am escaped alone to tell thee."

The meditative Epilogue of *White Jacket* (titled "The End") views a man-of-war as a counterpart of "this earth that sails through the air." "Outwardly regarded," the narrator observes, "our craft is a lie; for all that is outwardly seen of it is the clean-swept deck, and oft-painted planks comprised above the water-line; whereas, the vast mass of our fabric, with all its storerooms of secrets, forever slides along far under the surface" (VI, 503). This passage could well serve as the motto of *Billy Budd*. The storerooms of secrets aboard the *Bellipotent* are lodged in the hearts of Master-at-Arms Claggart ("Pale ire, envy and despair") and Captain Vere ("in earnest encounter with a fellow-man, a veritable touch-stone of that man's essential nature"). Vere, normally capable of seeing through deception, is alert to the possibility of Claggart's perfidy – but is at a loss to know how to proceed. He is reluctant to call for the "substantiating proof" that Claggart claims is close at hand because "such a proceeding would result in the matter at once getting abroad, which in the present stage of it, he thought, might undesirably affect the ship's company" (p. 90). But if Billy had not been afflicted with a speech impediment and had been capable of defending himself with words instead of an involuntary blow, what light on Claggart's reliability would have been shed by his denial, however circumstantial and eloquent? Vere's suspicions about Claggart would have become a near-certainty that his Master-at-Arms was a dangerous troublemaker – but further inquiry would still have been necessary. That a guilty Billy Budd might lose his composure and betray himself to Vere is a possibility. The confrontation, however, is primarily aimed at Claggart (". . . heed what you speak," the captain warns Claggart after first hearing his accusation; the penalty for bearing false witness is death by hanging, he reminds him [p. 89]).

Vere substitutes a confrontation that cannot possibly lead to the truth for the discreet inquiry into the reliability of Claggart's testimony he initially considered and rejected. The drama enacted aboard the *Bellipotent* focuses on Vere's blindness, not his stupidity or criminality. "Starry" Vere blunders at a crucial moment because he fails to pursue a practical and prudent inquiry into Claggart's reliability as a witness. Once the fatal blow has been struck, Vere blunders by becoming a caricature of a king's man, ready to answer every alternative to an immediate execution with unanswerable legalism and a dubious assessment of the immediate dangers to the ship.

When asked by a member of the drumhead court whether it would not be possible to "convict and yet mitigate the penalty," Vere unhesitatingly rules out such clemency, for the ship's crew would account it "pusillanimous" (p. 108). Such a response from the crew, however, could be a real possibility only if Claggart had not borne false witness – if there were indeed a mutinous conspiracy among the men. To the troubled suggestion of the officer of the Marines that it might be possible, by questioning members of the ship's company, to "shed lateral light, if any is to be had, upon what remains mysterious in this matter," Captain Vere is sympathetic – but undeviatingly certain of his ground. The light that would be shed, he insists, has nothing to do with a military court but is, rather, "a matter for psychologic theologians to discuss"; further, he adds, Claggart's death (". . . the lasting tongue-tie of him – in yonder") makes impossible such an inquiry. "The prisoner's deed," he insists, "– with that alone we have to do" (p. 104).

Vere's responses are self-contradictory. It would have been possible to gather "lateral light" in a prudent way despite the fact that Claggart was dead; such light might have made it possible to "mitigate the penalty" – as the junior Lieutenant had suggested. But it is rigid legalism that prevails. In His Majesty's navy, in wartime at sea, a blow struck by a sailor at a superior officer, apart from its effect, is a capital crime. Captain Vere's heart is genuinely moved ("I feel as you do for this unfortunate boy"); his sympathy notwithstanding, Billy Budd must – and does – hang at dawn, his blessing on Captain Vere echoed by the crew.

When the rebellious old Ushant in *White Jacket* alone keeps his beard and suffers a flogging ordered by Captain Claret, Jack Chase is terribly tempted to strike his captain ("'Better not,' said a topmate; 'it's death, or worse punishment, remember'"). Chase holds back his blow but cannot bear the sight of old Ushant being whipped (". . . with moist eyes Jack forced his way to one side") (VI, 461).

The "great heart" of "Jack Chase, Englishman" is visibly manifested in *White Jacket* and is a hovering presence in *Billy Budd*. And it had made itself felt in *Moby-Dick*. "Oh, my Captain! my Captain! noble soul! grand old heart," exclaims Starbuck to Ahab in a rare moment of tenderness and in a final attempt to call a halt to the imminent fatal encounter with the white whale. For a brief time, Ahab responds with thoughts of his wife and son – then reverts to his former obsession:

What is it, what nameless, inscrutable, unearthly thing is it; what cozening, hidden lord and master, and cruel, remorseless emperor commands me; that against all natural lovings and longings, I so keep pushing, and crowding, and jamming myself on all the time; recklessly making me ready to do what in my own proper, natural heart, I durst not so much as dare? (p. 445)

The two captains have surrendered the humanity of Star-buck and Jack Chase to their obsessions: the American Ahab to an anarchic defiance of God's rule; the British Vere to an inflexible defense of the king's rule.

Two voices: Shakespearian sonorities and "sinewy Saxonisms"

Hemingway described Melville as one of America's early "writers of rhetoric who had the good fortune to find a little . . . of how things, actual things can be, whales for instance, and this knowledge is wrapped in the rhetoric like plums in a pudding." Occasionally, the knowledge is made available "unwrapped in pudding" and that is praiseworthy; but Mel-ville is praised by the critics for his unimportant rhetoric and for "a mystery which is not there."[25] For Hemingway, there are no important American writers before Mark Twain and his famous pronouncement ("All modern American literature comes from one book . . . called *Huckleberry Finn*") has done almost as much to promote that classic as Twain's devastating attack on Cooper has accomplished in undermining the Leatherstocking saga.

William Faulkner has a different view of Melville and his masterpiece. "I think that the book which I put down with the unqualified thought 'I wish I had written that' is Moby Dick," he wrote in 1927 in reply to a question from a literary editor. His enthusiasm was in part directed at Melville's power-ful representation of Ahab's tragedy ("a sort of Golgotha of the heart") as he drags down those around him amidst the timelessness of the sea and "the symbol of their doom: a White Whale." But it is Melville's language as well as his theme that arouses Faulkner's wonder: "A White Whale. White is a grand word, like a crash of massed trumpets; and leviathan himself has a kind of placid blundering majesty in his name. And then put them together!!!"[26] Faulkner read *Moby-Dick* at frequent intervals all of his life;[27] he saw in it mysteries worthy of his lifelong attention – and a language evocative of those mysteries. Faulkner saw not only the grand myth-making and soaring language ("a crash of massed trumpets") but also the pervasive serio-comic effects in *Moby-*

Dick – effects that expand the balloon to cosmic proportions by suddenly puncturing it. These are effects first fully developed in Neal's *Brother Jonathan* (the hero's response to a keg of dynamite and careless smokers during a stagecoach crash) and clearly visible in Poe (the framework of *Pym*), *Moby-Dick* (the final sentence of "Stubb Kills a Whale") – and, in our time, in Faulkner (the birth of a baby in a snake pit at the crest of a flood in "Old Man") and Bellow (Mr Sammler's strugglings – in the midst of a flooded house and other man-made disasters – to reach the bedside of his dying nephew).

Several years before his death Faulkner was asked to name "the single greatest book in American literature" and – insisting that his answer did not convey unqualified certainty – said it was *Moby-Dick*. He placed it over Mark Twain's masterpiece for the same reason that "I rate [Thomas] Wolfe higher than Hemingway." *Huckleberry Finn* was completely shaped and controlled, while *Moby-Dick* is only partly successful, for "it was bigger than one human being could do." To Faulkner, "the gallantry of the effort" was all-important – and it was more important to achieve a gallant failure than a safe success.[28]

A deep sense of the futility of ever completing his explorations of the human condition or adequately conveying its mystery and power are at the heart of Faulkner's observations on his own writings and those of others. Faulkner's one-volume Shakespeare was a perennial companion all of his life and, as he wrote to a friendly critic, he infinitely preferred Shakespeare with all his flaws to Walter Pater with all his polish.[29] His awe and wonder at Shakespeare's achievement resemble Melville's passionate response most forcibly conveyed, during the composition of *Moby-Dick*, in his "Mosses" essay. There Melville sees Shakespeare, "in this world of lies," as the master "of the great Art of Telling the Truth, – even though it be covertly and by snatches" (p. 542). Through such "dark" characters as Hamlet, Lear, Timon and Iago, Shakespeare "craftily says, or sometimes insinuates the things, which we feel to be so terrifically true, that it were all but madness for any good man, in his own proper character, to utter or even hint of them" (pp. 542–3). (Ten years earlier, Sören Kierkegaard had described Shakespeare as "the great master of irony" – one who has mastered his ironic vision so thoroughly

that "insofar as his lyricism sometimes culminates in madness
there is in this madness nevertheless an extraordinary degree
of objectivity.")[30]

In *Moby-Dick*, Melville's mastered irony enables him to
transform Ahab into an American Lear – the Shakespearian
trappings carelessly laid about (on occasion, complete with
stage directions), the rhythms of Shakespeare's grandiloquence
pervading not only Ahab's speech but, to a lesser extent, the
talk of other Yankees among the crew. Though Ahab's
Shakespearian sonorities ring hollow on occasion, there are
times when they strike home – especially so in the speeches
involving Pip.

After the Manxman berates and roughly handles the demented Negro boy, Ahab intervenes (and reveals some of his
buried humanity):

"Hands off from that holiness! Where sayest thou Pip was, boy?"
"Astern there, sir, astern! Lo, lo!"
"And who art thou, boy? I see not my reflection in the vacant
pupils of thy eyes. Oh God! that man should be a thing for im-
mortal souls to sieve through!" (p. 427)

Contributing to the poignancy of this and other Ahab–Pip
exchanges are verbal felicities that set the stamp on Ahab as a
Nantucketer as well as a quasi-Shakespearian tragic hero. His
vocabulary rarely contains the Yankeeisms that were an
abomination to some British (and American) reviewers, but
they occasionally conveyed Melville's keen ear for distinctive
American expressions. The word *sieve* (in the sense of "to pass as
through a sieve") in Ahab's just-quoted speech to Pip is an Ameri-
canism not recorded in the *Dictionary of American English*.[31]

"(*Enter Ahab: Then, all*)" is the Shakespearian stage direction
introducing the "Quarter-Deck" chapter; but what follows
is a profusion of salty nautical talk from Ahab as the shrewd
captain works up his crew to a fever-pitch of excitement about
the white whale. The feelings of the men mount as they
respond to Ahab's barrage of questions ("What do ye do when
ye see a whale, men?" "And what do ye next, men?" "And
what tune is it ye pull to, men?"); and Ahab's own reply to
the questions of his harpooneers reaches an emotional (and
colloquial) crescendo:

"Corkscrew!" cried Ahab, "aye Queequeg, the harpoons lie all twisted and wrenched in him; aye, Daggoo, his spout is a big one, like a whole shock of wheat, and white as a pile of our Nantucket wool after the great annual sheep-shearing; aye, Tashtego, and he fan-tails like a split jib in a squall. Death and devils! men, it is Moby Dick ye have seen – Moby Dick – Moby Dick!"

All this and more is followed by an invitation to the crew that smacks more of a whaling vessel's deck than an Elizabethan stage: "What say ye, men, will ye splice hands on it, now? I think ye do look brave" (pp. 140–3).

The two voices of Ahab (the first Shakespearian, the second nautical and homespun) are counterbalanced by the many voices of Ishmael. Ahab is central but he is encompassed – and overshadowed – by Ishmael. Ishmael's voices speak with compelling authority for many reasons; of central importance is their Americanness.

In *Moby-Dick* Melville assimilated the styles of many writers to shape his own: Rabelais, Burton, Browne, Milton, Coleridge, Carlyle – among others. Shakespeare looms largest among the writers to whom a name can be assigned; and the Bible looms larger than Shakespeare. It is not surprising that, in his mind, these two great influences should be conjoined: in an 1849 letter to his friend Duyckinck, Melville compared "the divine William" to Jesus and suggested that "if another Messiah ever comes twill be in Shakespeare's person."[32] In his "Mosses" essay, Melville referred to a new Messiah in American literature ("this American Shiloh, or 'Master Genius,' as Hawthorne calls him" [p. 550]) – no doubt aware of the fact he was himself writing a new American testament at the time. ("Though I wrote the Gospels in this century," he informed Hawthorne shortly before *Moby-Dick* went to press, "I should die in the gutter.")[33]

The English edition of *Moby-Dick* (titled *The Whale*) was set from proof sheets of the American edition mailed to Richard Bentley, Melville's British publisher, on September 10, 1851.[34] To these sheets, Melville added – to a description of a herd of whales in a state of panic – a long footnote on the whaling term "gally, or gallow."[35] In his note, specifically aimed at his English readers, Melville proudly throws down an American gauntlet in defense of "sinewy Saxonisms" which may sound to a polite landsman's ears like a whaleman's "self-derived savageries" but are actually proud descendants of aristocratic English words now "democratized" in the New World:

*To *gally*, or *gallow*, is to frighten excessively, – to confound with fright. It is an old Saxon word. It occurs once in Shakespeare: –

> "The wrathful skies
> *Gallow* the very wanders of the dark,
> And make them keep their caves."
>
> *Lear*, Act iii, sc. 11

To common land usages, the word is now completely obsolete. When the polite landsman first hears it from the gaunt Nantucketer, he is apt to set it down as one of the whaleman's self-derived savageries. Much the same is it with many other sinewy Saxonisms of this sort, which emigrated to the New-England rocks with the noble brawn of the old English emigrants in the time of the Commonwealth. Thus, some of the best and furthest-descended English words – the etymological Howards and Percys – are now democratised, nay, plebeianised – so to speak – in the New World. (p. 322)

Melville's contention that these "sinewy Saxonisms" are neither American corruptions nor American inventions but are American preservations of the very language of Shakespeare echoes a view widely held in nineteenth-century America – and most vigorously promoted by James Russell Lowell.[36] However inaccurate (it has been repudiated by modern authorities on the history of American English), it reflects Melville's (and America's) deep need for British roots; but his lengthy footnote may also reflect his anticipation of the thoroughgoing bowdlerization (or bentleyization) his *Moby-Dick* proof sheets would be subjected to before its London publication, in three blue-cloth volumes, as *The Whale*.

The vigorous colloquialisms of *Moby-Dick* surrender to British sedateness:

Moby-Dick Who aint a slave?
The Whale Who is not a slave?
Moby-Dick thinks I to myself, I wonder now if this here has any effect on the head?
The Whale thinks I to myself, I wonder now if this has any effect upon the head?

Moby-Dick	True, they rather order me about some
The Whale	True, they rather order me about
Moby-Dick	a sort of eating his own gums
The Whale	eating his own gums
Moby-Dick	but 'tis not me!
The Whale	but 'tis not I![37]

These and numerous other changes water down Melville's pungent Americanness into something more acceptable to what the English editor believed to be the greater delicacy of the English palate.

But it is in the realm of sex that the bowdlerizing proclivities of Bentley's editor become most apparent. A few instances convey the prevailing drift:

Moby-Dick	so that all deified Nature absolutely paints like the harlot, whose allurements cover nothing but the charnel-house within;
The Whale	[omitted]
Moby-Dick	affording Queequeg a fair chance for performing his agile obstetrics on the run, as you may say: Yes, it was a running delivery, so it was.
The Whale	affording Queequeg a fair chance for performing his agile dexterities on the run, as you may say. [following sentence omitted]
Moby-Dick	We saw young Leviathan amours in the deep.
The Whale	[omitted]
Moby-Dick	When overflowing with mutual esteem, the whales salute *more hominum*.
The Whale	[omitted]

Concerning religious matters, the English editor was equally if not more touchy. Every biblical allusion or reference not strictly reverential must be cut out. "Poor Paul" in *Moby-Dick* becomes "St Paul" in *The Whale*; "God" becomes "the Almighty," "that's Christianity" becomes "that's the right sort." A humorous approach to Adam and Eve will simply not do – any more than Ishmael's tolerant meditation on Queequeg's wooden idol:

| *Moby-Dick* | The act of paying is perhaps the most uncomfortable infliction that the two orchard thieves entailed upon us. But *being paid* – what will compare with it? |
| *The Whale* | [omitted] |

Moby-Dick	Thought I. Do you suppose now, Ishmael, that the magnanimous God of heaven and earth – pagans and all included – can possibly be jealous of an insignificant bit of black wood? Impossible!
The Whale	[omitted]

Ishmael's expressions of democratic humanism undergo a sea change:

Moby-Dick	The great God absolute! The centre and circumference of all democracy! His omnipresence, our divine equality!
The Whale	[omitted]
Moby-Dick	thou great democratic God!
The Whale	thou great God!

And the English editor was most deeply offended by chapter 25 in *Moby-Dick* – one that deals in a somewhat less than solemn and respectful way with the coronation of British kings and queens. He cut it out completely from *The Whale* and – since it is short and significant – it is reproduced here in full:

Chapter 25

POSTSCRIPT

In behalf of the dignity of whaling, I would fain advance naught but substantiated facts. But after embattling his facts, an advocate who should wholly suppress a not unreasonable surmise which might tell eloquently upon his cause – such an advocate, would he not be blameworthy?

It is well known that at the coronation of kings and queens, even modern ones, a certain curious process of seasoning them for their functions is gone through. There is a saltcellar of state, so called, and there may be a caster of state. How they use the salt, precisely – who knows? Certain I am, however, that a king's head is solemnly oiled at his coronation, even as a head of salad. Can it be, though, that they anoint it with a view of making its interior run well, as they anoint machinery? Much might be ruminated here, concerning the essential dignity of this regal process, because in common life we esteem but meanly and contemptibly a fellow who anoints his hair, and palpably smells of that anointing. In truth, a mature man who uses hair-oil, unless medicinally, that man has probably got a quoggy spot in him somewhere. As a general rule, he can't amount to much in his totality.

But the only thing to be considered here, is this – what kind of oil is used at coronations? Certainly it cannot be olive oil, nor macassar oil, nor castor oil, nor bear's oil, nor train oil, nor cod-liver oil. What then can it possibly be, but sperm oil in its unmanu-factured, unpolluted state, the sweetest of all oils?

Think of that, ye loyal Britons! We whalemen supply your kings and queens with coronation stuff! (p. 102)

The drastic cuts and changes in *Moby-Dick* administered by the House of Bentley do not permit generalizations about British prudishness as contrasted to American openminded-ness. There were many American publishers as cautious and timid as Bentley. One of them, Wiley and Putnam, insisted on numerous changes in Melville's first book, *Typee*. Deleted from the British edition (published by John Murray), for example, was an anecdote concerning a native queen who flings up her skirts to reveal some hieroglyphics "on her own sweet form" – to the consternation of some French officers (and Mr Wiley, of Wiley and Putnam). Still unsatisfied, the very proper Mr Wiley insisted on a "Revised Edition" from which more of the "raciness" and all critical comments on missionaries were deleted.[38] Melville's dealings with publishers were troublesome on both sides of the Atlantic.

Despite the deletions of many of its most pungent collo-quialisms, a reviewer of *The Whale* in the London *Britannia* complained about those "few Americanisms" that mar for him language that is "appropriate and impressive"; another reviewer, for *John Bull*, is patronizing ("all that is idiomatically American in the tone of his sentiments, and in the slang which runs through his discourse, we are most willing to forgive him"); still another reviewer, in the London *Morning Chronicle*, has reservations about the "moonstruck lunacy" of portions of the novel – but the highest praise for the "rare imaginative power and noble might of expression" of the book as a whole.[39]

Some of the most searching praise for *Moby-Dick* came from British critics – but the book was a financial failure in Britain as well as America. Melville turned away from sea subjects to a land-based romance centering on misguided love and author-ship, *Pierre: or the Ambiguities*, offering it to Bentley as a work "very much more calculated for popularity" than his previous works ("a regular romance, with a mysterious plot to it, & stirring passions at work, and withall, representing a new & elevated aspect of American life"). Bentley was not impressed and would agree to accept Melville's new novel only if the American author would accept smaller royalties and agree to the alterations of "a judicious literary friend" – alterations that both *Mardi* and *The Whale* would have profited from. If in those novels, wrote Bentley to Melville, "You had . . . restrained your imagination somewhat and had written in a style to be understood by the great mass of readers – nay if you had not sometimes offended the feelings of many sensitive readers you would have succeeded in England."[40] Melville broke off his negotiations and Bentley never published *Pierre*, or any other work by Melville. Two other Melville books – *The Piazza Tales* (1856) and *The Confidence-Man* (1857) – did find British publishers. It was apparent, however, that his bid for critical recognition and financial reward from England or his native land had failed. At the age of thirty-seven, Melville was at the end of his public career as a writer of fiction.

Two revivals: Leicester and London

In 1884, Melville was an almost totally forgotten writer in his native land. Though philosophical and resigned about the literary oblivion to which he had been consigned by his contemporaries, he nonetheless had some feelings about that oblivion: when invited to assist in the founding of the Authors' Club, a year earlier, Melville had declined – and when he did make an appearance, a young member remembered him as "an unobtrusive personality" whose name "meant little to me then, and I gave him only a casual glance."[41] (The young member, Brander Matthews, was recalling the encounter almost four decades later, at the beginning of the Melville revival.) About the same time as Melville's unenthusiastic and virtually unnoticed visit to the Authors' Club in New York City, a young Englishman wrote from his native town of Leicester to thank Melville

for an immense deal of good I have derived from reading your works & can assure you that here in Leicester your books are in great request. We have had a great deal of trouble in getting them . . . [and] as soon as one is discovered (for that is what it really is with us) it is eagerly read & passed round a rapidly increasing knot of "Melville readers."

Melville's admirer was James Billson, twenty-six years old and three years out of Oxford, where he had taken honors in his study of the classics; in Leicester he combined a law practice with informal instruction of working-men in Greek and Latin literature. Billson informed Melville, in his letter, that he and his circle had, with great difficulty, unearthed and read with delight nine of his books; he listed them and asked for the titles of any other books by Melville not on his list.[42] Billson's list included (in the order he gave them) *Mardi, Typee, The Confidence-Man, The Piazza Tales, Omoo, Redburn, Moby-Dick, Israel Potter* and *Pierre*. It is possible (if not probable) that, in 1884, there were as many (if not more) devoted and knowledgeable readers of Melville's writings in the town of Leicester than in the whole of America. Melville's reply was grateful and gracious and a friendly correspondence followed; in the course of it, Melville sent Billson a copy of *Clarel*, "the sole presentation-copy of the issue."[43]

During the same year in which James Billson initiated his correspondence with Melville, another Englishman searched in vain for the novelist in New York City – and conveyed his dismay at America's neglect of "this Titan." Robert Buchanan, an ardent admirer of Walt Whitman, published in the London *Academy* a poetic tribute to Whitman, "Socrates in Camden" – with prominent reference, in a lengthy passage, to Melville ("my sea-magician"). In a footnote to the poem, Buchanan tells of his vain search for Melville and complains: "No one seemed to know anything of the one great imaginative writer fit to stand shoulder to shoulder with Whitman on that continent." Billson sent Melville a copy of the *Academy* containing Buchanan's poem; the novelist conveyed his pleasure ("The tribute to Walt Whitman has the ring of strong sincerity") – with the suggestion that the praise directed toward him is undeserved ("tho' I am alive to the spirit that dictated it").[44]

Other British admirers conveyed their appreciation (among them, W. Clark Russell, John W. Barrs, Henry S. Salt) and it may well have been the encouragement provided by the Melville coterie in Leicester that moved the novelist-turned-poet to turn again in the last years of his life to fiction. The manuscript of *Billy Budd* opens with a notation ("Friday November 16, 1888 / Began") and closes with another ("End of Book / April 19th 1891") – notations that reflect, in part, the enthusiasm and understanding he was receiving from England. After three decades, he had returned to fiction – to a novel about a British captain and British naval vessel – dedicated to "Jack Chase / Englishman."

At the time of Melville's death five months later, the manuscript of *Billy Budd* remained unpublished among his papers. "Publication – is the Auction / Of the Mind of Man –" wrote Emily Dickinson, who carefully preserved her poems in manuscript – discovered in a locked box shortly after her death in 1886. Herman Melville, who had learned all too well Dickinson's lesson, made no attempt in the time remaining to him after its completion to arrange for the publication of *Billy Budd*.

In 1906, Frank Jewett Mather sought out Melville's daughter Elizabeth at the Florence, an old-fashioned apartment house in lower New York. She brought out a japanned tin cakebox and Mather read through portions of Melville's travel diaries and the manuscript of *Billy Budd*. He approached a number of American publishers with a proposal for a modest biography but the response was uniformly and decisively negative: "Herman Melville was a hopelessly bad risk, and one that no prudent publisher could undertake even to the extent of a few hundred dollars." Thirteen years later, Raymond Weaver traced Melville's granddaughter to her home in Wellesley Farms and rediscovered "the most precious of cake boxes."[45] Weaver's *Herman Melville: Mariner and Mystic* (1921) was the first biography and provided impetus to the rediscovery of Melville. But by 1921, D. H. Lawrence had already written two extraordinary essays on Melville (he had expressed admiration for *Moby-Dick* as early as 1916); other British tributes (by John Masefield, F. C. Owlett, Viola Meynell, E. L. Grant Watson) also appeared before Weaver's biography. H. M. Tomlinson, who hailed Melville and heralded the Melville revival in a series of articles in British journals, saw the publication, in 1920, of *Moby-Dick* in the World's Classics series of Oxford University Press, with a preface by Viola Meynell, as the event that "dates the accession of Herman Melville."[46] But the event that most certainly dates the accession of Herman Melville took place in London between 1922 and 1924: the publication by Constable and Company of *The Works of Herman Melville* in a handsome sixteen-volume set; it was fitting that *Billy Budd* should make its first appearance in print (as volume 13) in England. The long-forgotten writings that James Billson and his friends in Leicester had tracked down and collected with great difficulty and devotion in the early 1880s were now readily available to England and to the rest of the world. The Melville revival was now truly on – in England and throughout the world.

Part Two

FORAYS AND FRIENDSHIPS

8

God's ambassador: Harriet Beecher Stowe and Old England

God's Book and Byron's presence

In mid-June of 1852, three months after the publication of *Uncle Tom's Cabin,* Harriet Beecher Stowe told a friend about a recent letter from her brother expressing concern that the great praise and publicity she was receiving might "induce pride and vanity" and do harm to her Christian character. Her brother had no need to be troubled, the author told her friend, for "I did not write that book." It had all come "before me in visions one after another, and I put them in words." The first vision had come upon her in February 1851 during a communion service in the Bowdoin College church. She saw before her, "like the unrolling of a picture," an old slave being whipped to death. She was witnessing, in terrible detail, the death of Uncle Tom. On returning home, she immediately wrote out what she had seen – and read the account to her children. They wept, and Uncle Tom was ushered into the world.[1] A month later she wrote to the editor of the *National Era* about her story, "a series of sketches" that might run for three or four installments. It grew involuntarily and unpredictably, and took forty installments of increasing length to run its course.[2]

When Lord Carlisle wrote to praise her book, Mrs Stowe's reply was characteristic:

The subject is one so grave, so awful – the success of what I have written has been so singular and so unexpected – that I can scarce retain a self-consciousness and am constrained to look upon it all as the work of a Higher Power, who, when He pleases can accomplish his results by the feeblest instruments.[3]

And this is the account of the book's origin that she presented throughout her life. In her old age, when an admirer of *Uncle*

Tom's Cabin asked permission "to shake hands with you, Mrs Stowe, who wrote it," she shook his hand – but disclaimed any credit as writer. "God wrote it," she insisted; "I merely did his dictation."[4]

From Brunswick, while her novel was growing in the pages of the *National Era*, she wrote to Frederick Douglass to enlist his help in making her scenes on a cotton plantation authentic in its details. In the course of her letter she objected to his view that the Church was "pro-slavery." While in a sense true, Mrs Stowe felt the charge to be unfair, in that a majority of the abolitionists were in the Church. She spoke with authority as "a minister's daughter, and a minister's wife, and I have had six brothers in the ministry." Her father and brothers were, as long as she could recall, passionately dedicated to the anti-slavery movement. She and her husband, as residents on the border of a slave state for seventeen years, had helped innumerable fugitives, and had received the children of liberated slaves into a family school where they were taught by her alongside her own children.[5]

Young Harriet's New England childhood, predictably steeped in Puritan piety, had also a strong admixture of poetry and storytelling. She encountered at an early age the ballads of Walter Scott and Burns, *The Arabian Nights*, Cotton Mather's *Magnalia* – wonderful stories "about my own country . . . that made me feel the very ground I trod on to be consecrated by some special dealing of God's providence."[6] Though novels were generally regarded with suspicion, those of Walter Scott were set apart as superior (and acceptable) by the Reverend Dr Lyman Beecher and, in one summer, young Harriet and her brother "went through 'Ivanhoe' seven times, and were both of us able to recite many of its scenes, from beginning to end, verbatim." But the writer who left the deepest impression on her young childhood was Lord Byron.

One day, she came upon a stray volume of his poetry in her aunt's room:

It was the "Corsair." I shall never forget [Harriet Beecher Stowe wrote late in life] how it astonished and electrified me, and how I kept calling to Aunt Esther to hear the wonderful things that I found in it, and to ask what they could mean. "Aunt Esther, what does it mean – 'One I never loved enough to hate'?"

Her aunt could tell her only that it was one of Byron's strong expressions. She thought much about the poet – a preoccupation strengthened by the fascination he aroused in those around her. Among those drawn to him was her father, and she recalls overhearing at the dinner table his account of the poet's separation from his wife. When Harriet was thirteen there was a day when Dr Beecher said to his wife, "with a sorrowful countenance, as if announcing the death of some one very interesting to him, 'My dear, Byron is dead – *gone*.'" After a long pause, the minister expressed regret that the poet had not lived "to do something for Christ." "What a harp he might have swept!" exclaimed her father in a conversation that struck young Harriet as "solemn and painful" – one that stayed vividly in her mind for the rest of her life. (Three decades later she told Lady Byron of the solitary hours she spent on a lonely hill the day she heard the news.) And she remembered equally well the sermon her father preached the following Sunday, a funeral sermon on the text: "The name of the just is as brightness, but the memory of the wicked shall rot." He presented a sketch of Byron's career, an evaluation of his writings (some imperishable as brass, others – marred by impurities – doomed to oblivion), and concluded with an "eloquent lamentation over the wasted life and misused powers of the great poet." Young Harriet did not understand most of her father's sermons – "but this I understood perfectly, and it has made an impression on me that has never been effaced."[7]

A year later, during the summer of 1825, her father preached another sermon that – unlike his usual unintelligible discourses on doctrine – "sprung out of the deep feeling of the occasion" and had as its text the declaration of Jesus: "Behold, I call you no longer servants, but friends." Moved as she had never been before by Dr Beecher's "direct, simple, and tender language" and his picture of Christ as a compassionate comrade, young Harriet became aware of her great need – and was suddenly convinced that if she was required to have a conviction of sins that she had never heretofore experienced: "He was able to give me even this also." She never forgot the expression on her father's face when she came to him in his study "and fell in his arms saying, 'Father, I have given myself to Jesus, and He has taken me.'"[8]

There was no contradiction between Harriet's intense piety and her enthusiasm for the adventurous and sinful Byron. And there was a temperamental affinity between the forty-year-old author of *Uncle Tom's Cabin* and the dead Byron. It manifested itself in her creation of what may be one of the most vivid characters in the novel, the aristocratic southern slaveholder Augustine St Clare.

Uncle Tom has rescued Eva from a watery death and her father negotiates with the slave-trader Haley to purchase him. St Clare has Eva's "noble cast of head, the same large blue eyes" – but St Clare's expression (unlike Eva's dreaminess) is clear and bold, with "a light wholly of this world: the beautifully cut mouth had a proud and somewhat sarcastic expression, while an air of free-and-easy superiority sat not ungracefully in every turn and movement of his fine form" (153–4).[9] This is a portrait of Byron – his physical appearance, his sardonic serio-comic stance simultaneously expressive of hopelessness and faith. St Clare is a sufferer who has lost his true love (through treachery) and is hopelessly trapped in a loveless marriage. His New England cousin, Miss Ophelia St Clare (an exaggeratedly stern caricature of the author), walks so unswervingly in the path of duty that she displays "a severe and somewhat gloomy cast to her religious character." How, asks the narrator, can we explain her close relationship to Augustine, whose skepticism is at odds with "every one of her most cherished habits and opinions?" We are told simply that she has cared for him during his childhood and that she loves him. But more, she has an understanding of that side of him that he usually hides from the world. When St Clare rhapsodizes about what Uncle Tom means to Eva ("his songs and Methodist hymns are better than an opera, and the . . . little bits of trash in his pocket a mine of jewels"), Miss Ophelia responds:

"It's strange, cousin," said Ophelia; "one might almost think you were a *professor*, to hear you talk."
"A professor?" said St. Clare.
"Yes; a professor of religion." (184)

On another occasion, St Clare confides to his cousin his earlier dreams of being something more than a drifter: he once had "vague, indistinct yearnings to be a sort of emancipator, – to free my native land from this spot and stain." And he tells how, in a fortnight, he was able to tame a rebellious slave ("a regular African lion" called Scipio) who had successfully rebelled against all the overseers and masters. St Clare dressed Scipio's wounds, tended the slave in his own room, and offered him his freedom. In turn, Scipio tore up his freedom papers, embraced Christianity and soon after laid down his life for his new master (238–40). St Clare's account is not a commentary on the efficient handling of slaves; it tells of the extraordinary efficacy of Christian love and of Christ-like traits for the most part buried within himself.

St Clare is a dreamer and talker, not a doer. He sees clearly and talks lucidly about the enormous task of education that lies ahead after emancipation – but transacts Topsy's freedom papers only when Miss Ophelia's Yankee insistence on immediate action cannot be ignored. And the fatal stab wound inflicted when he attempts to prevent bloodshed during a drunken brawl seems an appropriate conclusion to an inconclusive life. While attempting to wrest a bowie knife from one of the brawlers, he receives a fatal stab in the side. It is a trivial, sordid happening; but St Clare has acted. And he dies recalling the phrases from the "Dies Irae" that speak of Jesus' sacrifice for him; with Tom's hand in his, St Clare dies in joyous acceptance of Christ's acceptance of him.

St Clare, in his inability to act on his abhorrence of slavery, stands sharply apart from the author who sees her book as God's instrument designed to effect change where the possibility of change appears non-existent. Her book was nothing if not an act, a blow for freedom. Mrs Stowe had little patience with what she referred to as "cold art"; her book, she states in her preface, seeks to strike a note "in unison with the great master chord of Christianity, 'good will to man.'" Her book was an act of faith with little hope or expectation of success; she had no choice but to write it.

Byron had expressed, in 1821, similar views on the need to act, however uncertain the outcome:

They mean to *insurrect* here [at Ravenna], and are to honour me with a call thereupon. I shall not fall back; though I don't think them in force or heart sufficient to make much of it. But, *onward*!

– it is now time to act, and what signifies *self*, if a single spark of that which would be worthy of the past can be bequeathed unquenchedly to the future? It is not one man, nor a million, but the *spirit* of liberty which must be spread.[10]

Byron was much more of a lapsed Calvinist than Stowe; his campaigns for the spirit of liberty are not infused with the redemptive Christianity that pervades *Uncle Tom's Cabin*. But, less than a year before his death, he expressed sentiments that place him within the range of sentiments conveyed by Augustine St Clare shortly before his death – and close to those of the narrator of the novel. Byron told Dr James Kennedy that "he was very desirous to believe, as he experienced no happiness in having his religious opinions so unsteady and unfixed." But he was troubled by an inability to understand the Scriptures and by the vast gulf he had observed between the principles and the conduct of professed believers. Byron was sorry to report that "he had seen few, if any, whom he could rely upon as truly and conscientiously believing the Scriptures."[11] (It was these lengthy conversations on religion between Byron and Dr Kennedy – published by Kennedy in 1830 – that Harriet Beecher Stowe would recall to Lady Byron during a fateful meeting in London in 1856.)

The gap between "the great principles of Christian brotherhood" and the active or passive support of slavery by those who professed to be true believers was the mighty subject of *Uncle Tom's Cabin*. St Clare, however, is closer to the gloomy, disillusioned hero of *Childe Harold's Pilgrimage* than the fighter for freedom that Byron eventually became. His disillusion is lifted in his dying hour as he reaches out his hand to Uncle Tom; and it is Tom's Christian martyrdom that sums up God's blow for freedom. Harriet Beecher Stowe knew well both aspects of Byron's genius: the creator of the melancholy Harold – and "the Trumpet Voice of Liberty." During her own brief pilgrimage to Europe in 1853 – shortly after her triumphal tour of England – it is not surprising that the author of *Uncle Tom's Cabin* "read Childe Harold on the Rhine."[12]

"The good land of my fathers": triumphal tour

Harriet Beecher Stowe did not see her divine mission as completed with the completion of her book. Shortly after sending in the last proof sheet, she read with dismay Horace Mann's eloquent (and vain) plea on behalf of a number of young men and women about to be consigned to a slave warehouse in Virginia. "It seemed [she wrote in the introduction to a later edition of *Uncle Tom*] that there was no hope, that nobody would hear, nobody would read, nobody pity; that this frightful system, that had already pursued its victims into the free States, might at last even threaten them in Canada." It occurred to her that a direct appeal to influential Englishmen might enlist their help in the anti-slavery cause – and reduce the possibility of Canada being closed as a haven to fugitive slaves. She wrote letters to those known to be interested in the suffering of the slaves: Prince Albert, the Duke of Argyll, the Earls of Carlisle and Shaftesbury, Macaulay, Dickens, Charles Kingsley – and many others. A presentation copy of the novel accompanied each letter.[13]

Her lengthy response to Lord Carlisle (a portion of which has already been quoted) helps to clarify why she was directing her particular attention to England. More was involved than the danger of losing Canada as a haven for runaway slaves. She was witnessing what she believed to be the moral disintegration of the American people, whose leaders privately proclaimed slavery an abomination, yet publicly united in giving support to the Fugitive Slave Law. She had become blunted in her own feelings: "In dealing even for the ransom of slaves, in learning market prices of men, women, and children, I feel that I acquire a horrible familiarity with evil." Nothing had made the atrophy of the American conscience more evident than the fact that the English had responded with "much more keenness" to the crimes exposed in her book. Mrs Stowe saw in England a kindred spirit – "but disembarrassed from our temptations" and free from "the thousands of influences that blind and deaden us." She looked for a lively and healthful surge of English feeling on the subject that would bring back to life America's "paralyzed vitality."

Enthusiastic letters poured in from both sides of the Atlantic –

but in England there was also a call for action. A group of women representing the social, philanthropic and literary worlds met at Stafford House, the Duke of Sutherland's London residence, and approved a document composed by Lord Shaftesbury – *An Affectionate and Christian Address from the Women of Great Britain to the Women of America*. It called for the abolition of slavery – and, in the interim, for the elimination of those American laws which, "in direct contravention of God's own law," denied the slave, first, a family life secure from arbitrary separation and, second, a Christian education. By the end of the winter of 1852–3, more than half a million British women had signed the document; twenty-six huge volumes containing their signatures were eventually sent to Harriet Beecher Stowe as spokeswoman for all the women of America. The closing paragraph of the document made it clear that this was not a British indictment of America – that England must also accept a part of the blame:

We acknowledge with grief and shame our heavy share in this great sin. We acknowledge that our forefathers introduced, nay, compelled the adoption of, slavery in those mighty colonies. We humbly confess it before Almighty God; and it is because we so deeply feel and unfeignedly avow our own complicity, that we now venture to implore your aid to wipe away our common crime and our common dishonour.[14]

It was in a grateful and responsive mood that Harriet Beecher Stowe received a letter in December 1852 from Dr Ralph Wardlaw, on behalf of two Glasgow anti-slavery organizations, extending an invitation to Mrs and Professor Stowe to visit the British Isles at their expense. In February, she wrote to Eliza Fullen (an American on an extended visit to London) about her invitation:

It seems so odd and dream-like that so many persons desire to see me, and now I cannot help thinking that they will think, when they do, that God hath chosen "the weak things of this world."

If I live till Spring I shall hope to see Shakespeare's grave, and Milton's mulberry-tree, and the good land of my fathers, – old, old England! May that day come![15]

The day came; on April 10, 1853, the steamer *Niagara* dropped anchor in Liverpool after eleven days at sea. Mrs Stowe, accompanied by her husband and brother, was surprised to find "quite a crowd on the wharf, and we walked up to our carriage through a long lane of people, bowing and looking very glad to see us."[16] They were, in fact, there to see the woman who had produced America's most electrifying book. It was a scene that would be repeated again and again throughout Scotland and England during the next two months. (Sydney Smith's contemptuous query had been answered: in England, *everyone* was reading an American book!)

The remarks of the Reverend Mr George Gilfillan on behalf of the Dundee Antislavery Association are characteristic in their fervent tribute to Mrs Stowe's "transcendent literary merit and moral worth." Gilfillan's tribute, however, incorporated some observations on American writers that may have made her more than a little uneasy. "We have long been accustomed to despise American literature – I mean as compared to our own," he observed. "It was thought that [Americans] lived entirely on plunder – the plunder of poor slaves, and of poor British authors." The text of Gilfillan's address indicates that "Loud cheers" erupted at this point; but it is doubtful that the enthusiasm was shared by the American author to whom this talk was directed – even though her success was extravagantly hailed by Gilfillan as one "altogether unparalleled, and in all probability never to be paralleled in the history of literature." Heretofore, Gilfillan remarked, American writings "have been treated either with contempt or with patronizing wonder"; but the time for such treatment was past. "Let us hear no more of the poverty of American brains, or the barrenness of American literature," he proclaimed, for *Uncle Tom's Cabin* alone saves America from all such contempt – as surely as *Don Quixote* would have rendered Spain illustrious had it produced no other work.[17] This was praise that did not conceal a deep hostility. (A former admirer of Emerson, Gilfillan had recently come to regard the American as a dangerous enemy of Christianity.)

The book and Mrs Stowe were received in Scotland and England with unprecedented enthusiasm. About the time Mrs Stowe reached England, more than two and a half million copies of *Uncle Tom's Cabin* had been sold in all countries – one and a half million of them in Great Britain and its colonies alone; and this *before* the author had set foot on British soil. The sale in the United States was enormous – 305,000 copies from April through December of the first year – but scarcely as impressive as the staggering totals abroad.[18] The British sales, of course, reflected the fact that the novel, unprotected by copyright, was being issued in numerous cheap editions. But it would not have been possible to give away free copies of a book that people did not want to read – and almost everyone (especially in England) was eager to read *Uncle Tom's Cabin.*

Mrs Stowe was, of course, in tremendous demand for public meetings and social occasions. In the midst of all the adulation, she was calm, insisting that these displays were the manifestations of universal revulsion at the evils of slavery rather than a personal tribute.

Accompanying the adulation were, as in Dundee, unpleasant rumblings. Old animosities had a way, on occasion, of transforming anti-slavery sentiment into anti-American sentiment. On May 16, four thousand people crowded into Exeter Hall to catch a glimpse of Mrs Stowe. "The character of the speeches at this meeting, with the exception of Lord Shaftesbury's [the author wrote to her father] was more denunciatory, and had more to pain the national feelings of an American, than any I had ever attended." Professor Stowe, unable to restrain himself, took the floor to point out that England could put an end to American slavery by insisting on free-grown cotton; it now consumed four-fifths of the American slave-grown cotton. "Are you willing to sacrifice one penny of your own profits for the sake of doing away with this cursed business?" he asked. A London representative of *The Observer* reported that the Exeter Hall fanatics would have created some unpleasantness for the professor if he were not the husband of Harriet Beecher Stowe.[19]

Lord Carlisle, in his first letter of praise in response to *Uncle Tom's Cabin,* had expressed some unhappiness about what he felt to be the book's unfair attacks on England. St Clare had compared the crime of slavery to the exploitation of the poor in England:

Look at the high and low, all the world over, and it's the same story, – the lower class used up, body, soul and spirit, for the good of the upper. It is so in England; it is so everywhere; and yet all Christendom stands aghast, with virtuous indignation, because we do the thing in a little different shape from what they do it.

Miss Ophelia's response is brief: "It isn't so in Vermont" – and St Clare concedes that "in New England, and in the free states, you have the better of us, I grant" (219). Lord Carlisle grants no such thing about England in his letter to Mrs Stowe. "Whenever you speak of England and her institutions," he complains, "it is in a tone which fails to do them justice." The parallel drawn between British aristocracy and capitalists and southern slaveholders is "wholly inapplicable." "Our capitalists," he suggests, "are very much the same sort of persons as your own in the Northern States."[20]

Lord Carlisle's objection notwithstanding, the parallel was frequently drawn – most dramatically at the Lord Mayor's banquet in London on May 2. Charles Dickens had been invited as England's literary representative and, as Mrs Stowe reported in a letter to her sister, Mr Justice Thomas Noon Talfourd proposed a toast to "the literature of our two countries, under the head of 'Anglo-Saxon Literature.' He made allusion to the author of Uncle Tom's Cabin and Mr. Dickens, speaking of both as having employed fiction as a means of awakening the attention of the respective countries to the condition of the oppressed and suffering classes."[21] After some further praise for Mrs Stowe and a tribute to the works of Dickens, Judge Talfourd concluded by proposing "Mr. Charles Dickens and the literature of the Anglo-Saxons." In his reply, Dickens observed that "he could not forget he was in the presence of a stranger who was the authoress of a noble book, with a noble purpose. But he had no right to call her a stranger, for she would find a welcome in every English home."[22] Dickens then went on to respond in a humorous vein to a previous speaker's defense of the Court of Chancery (and veiled criticism of *Bleak House*). Mrs Stowe, who was sitting opposite Dickens, overheard a later conversation between the author and "a gentleman of the bar" who insisted that improvements in the legal system had greatly speeded things up – "that a case not extraordinarily complicated might be got through with in three months." Dickens was glad to hear this but seemed, Mrs Stowe reported, not entirely convinced.

She commented on the "good-natured and agreeable" tone of the exchange – in favorable contrast to the bitterness of American controversy.[23]

Mrs Stowe seems to have been unaware that Dickens' easy and agreeable manner was a courteous façade; several months earlier, Dickens had been subjected to a series of scathing criticisms in the London *Standard* by Lord Denman, former Lord Chief Justice of England and heretofore a good friend of the author. Dickens had, in *Household Words*, referred to *Uncle Tom* as "a noble work" but one seriously marred by "overstrained conclusions and violent extremes."[24] Lord Denman took strong exception to Mrs Jellyby in *Bleak House*, "a disgusting picture" of a woman full of zeal for Africa while creating a life of misery for her own children. Angered by what he felt to be advocacy of the slaveholder's cause, Lord Denman attacked the novelist's exposure of the abuses of Chancery for coming after – instead of before – the recent successful campaign on behalf of Court reform. And he was especially vehement in his attack on Dickens' faint praise and adverse criticism of *Uncle Tom*. The "violent extremes" referred to by Dickens, Lord Denman insisted, existed only in "the capricious cruelty of masters, and the extreme suffering of the oppressed." Harriet Beecher Stowe, Lord Denman announced rather pointedly, was an author without equal – with "graphic skill and pathetic power" beyond the reach of all living writers.

Dickens did not respond publicly to these attacks but, in letters to friends, continued to express both admiration for and dissatisfaction with *Uncle Tom's Cabin* and its author. Uncle Tom seems "a little too celestial"; St Clare is "conceived with great power and originality" and would be unexceptionable if he had not "a Grecian outline of face" which already had become a little tiresome to him, in his infancy. Further, Mrs Stowe "is a leetle unscrupulous in the appropriatin' way"; Dickens sees someone very much like himself "peeping very often through the thinness of the paper."[25] To Lord Denman's daughter – who had written a letter of explanation and apology shortly after her father suffered a paralytic stroke – Dickens wrote a lengthy defense of *Bleak House* and Mrs Jellyby, and of his criticism of *Uncle Tom's Cabin*.[26]

All this was a preamble to the Lord Mayor's banquet.
Harriet Beecher Stowe's most detailed biographer notes, without explanation, that Dickens' remarks on that occasion
represented "the most restrained praise of herself and *Uncle
Tom's Cabin* Harriet was to hear publicly expressed in the
course of her entire British visit."[27] But Dickens' "restrained
praise" was not very surprising; though Lord Denman was
not present at the banquet, Dickens must have been very much
reminded of him – and his hostile criticisms.

My account of the Stowe–Dickens relationship has been
based in part on the letters Mrs Stowe wrote to friends and
relatives during her visit – collected and printed in 1854 as
Sunny Memories of Foreign Lands. About this book, Dickens
conveyed sentiments that can scarcely be termed "good-
natured and agreeable." He writes a friend that Mrs Stowe's
book is pleasant but "a little conceited in its affectation of
humility. Her Moony Memories are very silly I am afraid."[28]
Dickens could not have failed to notice in *Sunny Memories* Mrs
Stowe's warm tribute to Lord Denman and the series of letters
he had written in response to "some palliations of [slavery]"
that appeared in certain English papers – an exertion that
caused a breakdown in his delicate state of health.[29] The six
articles had been reprinted as a pamphlet dedicated to Mrs
Stowe and titled *Uncle Tom's Cabin, Bleak House, Slavery and
Slave Trade. Six articles by Lord Denman, Reprinted from the
Standard* (London, 1853).[30] Dickens is not mentioned in Mrs
Stowe's comments on Lord Denman's articles – though the
pamphlet dedicated to her must have been known to her.
Mrs Stowe's silence in *Sunny Memories* about the central target
of Lord Denman's pamphlet was, consequently, a very eloquent one to Dickens – one that contributed to his comments
on "Moony Memories" and its author. These remarks, however, were positively good-natured and agreeable compared
to his expressions of feeling in 1869, when Mrs Stowe's
revelation about Lord Byron appeared.

Despite the anti-American clouds that darkened some of the
public meetings and the chilly undercurrents of Mrs Stowe's
relationship to Dickens, her tour of Great Britain was a
triumph. She found time for pilgrimages to the great architectural monuments of the past. Much of Scotland she saw

through the eyes of Scott – reminded on frequent occasions of his presence amidst the wild loveliness of Scottish landscapes, castles and abbeys. At Glamis Castle she reflected on the tragedy of Macbeth and on the night, in 1793, that Scott spent in the castle. She quotes at length from Scott's account (in his *Letters on Demonology*) of what proved to be a terrifying experience – "mingled at the same time with a strange and indescribable pleasure."[31] After a long visit to Abbotsford, Mrs Stowe was ferried across the Tweed (whose white, pebbled bottom was "just like our New England mountain streams") to Scott's burial place in Dryburgh Abbey. The boatman invited the author and her party to his cottage, where she discovered that "he and all the household, even the old grandmother, had read *Uncle Tom's Cabin*, and were perfectly familiar with all its details." She was told that everyone in the vicinity had read her book. When Mrs Stowe mentioned that she was going to Dryburgh to see Scott's grave and asked whether he was a favorite, she was told that Burns was more popular than Scott among the working-people. Mrs Stowe, reflecting on this phenomenon on another occasion, came to the conclusion that Scott belonged more "to a past, and not to the coming age"; that "He loved and worshipped in his very soul institutions which the majority of the common people feel as a restraint and a burden." Free Americans, far removed from feudalism, were moved by the picturesque aspects of these institutions, while those who had suffered under them "have quite another impression."[32]

She became aware of Byron's presence in Scotland – and elsewhere. In Aberdeen, at the famous bridge of Balgounie, Mrs Stowe meditated on the way in which these lovely surroundings had helped shape "the sensitive mind of Byron, who lived here in his earlier days." But it was at a luncheon in London on May 24 that she had an experience that brought Lord Byron out of the world of shadowy imagination into the immediate present: she met Lady Byron.[33]

Byron's widow was, in Mrs Stowe's eyes, a fragile beauty of sixty-one, slender and slight, graceful and decisive, her bright eyes "full of interest and quick observation." While they were being introduced, Byron's words came to Mrs Stowe's mind:

There was awe in the homage that she drew;
Her spirit seemed as seated on a throne.

Their talk, after some initial playfulness, turned to the slavery
question and Mrs Stowe was impressed by Lady Byron's
incisiveness and knowledge – and by a moral vision "higher
and deeper than the common sentimentalism of the day." It
was a decisive occasion for both women, one that would have
explosive consequences.

Eleven days after this eventful meeting, Harriet Beecher
Stowe was in Paris, at the beginning point of a three-month
tour of the Continent. She had been in Great Britain less than
two months and was to spend three months in Europe; but
her *Sunny Memories of Foreign Lands* devotes three-fifths of its
750 pages to England. On her return from the Continent,
there was a last week in London (where the simplicity of a
service in Westminster Abbey conducted in the English
language was a welcome change from the dramatic effects of
the Roman Catholic rites of Italy) and, soon after, her departure from Liverpool for home on September 7. Her Liverpool
friends waved farewell as she boarded a tender for the trip
down the Mersey to the S.S. *Arctic*. "And thus, almost sadly
as a child might leave home [she writes to conclude her
account of her first visit], I left the shores of kind, strong Old
England – the mother of us all."[34]

Byron's persistence: revelation and outcry

Three years later, Harriet Beecher Stowe visited England
again – this time to obtain the British copyright for her new
anti-slavery novel *Dred*. Aside from this practical purpose,
Mrs Stowe looked forward to a renewal of her acquaintance-
ship with Lady Byron – "one of the brightest anticipations
held out to me in this journey."[35] Their first meeting had
resulted in a correspondence and, in one of her letters, Lady
Byron referred to her failing health and her desire to discuss
some of her religious views "personally with you; for it would
be *soul to soul*." One of Mrs Stowe's first acts on reaching
London was to write to her friend; Lady Byron responded
from her sick-bed urging Mrs Stowe to visit her at once
despite the awkwardness of her situation ("It is not a time for

small personalities, if they could ever exist with *you*"). They talked at great length about the anti-slavery campaign, religion, a variety of other topics. Soon after, Lady Byron wrote to convey her impressions of *Dred* – a book she feels "must prove a great moral force; perhaps not manifestly so much as secretly." She anticipates hostility to the book ("there will be a strong disposition to resist on the part of all hollow-hearted professors of religion, whose heathenisms you so unsparingly expose"), but cites Lord Byron's view that fiction survives to the extent that it contains truth to back up her faith in a long life for *Dred*. Lady Byron told of a strange dream she had experienced after reading the book until a late hour – a dream that brought horrible specters and an agony of fear, followed by a new sense of courage and a renewed trust in God. "Did you do this?" she asks, and says in closing that "I know more than ever how to value communion with you."

In their next meeting, Mrs Stowe told Lady Byron how much the mention of Lord Byron had affected her. They talked at length about Byron, with special reference to the poet's serious conversations about religion with Dr Kennedy – conversations that had long been of special interest to Mrs Stowe. The American told of Byron's powerful influence on her from childhood on – and how deeply, as a girl, she had been affected by the news of his death. To these confidings, Lady Byron responded with the fact that she had already heard of all this from a friend – "and it was one of the things that made me wish to *know* you. I think *you* could understand him."

Their friendship deepened and Lady Byron entertained Mrs Stowe and her family at a lunch soon after. Invited to the party for the sake of Mrs Stowe's young son Henry was Lady Byron's grandson Lord Ockham. The author was moved by Lady Byron's sympathetic and perceptive discussion of her grandson's eccentricities – and her genuine interest in Henry Stowe and her other children.

There came an afternoon in the fall of 1856, shortly before Mrs Stowe was scheduled to leave England for the Continent, set aside by Lady Byron for a confidential talk with her American friend. She had found a true friend and she was moved to tell her an untellable thing about Lord Byron for reasons that Mrs Stowe would fully understand – that she alone could fully understand. "The great fact upon which all turned [the author reported] was stated in words that were unmistakable: – 'Mrs. Stowe, he was guilty of incest with his sister.'" There followed – during the rest of the afternoon – the tangled story of a marriage undertaken by Byron to perpetuate and conceal an attachment abhorrent to the world. Byron had thrust this relationship on her and, when he saw that she could not accept it, insisted on a separation – and warned her that she would always bear the blame, that "The world will believe me, and it will *not* believe you." She had agreed to the separation and never revealed the truth about the rupture. But now she felt it necessary to make a decision about a question that had become increasingly insistent and burdensome: was it not her duty to "make a full and clear disclosure before she left the world?"

Lady Byron believed that it was a terrible thing to be an accomplice in falsehood, that a disclosure of the truth might be essential not only for her own sake but for Lord Byron's. He had always shown signs of remorse and "it was strongly impressed upon her mind that Lord Byron must suffer in looking on the evil consequences of what he had done in this life, and in seeing the further extension of that evil." In a real sense, withholding the truth and presenting him in a falsely sympathetic light had contributed to England's moral decay – a decay accelerated by the numerous cheap editions of Byron's poems that were beginning to flood the market. "It has sometimes strongly appeared to me," Lady Byron told her friend, "that he cannot be at peace until this injustice has been righted."

From Paris a month later, Mrs Stowe conveyed her opinion about what Lady Byron's course of action should be in this terrible matter. She advised, for the present, silence. A revelation at this time would leave vulnerable all that she loved and revered to the unworthy and unjust judgments of this world, to the world's "harpy class, which pollutes what it touches." The day would yet come when all would be revealed – when justice would prevail.

That day came very much closer when Harriet Beecher Stowe was shaken to the center of her being by the publication, in 1869, of *My Recollections of Lord Byron* by Countess Guicciolli, Byron's last mistress, and – far worse – a laudatory review of the book in *Blackwood's Magazine.*[36] The book, a rapturous tribute to the poet and a caustic commentary on his wife ("Lady Byron was an only and a spoilt child, a slave to rule") is surpassed in its animosity only by the *Blackwood's* reviewer ("whatever real or fancied wrongs Lady Byron may have endured are shrouded in an impenetrable mist of her own creation – a poisonous miasma in which she enveloped the character of her husband").

Lady Byron died in 1860, four years after telling her terrible secret. Mrs Stowe had looked in vain for some memoir of this remarkable woman – one that would correct the false picture that Lord Byron and his admirers had perpetuated about her character. Instead, the slanders of Byron's mistress were being "eagerly gathered up and read by an undiscriminating community." Perhaps there were family reasons in England that prevented Lady Byron's friends from speaking out; but Lady Byron had an American reputation – and it was time for an American to refute the slanderous assaults.

There was another compelling reason for Mrs Stowe's defense of Lady Byron. On July 9, 1857, shortly after her return from England, Harriet Beecher Stowe suffered a terrible blow: Henry Stowe, her oldest son, drowned while swimming in the Connecticut River at Hanover, where he was a freshman at Dartmouth College. There were terrors more terrible than the sudden, accidental death of a son in the flower of his youth. Young Henry had not declared himself a Christian: what would be the fate of his eternal soul? She wrote to her sister Catherine: "If ever I was conscious of an attack of the Devil trying to separate me from the love of Christ, it was for some days after the terrible news came." But she had come through the perilous trial: God who made her capable of so total a devotion for her children that she would gladly sacrifice her eternal salvation for them did not create more love in her than He had within himself. She struggled and to her youngest daughter Georgiana expressed the confident hope that "there is coming an inconceivable hour of beauty and glory when I shall regain Jesus, and He will give me back my beloved one, whom He is educating in a far higher sphere than I proposed."[37] To Lady Byron she reached out as a sister-sufferer who knew "everything that sorrow can teach: you whose whole life has been a crucifixion, a long ordeal." God had linked Lady Byron to one "strangely gifted" and "fearfully tempted"; God would, when she left this earth, reward her lifelong trial and love by a sight of her husband, "set free from sin and glorified" through her efforts. Lady Byron's reply (delayed because of her illness) expresses sympathy for her friend's calmness in affliction and, linking Mrs Stowe's loss to her own, offers the consoling thought that "As long as *they* are in God's world, they are in ours."

All this and more led Mrs Stowe to publish in England and America (in *Macmillan's* and the *Atlantic Monthly*) "The True Story of Lady Byron's Life," an article that aroused a tremendous controversy on both sides of the ocean. For three months, reported John Paget in *Blackwood's*, "every newspaper has been filled, and every household in the kingdom inundated" with discussions on matters rarely if ever mentioned by a large segment of the population. Reluctantly, but out of a sense of duty, Paget examined the American novelist's revelations ("We have no more right to shrink from the investigation of Mrs. Stowe's disgusting story than a surgeon has from the examination of a foul disease"). That examination led him to conclude that Lady Byron's charges were totally without foundation. As to Mrs Stowe, "one universal cry of indignation has risen on both sides of the Atlantic. All who glory in the fame of Byron . . . – all who would guard the purity of home from pollution, and the sanctity of the grave from outrage – have joined in one unanimous chorus of condemnation."[38] Dickens conveyed his feelings succinctly in a letter to his good friend James T. Fields, editor of the *Atlantic Monthly* in which Mrs Stowe's article appeared: "Wish you had nothing to do with the Byron matter. Wish Mrs. Stowe was in the pillory." A few weeks later, addressing himself to another friend, he summed up his feelings with even greater energy (in what proved to be his last recorded remarks about Mrs Stowe): "It seems to me that to knock Mrs. Beecher Stowe on the head, and confiscate everything about it [the Byron scandal] in a great international bonfire to be simultaneously lighted over the whole civilized earth, would be the only pleasant way of putting an end to the business."[39]

"This is war to the knife," Mrs Stowe wrote to her

publisher James R. Osgood; "The enemy are perfectly un-scrupulous." Why, she complained, was everyone wildly and distractedly calling on her for proof: "Nobody ever called for proof from any of the numberless writers who reported their conversations with Byron." Her proof, she said, was founded on Lady Byron's known character – and she pointed out that "reliable human testimony is the only proof of the facts which we rest on, in anything."[40]

The central fact is that Harriet Beecher Stowe loved Lady Byron and had unquestioning faith in her story. Her deter-mination was such that she persuaded two hardheaded pub-lishers, one a close friend of Dickens, to publish her article in the *Atlantic Monthly*. And – despite the furor (accompanied by a flood of cancelled subscriptions) – their faith in Mrs Stowe was such that they were persuaded to publish *Lady Byron Vindicated* the year following – a book that elaborates the charges she brought to light in her explosive article. Years later, she said of this book that "the devil and all of his angels could never make me sorry I wrote it." When someone you love is slandered, there is no choice about your course – what-ever the price.[41] It was as necessary – and inevitable – for her to write *Lady Byron Vindicated* as it had been for her to bring forth *Uncle Tom's Cabin*. She was God's instrument.

God's voice as American woman's voice

Two days after the funeral of her son Henry, Harriet Beecher Stowe and her husband visited his college, saw Henry's friends and his room – kept just as it was the day he left it. They walked down to the river, to the bathing place where, "into the pure, clear water he plunged, little dreaming that he was never to come out alive." In a letter to the Duchess of Sutherland (who had lost a son close to Henry's age), Mrs Stowe told how, during their visit, "a poor, deaf old slave woman, who has still five children in bondage, came to com-fort me."

"Bear up, dear soul," she said; "you must bear it, for the Lord loves ye." She said further, "Sunday is a heavy day to me, 'cause I can't work, and can't hear preaching, and can't read, so I can't keep my mind off my poor children. Some on 'em the blessed Master's got, and they's safe; but, oh, there are five that I don't know where they are."

"What are our mother-sorrows to this!" exclaimed the bereaved Mrs Stowe to her English friend. The campaign against slavery, she said, seemed hopeless; but every sorrow she had, every lesson about family love, made her more determined than ever to fight against "this dreadful evil that makes so many mothers so much deeper mourners than I ever can be."[42]

The vision of a slave being beaten to death (experienced during a communion service in a Brunswick church) was the first picture she sketched for *Uncle Tom's Cabin*; but the real beginning of the novel took place during the terrible summer of 1849, at the deathbed of her eighteen-month-old son Charles. While her husband was away in Brattleboro for an extended health cure, Cincinnati was visited by a terrible epidemic of Asiatic cholera. Eleven-year-old Henry began vomiting in the middle of the night, but it was "My Charley – my beautiful, loving gladsome baby" – who finally succumbed. She watched over him in his death agony for four days, "looked on his imploring face [she wrote her husband] when I could not help nor soothe nor do one thing, not one, to mitigate his cruel suffering, do nothing but pray in my anguish that he might die soon."[43] On the eve of Mrs Stowe's first visit to England, she reported (in her long letter to Mrs Follen) that it was at her son's "dying bed and grave that I learned what a poor slave mother may feel when her child is torn away from her." Her only prayer, at that terrible time, was that "this crushing of my own heart might enable me to do some great good to others." She believed that *Uncle Tom's Cabin* "had its root in the awful scenes and bitter sorrows of that summer."[44]

It was this depth of a mother's feeling coupled with an authentic gift for storytelling that enabled Mrs Stowe to serve as God's agent in the production of a masterpiece. In her very first published story, "A New England Sketch" (1834), she had demonstrated an unerring eye and ear for the shadings of regional character and speech; more important, her earliest work displays examples of the effortless fusion of understated wit and compassion to be found in her later, more mature achievements. The main character, Lot Griswold, is an old Yankee whose taciturn, gruff exterior inadequately hides his warmth and vulnerability. The plot, such as it is, has to do with the old man's inability to accept the untimely death of his son – and with his eventual coming to terms with his loss. In the introductory remarks prefacing this story, the narrator pays tribute to "my own land – my own New England . . . the land often spoken against, yet always respected; 'the latchet of whose shoes the nations of the earth are not worthy to unloose.'" She pokes fun at her own "breeze of patriotism," suggesting that each one of us cherishes remembrances of all we loved in the land of our childhood – and invites the reader to substitute "'Old Kentuck,' Old England," or any other place that might make her rhapsodic flight seem more rational. In 1843, Harriet Beecher Stowe published her first book, *The Mayflower*, a collection of fifteen stories and sketches of New England life – and included "Uncle Lot" (the new title of her first story) as the first story in the volume; each of these pieces combined serious emotion (bordering on pious sentimentality) with keen and humorous observations of Yankee foibles.[45]

In her willingness to ridicule her own sentimental attachment to New England, Mrs Stowe exhibited a tough-minded wit that is an important dimension of her first novel – one that makes her accompanying sense of outrage so compelling and contagious. A facet of this tough-mindedness is an appreciative ear for live talk, so fully developed in *Uncle Tom's Cabin* that the novel is, in many ways, a direct forerunner of *Adventures of Huckleberry Finn*. Old Prue responds to Tom's promise of heaven in terms that directly anticipate Huck ("an't thar where white folks is gwine?" she asks; "I'd rather go to torment, and get away from Mas'r and Missis"); and the shadings of vernacular expression are conveyed not only in uneducated white and black characters but – to the dismay of the British poet Coventry Patmore – in the affluent and educated as well. ("Suppose we sell one of your farms, and pay up square," says Mrs Shelby to her slave-owner husband when she learns of his decision to sell Tom; Patmore cites this and many other colloquialisms to illustrate what he calls a "remarkable vulgarity of language" and "an unEnglish tone of conversation.")[46]

The live talk that pervades the novel is related to another dimension of *Uncle Tom's Cabin*: the author's uncanny ability to seem – to *be* – not the creator but the recorder of these scenes. In a letter Mrs Stowe wrote to her father during her first trip to England, the three great writers she held up as models for the use of the English language were Shakespeare, Bunyan and Defoe – admirable in their exhibiting "the solid grain of the English oak, not veneered by learning and the classics." And it is Defoe who is "the most suggestive writer to an artist of fiction that the English language affords." She refers to his gift for producing an impression of reality – so great in *A Journal of the Plague Year* that medical men cited it as an authentic narrative. (It is possible that she read or reread Defoe's work shortly after the Cincinnati cholera epidemic and that his method of combining documented reports with his own reminiscences and visions suggested to her a powerful method for her narrative.)[47]

In the opening chapter of *Uncle Tom's Cabin* we are plunged immediately into the compassionate heart of the book: the separation of a mother from her child. In the foreground are the slave-trader, Haley, and the kindly Mr Shelby, a humane master hopelessly entrapped by financial indebtedness to Haley. Tom is the chief item for negotiation and Haley concedes that "religion [is] a valeyable thing in a nigger, when it's the genuine article, and no mistake." When Eliza's little son Harry demonstrates his cleverness and becomes an item for trade, the mood changes. We know about Tom, thus far, only through his master's affectionate, respectful description; but we are given a direct and vivid picture of Harry – and shortly thereafter we see his mother, hovering anxiously in the vicinity of her son. The beautiful Eliza, in turn, becomes an object of interest to the trader (whose quick eye is "well used to run up at a glance the points of a fine female article"). Haley is no cardboard villain: he knows how to trade and how to manage the emotional complications that clutter a transaction. When he hears of Mrs Shelby's intractable opposition to the sale of Eliza, he proposes "watches, feathers, and trinkets" to smooth the way. When confronted by an irreversible rejection of his bid for Eliza, he is always the businessman – and moves on to negotiate for the boy. As for separating little Harry from his mother, he knows how such things need to be done: you get the girl away for a time – and: "Your wife might get her some ear-rings, or a new gown, or some such truck, to make up with her." Haley provides illustrations of his humane methods as they contrast with those of other traders and suggests that "humanity, sir . . . is the great pillar of *my* management." Shelby is amused – but is left with the grim task of informing his wife that Tom and Eliza's child must be sold. "I would as soon have one of my own children sold," Mrs Shelby tells Eliza to remove her fears. She speaks in good faith before she learns about the financial circumstances that make the sale of Uncle Tom and little Harry, in her husband's view, an absolute necessity.

All this, in a few pages, provides the reader with the living materials for all that follows: the story of Eliza's flight to freedom with her child (and of her eventual reunion with her husband); and the story of Uncle Tom's martyrdom. Though warned by Eliza of his impending fate, Tom chooses submission ("It's better for me alone to go, than to break up the place and sell all") – but he fully understands Eliza's flight ("it's her right! . . . – 'tan't in *natur* for her to stay"). The two strands of the novel are laid out clearly and forcefully at the outset and each complements the other as both proceed, in alternative stages, to the bitter, triumphant end.

One of the most poignant episodes in the book (in chapter XII, "Select Incident of Lawful Change") illustrates the interaction between the two strands. Trader Haley, through a bit of adroit management, sells a young woman's ten-month-old son and gets the infant ashore while the river boat is docked at Louisville – and the young mother is asleep. She awakes, bewildered, to the terrible truth.

"Lucy," said the trader, "your child's gone, you may as well know it first as last. You see, I know'd you couldn't take him down south; and I got a chance to sell him to a first-rate family, that'll raise him better than you can."

The trader had arrived at that stage of Christian and political perfection which has been recommended by some preachers and politicians of the north, lately, in which he had completely overcome every human weakness and prejudice. His heart was exactly where yours, sir, and mine could be brought with proper effort and cultivation. The wild look of anguish and utter despair that the woman cast on him might have disturbed one less practised; but he was used to it. He had seen that same look hundreds of times. (134)

Tom looks on helplessly and understands all. He weeps at Lucy's suffering and speaks of "a pitying Jesus, and an eternal home; but the ear was deaf with anguish, and the palsied heart could not feel." The night wears on and Tom hears, at intervals, a smothered cry and sob. At midnight he wakes to a movement near him – and a splash in the water. The trader is not shocked when he hears the news for it is part of the uncertainties of his business; he sits down with his account book and puts down "the missing body and soul under the head of *losses*!" Should we be shocked at the trader? the narrator asks. Who makes the trader? Should we blame the trader or the system (and those who support the system) that support him and make him inevitable? Uncle Tom is a helpless witness to Lucy's suffering and destruction; the narrator is an outraged witness – and her outrage makes more palpable and visible the presence and suffering of Lucy and Tom that she (and we) are witnessing.

The narrator of Defoe's *Journal of the Plague Year*, outraged at the callous and blasphemous language and behavior of some tavern roisterers – directed in part at himself – prepares for sleep that night by "set[ting] my Mind seriously, and with utmost Earnestness, to pray for those desperate Wretches, that God would pardon them, open their Eyes, and effectually humble them."[48] The narrator of *Uncle Tom's Cabin*, after Lucy's fatal plunge into the river, calls for patience from those who are outraged by wrongs like these, for: "Not one throb of anguish, not one tear of the oppressed, is forgotten by the Man of Sorrows, the Lord of Glory" (136). Like Defoe's narrator, Stowe's is a witness–participant who sees horrifying instances of cruelty, makes visible and tangible what she sees, finds Christian consolation in the midst of these outrages, and at the same time conveys a righteous wrath that reflects (in the language of Defoe's narrator) a "real Zeal for the Honour of God," separate and separable from "the Effects of . . . private Passions and Resentment." But, unlike Defoe's narrator, who is a direct participant as well as witness, Mrs Stowe's is a hovering, invisible presence who speaks for God in the voice of an American woman steeped from earliest childhood in the persuasive strategies of sermon oratory. (At its most eloquent moments, Mrs Stowe's narrator has a kinship with the hovering, invisible narrator of a new American book then in the making, *Leaves of Grass* – the creation of a poet almost equally conversant with sermon oratory and the Bible.)

Cassy's story, toward the close of the novel, further illustrates the skillful interaction between the two strands – and the central position of Eliza's story (of the story of womankind) in the novel. The badly-beaten Tom is ministered to by Cassy who gives an account of a lifetime of sexual exploitation and cruelty that has brought her to believe – to Tom's horror – that "there isn't any God, I believe; or, if there is, he's taken sides against us." When she had resisted sexual submission in the past, the threat was always that her children would be sold; but *after* submission, her children were sold after all. When she gives birth to a little boy who resembles a son she has lost, she makes up her mind never to let him grow up. She kisses her two-week-old infant, cries over him, gives him a fatal dose of laudanum and holds him to her bosom while he sleeps away to death. "I am not sorry to this day," she tells Tom; "he, at least, is out of pain." When Tom earnestly asks her to turn to Christ, Cassy tells him that she "used to see a picture of him, over the altar, when I was a girl . . . but, *he isn't here!* there's nothing here, but sin and long, long, long despair!" (367-77). Tom, with all his genuine feeling and eloquence, could say nothing to ease the grief of Lucy – and can say nothing to Cassy, another "Rachel weeping for her children, and would not be comforted" (Jer. 31:15; a portion of the epigraph for chapter 12, in which Lucy's tragedy is enacted).

In her "Concluding Remarks," the narrator observes that her novel came into being from her desire, after the Fugitive Slave Act of 1850, to convey to men and women of good will the truth about slavery as "a *living dramatic reality*." She addresses herself to all Americans, north and south, but there is a passage – addressed to "you, mothers of America" – that confronts us with the origin of *Uncle Tom's Cabin* and the deepest source of its power:

By the sick hour of your child; by those dying eyes which you can never forget; by those last cries, that wrung your heart when you could neither help nor save; by the desolation of that empty cradle, that silent nursery, – I beseech you, pity those mothers that are constantly made childless by the American slave-trade. (454–6)

This is a direct evocation of the death of her small son Charley during the Cincinnati cholera epidemic in July of 1849; it is a forceful reminder that *Uncle Tom's Cabin* continues to wield its power long after the institution of slavery has disappeared because the novel's ultimate center is another, an older and continuing instrument of forcible separation: death. To come to terms with the death of Charley, Harriet Beecher Stowe looked with new eyes at her fellow-sufferers, the slave-mothers of America, and – in the closing pages of her novel – at her fellow-sufferers, the bereaved white mothers of America. To all these mothers – and to all who can identify with their suffering – a *"living dramatic reality"* is presented so that we can all join hands in repentance, justice and mercy – and in resistance to the forces of injustice and cruelty that, unchecked, "shall bring on nations the wrath of Almighty God!" (460).

In the second anti-slavery novel, *Dred* (1856), and a series of New England novels – most notably *The Minister's Wooing* (1859), *The Pearl of Orr's Island* (1862) and *Oldtown Folks* (1869) – Mrs Stowe displayed and elaborated the perceptions and narrative skills she had exhibited in *The Mayflower*. *Dred* has passages of great force but suffers from being several works in one; Mrs Stowe's New England novels have charm and depth but lack the sweep, the intensity and the overpowering immediacy of *Uncle Tom's Cabin*. The praise of the English novelist Charles Kingsley for Mrs Stowe's first novel ("a really healthy indigenous growth, 'autochthones,' free from all second and third hand Germanisms and Italianisms, and all other unrealisms")[49] suggests its force and importance for an emerging – emergent – national literature. Harriet Beecher Stowe believed to the core of her being that *Uncle Tom's Cabin* was written by God and it bears the stamp – as a whole, and on almost every page – of an authentic, distinctively American millenarian manifestation.

9

Emerson, Carlyle and "the two Englands"

A voyage of self-discovery

Soon after the death of his beautiful young wife, the grieving minister of the Second (Unitarian) Church in Boston was exhibiting increasing restlessness with his religious calling – and an actual distaste for his Church. The heart is the center of the universe, Emerson noted in his journal: "But how little love is at the bottom of these great religious shows; – congregations and temples & sermons – how much sham!"[1] His dissatisfactions found their focus in the doubts he increasingly felt over the long-established rite of the Lord's Supper; in September 1832 he sent an amicable letter of resignation to the proprietors of the Second Church. On Christmas Day, Emerson was a passenger on the brig *Jasper* on a trip to visit Europe and recover his health and spirits. His deepest desire was not to gaze upon the architectural splendors and landmarks of the past but to see some of the English writers who had meant most to him – Coleridge, Wordsworth, Landor and, above all, Carlyle.

Long before Emerson knew Carlyle's name he had recognized the distinctive style and viewpoint of a prolific and anonymous contributor to the *Edinburgh Review* and other periodicals, who spoke directly to his own wavering religious affiliation and unwavering spiritual conviction. In "Signs of the Times" (1829), Carlyle had lashed out at the modern age of machinery not only in the material world, but as it manifested itself in the realm of religion, education, morality, poetry. The great achievements of the past, he argued, were the spontaneous and instinctive efforts of individuals. "To reform a nation," wrote Carlyle, "no wise man will undertake; and all but foolish men know, that the only solid though a far slower reformation is what each begins and perfects on *himself*."

These "Emersonian" sentiments were greatly relished by Emerson; his sermon "A Future Life" (delivered at the Second Church on September 11, 1831) closed with a translation of a Goethe quatrain by Carlyle taken from the opening paragraph of "Signs of the Times."[2] Emerson was also deeply impressed by "Characteristics," in which Carlyle surveys the recent strugglings for religious faith in a mechanistic age and finds a renewed recognition of the eternal fact "that God not only made us . . . but is in us and around us; that the Age of Miracles, as it ever was, now is."[3] A journal entry in early October of 1832 expresses Emerson's gratification with "my Germanick new-light writer whoever he may be"; by October 19, he has learned his benefactor's name and records his gratitude – to which is added some characteristic trepidation:

If Carlyle knew what an interest I have in his persistent Goodness, would it not be worth one effort more, one prayer, one meditation? But will he resist the Deluge of bad example in England? One manifestation of goodness in a noble soul brings him in debt to all the beholders that he shall not betray their love & trust which he has awakened.[4]

On the whole, Emerson's trip was a great success. Despite his protestations against sightseeing, he enjoyed the sights of Europe and quickly recovered his health and spirits during the course of his travels. But his visits with the great men he came to see were something of a disappointment. Landor was given to brilliant observation, not to the give and take of conversation; this was even more true of Coleridge who "was old and preoccupied, and could not bend to a new companion and think with him." Wordsworth was warm and direct but narrow and tame in his views.[5] Emerson's most memorable and rewarding visit was to Craigenputtock, Carlyle's remote farmhouse in Dumfriesshire, southwestern Scotland.

On Sunday, August 18, 1833, Emerson preached a sermon at the Unitarian Chapel on Young Street, Edinburgh – the only sermon he preached in Britain. During the next few days, he wandered over the steep streets of the old town and talked literature with his young guide and companion Alexander Ireland until it was time, on August 21, to begin his pilgrimage

to Craigenputtock. It took some Yankee ingenuity and persistence but, on Sunday afternoon, Emerson's hired gig pulled
up to the farmhouse gate after a fifteen-mile journey from
Dumfries. Carlyle was expecting his American visitor and the
gig was dispatched with instructions to return the next day.
The next twenty-four hours were of great importance to both
men. "Jane says," Carlyle wrote to his mother two days later,
"it is the first journey since Noah's Deluge undertaken to
Craigenputtock for such a purpose." Emerson wrote in his
journal the following day: "A white day in my years."[6]

At Craigenputtock Emerson found the openness and sincerity he had been up to this time seeking in vain. "Truth &
peace & faith dwell with them and beautify them," he wrote
in his journal. To Alexander Ireland, several days later, he
wrote that Carlyle "is the most simple, frank amiable person"
and his wife "a most agreeable accomplished woman." The
two men walked over the hills for several miles and talked
about questions of government and society, about literature
and religion, without reserve on either side. But there were
some shadows on the horizon: Emerson had the feeling that
Carlyle's insight into religious truth was limited – and that his
friend's interest lay in greater governmental intervention to
solve the problems of pauperism. His views of current literature were "despairing or satirical." Emerson was puzzled by
Carlyle's lack of enthusiasm for Socrates; and by his enthusiasm for London. (In a letter to Alexander Ireland, Emerson
expressed the hope that the Carlyles would not leave the
moors: "tis so much better for a man of letters to nurse himself
in seclusion than to be filed down by the compliances &
imitations of city society.")[7]

Of the greatest significance to Emerson at Craigenputtock,
however, was the warmth of feeling he experienced in the
presence of Jane and Thomas Carlyle. A gauge of Emerson's
responsiveness to the Carlyles is that – perhaps for the first
time since leaving home – he was able to overcome his usual
reserve and talk to his new friends about his dead wife.[8] But
in Liverpool, waiting for his ship to sail for home, his mood
shifted. He reflected on the fact that all four of the writers he
had sought out (Landor, Coleridge, Wordsworth, Carlyle)
were deficient – "in different degrees but all deficient – in

insight into religious truth." He was strengthened and heartened by these encounters to follow his own convictions. He now gladly bade farewell to England ("the old, the rich, the strong nation, full of arts & men & memories") without regret in the presence of its best men that he was not an Englishman. He was as thankful that he was an American as he was thankful that he was a man.[9]

On September 5, Emerson watched, from the deck of the *New York*, "the last lump of England receding without the least regret." Off the coast of Ireland the following day, he recorded in his journal what seems to be the first reference to an important book in the making: "I like my book about nature & wish I knew where & how I ought to live. God will show me." At sea on Sunday, September 8, Emerson restated his belief that "the great men of England are singularly ignorant of religion"; a few days earlier, he had expounded his own creed: "The purpose of life seems to be to acquaint man with himself. He is not to live to the future as described to him but to live to the real future by living to the real present. The highest revelation is that God is in every man."[10]

An Anglo-American alliance

Three weeks after his return to Boston, Emerson spoke again from the pulpit of the Second Church to express his pleasure – after continual journeyings among the great cities of the world – that God has "blessed my eyes with the sight of my own land and my own friends."[11] (For the next three years he would continue preaching intermittently while embarking on his new career as lecturer.) In the sermons he delivered after his return there was a stronger emphasis on the God within man ("this amazing revelation of my immediate relation to God, is a solution to all the doubts that oppressed me");[12] in his earliest lectures, he turned to science to broaden his perspectives in reflections that anticipated *Nature*, "The American Scholar," "The Poet" – and such central poems as "Each and All."

The perception of beauty, he said, is an effortless function of the eye under the most ordinary circumstance: sunrise and sunset, the forms of vegetables and of the creatures of the earth – all invite our attention and pleasure. Our knowledge of the earth's history and development "make the stones speak and clothe with grace the meanest weed." The "in-structed eye," examining a blade of grass, sees a design in its form, color, smell, "in the very posture of the blade as it bends before the wind." ("A willow or an apple is a perfect being; so is a bee or a thrush. The best poem or statue or picture is not.") Of central importance is the "secret sympathy" which links man's inner world to external nature. The continual exercise of this sympathy preserves us from the great vice of overcivilized communities: imitation. "All American manners, language, and writing are derivative," based on borrowings from England. America's great inheritance of English litera-ture is both a strength and weakness, for there now exists "an immense floating diction" on which we inevitably draw and which alters and shapes our expression. A cure for this vice of imitation may come through the passage of time – and the triumph of materialism over literature. A better cure would be the study of Natural History – the study of things leading "back to Truth, to the great Network of organized beings made of our own flesh and with kindred functions and related organs and one Cause." But while they lead back to one great cause and are part of one great scheme, things in nature are sharply differentiated and Natural Science teaches the difficult and valuable art of "distinguishing between the similar and the same." It would be desirable for biographers to describe men so that they are also sharply differentiated ("instead of that equal and identical praise which enters into all biographies and spreads poppies over all").[13]

While delivering these lectures and meditating these new ideas, Emerson was reading in *Fraser's Magazine* the first four installments of Carlyle's *Sartor Resartus*, and was moved, in May 1834, to convey his gratitude to the author – tempered by some serious critical reservations. It was good, he wrote, "to have a new eye inspect our mouldy social forms, our politics, & schools, & religion." (These attacks on British institutions, Emerson observed, had equal force in America.) And he gave thanks for Carlyle's courageous defense of spiritual values. But why, asked the American, had he chosen to present his celestial truths and wisdom "in this grotesque teutonic apocalyptic strain" – those "involved glees" that hindered rather than helped its effect? At Craigenputtock, Carlyle had uttered sacred truths; his obligation was a sacred one, for "no poet is sent into the world before his time . . . nations & ages do guide your pen." Did the prophet so despair of finding an audience that he was driven to speak in "droll sounds"? Emerson looked impatiently to the time when the vehicle will be worthy of the spirit, the word as simple as the thought, the words as one with things.[14]

Emerson's criticism and Carlyle's response make clear their differing perspectives. Emerson's objections were "welcome and instructive" – but Carlyle reminded his friend that the old modes of addressing mankind were "as good as broken and abolished" – that finding a fit mode for "Solemnities that are *not* Mummeries" was a difficult task – "so one leaves the pasteboard coulisses, and three unities, and Blairs lectures, quite behind; and feels only that there is *nothing sacred*, then, but the *Speech of Man* to believing Men!" He is trying other methods for getting at the truth – but knows "no method of much consequence, except that of *believing*, of being sincere." (Emerson was also seeking for a new, "fit mode" – and would find it in an oracular wit and a pithy plain style far removed from the novelistic framework and ironic–satiric elaborations of Professor Teufelsdröckh.) Carlyle closed his letter with friendly references to his current project (a book on the French Revolution); their move to London from Craigenputtock and the hope that he may visit them again ("your old Bed stands in a new room here, and the old welcome at the door"); the possibility that he might come to America ("It occasionally rises like a mad prophetic dream in me that I might end in the Western Woods!").[15]

The correspondence during the following years richly expressed the warmth of feeling and diverging viewpoints of the two men. Carlyle's hint about an American visit was picked up by Emerson who welcomed the possibility of a lecture tour and quoted a friend's remark "that people were not here as in England sacramented to organized schools of opinion, but were a far more convertible audience." In place of this assessment, Carlyle proposes – in his response – that America is "mainly a new Commercial England, with a fuller pantry:

little more or little less." At Carlyle's request, Emerson wrote
in great detail about the practical side of the lecturer's life in
Boston and environs: subjects and audiences, lecture fees and
expenses, living expenses, living arrangements ("if we do not
make out a case strong enough to make you build your house,
at least you should pitch your tent among us"). But despite
his eagerness to visit ("Except the Annandale Farm where my
good Mother still lives," Carlyle wrote in 1841 to the second
Mrs Emerson, "there is no House in all this world I should
be gladder to see than the one at Concord"), Carlyle could not
or would not make the trip.[16]

They exchanged domestic news, bright and dark. Emerson
had come to isolated Craigenputtock from the city of Boston.
By late 1834, he had resettled in the rural tranquility of Concord; Carlyle in Chelsea, at the outskirts of teeming London.
Emerson wrote to tell of the death of his brother Edward, and
again, of his brother Charles (both of consumption), of his
forthcoming marriage to Lydia Jackson, of the death of his
five-year-old son Waldo ("you can never know how much of
me such a young child can take away").[17] Carlyle responded as
a kindred spirit, an understanding friend.

But their correspondence flourished and their friendship was
soon transformed into something resembling an Anglo-
American alliance when Emerson supervised an American
edition of *Sartor* – followed by American editions of *The French
Revolution, Miscellanies* and *Past and Present*. Carlyle, in turn,
helped (in a less active way) in the British publication of *Nature*
and the two volumes of *Essays*. These ventures in transatlantic
"bibliopoly" (as Carlyle called it) came to a halt when literary
piracy made them increasingly unprofitable.[18]

Despite Emerson's serious reservations about the satiric
structure and style of *Sartor*, he recommended the book to his
friends as "a noble philosophical poem" and Carlyle's fame
began to spread in New England and America.[19] In his review
of *The French Revolution*, Emerson praises Carlyle's treatment of
history as poetry and finds that "the noble and hopeful heart
of the narrator breathes a music through every part of the tale."
But he concludes his laudatory commentary with some unenthusiastic remarks about Carlyle's self-indulgent obscurity.[20]
Emerson's 1843 review (in *The Dial*) of *Past and Present* reveals

a widening gulf between himself and his mentor–friend. He paid tribute to Carlyle's "manly tenderness" and eloquent courage in exposing the absurdities and appealing to the conscience and honor of contemporary England. The basic fault, Emerson found, was in the historical method for contemporary questions: "The historian of to-day is yet three ages off. The poet cannot descend into the turbid present without injury to his rarest gifts." Nonetheless, Carlyle had responded with overpowering sympathy to the terrible conditions of the age and created a powerful tract – powerful but flawed in its stridencies ("the habitual exaggeration of the tone wearies while it stimulates").[21]

Emerson's response to Carlyle's historical approach is a predictable one for an author who deplored his age, in the opening sentence of *Nature*, as retrospective, and who believed that "the world lacks unity, and lies broken and in heaps . . . because man is disunited with himself." To restore the world, said Emerson, redeem the soul; the imperfection that we see in nature is in our own eye. (In "The Poet," Emerson observes that "we use defects and deformities to a sacred purpose, so expressing our sense that the evils of the world are such only to the evil eye.")[22]

Another ardent American admirer of Carlyle, Herman Melville, whose compassionate description of poverty in Liverpool is suggestive of Carlyle's illustrations of poverty in Manchester in *Past and Present*, pencilled in his copy of the *Essays* an impatient marginal comment alongside Emerson's reference to the evils of the world and an evil eye: "What does the man mean? If Mr. Emerson travelling in Egypt should find the plague-spot came out on him – would he consider that an evil sight or not? And if evil, would his eye be evil because it seemed evil to his eye, or rather, to his sense using the eye for instrument?"[23] Carlyle's response to Emerson's review of *Past and Present* was good-humored and gracious ("A decided likeness of myself recognizable in it, as in the celestial mirror of a friend's heart"). To Emerson's *Essays*, second series (including "The Poet") Carlyle objected more vigorously – and with a touch of Melville's asperity. He pictures Emerson as "a *Soliloquizer* on the eternal mountain-tops," isolated from all other men and their terrible need. And he provides a vivid criticism of Emerson's style. Emerson's sentences are very short and "did not . . . always entirely cohere for me. Pure genuine Saxon; strong and simple; of a clearness, of a beauty – But they did not, sometimes, rightly stick to their foregoers and their followers: the paragraph not as a beaten *ingot*, but as a beautiful square *bag of duck-shot* held together by canvas!"²⁴

To Carlyle's criticism of his "unconnected" style, Emerson pleaded guilty. He knew his limitations as a writer all too well and continued only because it seemed better than silence. About the charge "respecting the remoteness of my writing & thinking from real life," however, Emerson displayed some asperity of his own. He had heard the same criticism from his own countrymen but "I do not know what it means." Emerson suggested that "you Londoners" know little about the realities of country Lyceums – that his obligation is to "express the law & ideal right" to his own satisfaction without worrying about how "the last act of Congress" deviates from his viewpoint.²⁵

In the same letter in which he announced his imminent second voyage to England (for lectures in Liverpool and Manchester arranged by Alexander Ireland), Emerson referred diffidently to his volume of *Poems* – published in London in late 1846 by John Chapman – and to the fact that a copy should by now be in Carlyle's hands ("Poor man! you need not open them"). A first draft of Emerson's letter includes a sentence deleted from the letter received by Carlyle: "I reckon myself a good beginning of a poet very urgent & decided in my bent and in some coming millenium [*sic*] I shall yet sing."²⁶ Did he remove this sentence because it was uncharacteristically aggressive – or did he accurately anticipate Carlyle's lack of enthusiasm for his poems? In his essay "The Poet" Emerson had proclaimed that "each new age requires a new confession, and the world seems always waiting for its poet"; and in his poem "Merlin" he calls for "The kingly bard" who smites the chords "rudely and hard" to give us "Artful thunder."²⁷ Such proclamations (and poetic embodiments) had little appeal to Carlyle, who praised Emerson's "Eternal Melodies" but complained that "You do not fall on me . . . like floods of sunlight, but with *thin* piercing radiances which affect me like the light of the *stars*." He wished Emerson "would become *concrete*, and write in prose the straightest way."²⁸

A British friend who would have responded with greater enthusiasm and understanding to Emerson's poems did not live to see them. John Sterling, poet and contributor of tales and criticism to *Blackwood's Magazine* and other journals, was a close friend of Carlyle – perhaps his closest. In late 1837, seven years before his death from the consumption that was already taking its toll, Sterling chanced on a copy of *Nature* in Carlyle's house and took it and its author to his heart. Carlyle understood Sterling's feeling for Emerson; he linked the two men and conveyed his deep feeling for both in the letter he wrote to his American friend about his new enthusiast: "There is a man here called John Sterling (*Reverend* John of the Church of England too) whom I love better than anybody I have met with, since a certain sky-messenger alighted to me at Craigenputtock, and vanished in the Blue again."[29] (Like Emerson, Sterling had resigned from his ministry.) Emerson and Sterling never met face to face but their correspondence was an intimate and enlightening one – one that sheds valuable light on both men and on Emerson's widening differences with Carlyle.

A dying friend

Several years before John Sterling's discovery of Emerson's writings and (through correspondence) of Emerson himself, Sterling had expressed dissatisfaction with Carlyle's vision and style in *Sartor Resartus* in language that strongly resembled Emerson's criticism. In a letter to Carlyle written just a year after Emerson had complained about "this grotesque teutonic apocalyptic strain of yours," Sterling conveyed his displeasure about the "headlong self-asserting capriciousness" and the "lawless oddity" of Teufelsdröckh's "memoirs." Sterling saw wanting in Carlyle's protagonist "the calm and cheerful reliance which would be the spring of active exertion" and found instead an aloofness "in savage isolation" – almost a "stern joy" at the prospect of the victory of the catastrophic elements in society.[30] That calmness and radiant confidence he found in Emerson.

After learning of his high regard for *Nature*, Emerson forwarded to Sterling (through Carlyle) copies of "The American Scholar" and "Literary Ethics" – and, after Sterling

initiated a correspondence, his newly-published *Essays*. To a
friend, Sterling wrote that the book seemed "far ahead in
compass and brilliancy of almost everything England has of
late years (generations) produced." To Emerson, he wrote that
"You are the only man in the world with whom, though unseen, I feel any sort of nearness." In another letter, he complained about an England as far removed from the truly
spiritual "as the camps of the Barbarians who deluged Rome."
Carlyle was "our one Man" – but he saw his function, "not to
build up . . . but to mourn, denounce, and tear in pieces."[31]

Sterling valued Emerson's essay on "Friendship" (along
with that on "Love") as "to me perhaps more delightful than
anything you have written."[32] Emerson required of a true
friendship "that rare mean betwixt likeness and unlikeness"
that moves each friend to express himself fully – "each with
the presence of power and of consent in the other party."
(He deplored in what passed for friendship an absence of
"manly resistance" – what he called "a mush of concession.")[33]
A letter from Carlyle to Sterling referred to Emerson in terms
that seemed to endorse this view of friendship – in terms that
explained the deep and enduring friendship of Carlyle and
Sterling and of Carlyle and Emerson, despite the differences
that set Carlyle apart from both these men: Carlyle valued
Emerson's *Essays* not because he agreed with its views (though
he did to a considerable extent) "but simply because it is his
own Book" – a genuine utterance and not an echo ("*Ach Gott*,
it is frightful to live among echoes!"). ("Better be a nettle in
the side of your friend than his echo," wrote Emerson in
"Friendship.")[34]

Sterling was by no means a blind enthusiast about Emerson's
views; he found an unacceptable "abnegation of individualism"
in his oration "The Method of Nature."[35] But they were
temperamentally closer to one another than to Carlyle in that
they were both poets – a state of affairs that Carlyle greatly
deplored.

Carlyle asked Sterling: "Why *sing* your bits of thoughts, if
you *can* contrive to speak them?" His friend, further, had no
real music within him. Most important, the present convulsive
age called for: "Intelligible word of command, not musical
psalmody and fiddling."[36] Sterling persisted in his poetry –

and dedicated his verse *Tragedy of Strafford* to Emerson. Emerson expressed his gratification ("You have done me an honour to which I have not the least title") and praised the book for its "authentic expression of health and perfect manhood"; he arranged for Margaret Fuller to review *Strafford* in *The Dial* and forwarded (through Henry James) a copy of Ellery Channing's poems ("though young, the best poet we have").[37] Though he had been writing poetry all of his life and was entering the period of his strongest and most unconventional productions ("Each and All" and "The Problem" were published in 1839; "Merlin," "Bacchus" and "Hamatreya" were written in the mid-1840s), Emerson characteristically makes no mention of his own efforts – and Sterling did not live to see Emerson's extraordinary essay "The Poet" or his volume of *Poems* (1846–7).

Sterling was unenthusiastic about Channing's volume ("it seemed to show abundant receptivity, but of productivity little") and expressed his discouragement about the state of poetry in England. Was it otherwise in America? Carlyle, who hated all poetry, aimed only "at giving a poetic completeness to historic fact." He was, said Sterling, "the greatest of moralists and politicians, a gigantic anti-poet."[38]

This exchange of letters, in late 1843 and 1844, took place during Sterling's final ordeal. In June 1844 he wrote to say he was a dying man. Emerson's response was thoroughly human: he had been a negligent correspondent "and this is the punishment of my luxury, that you should be threatened, and I should know nothing of your danger and mine." (He had witnessed the similar grim ordeal of his beloved Ellen and of two brothers and must have known all along – and suppressed to all but himself – the bleak prospect for Sterling's recovery.) In his last letter, Emerson told of the great benefit he had gained from their friendship – and that now it was to be left behind "and I must think of that which you represent, and not of the representative beloved." The power and form must be disunited – but "the power is yet to be infinitely trusted." He asked Sterling, if he had the strength, to "write me, if only your name." But Emerson still hoped to see his face. Sterling lived long enough to express his thanks for Emerson's letter. "You and I will never meet in this world," he wrote in a final farewell, and expressed the hope that his friend would be helped by heaven to realize all his inspirations. His struggle was almost over: "But I fear nothing, and hope much." To Carlyle, Sterling sent a similar farewell note and his friend responded with a passionate letter ("My Friend, my brave Sterling! A right valiant man; very beautiful, very dear to me; whose like I shall not see again in this world!"). Four days before his death, Sterling wrote a seven-stanza poem, "To Thomas Carlyle" (dated September 14, 1844). To Carlyle's lengthy and loving account of Sterling's last days, Emerson could say little ("I had no heart to answer") – but he added a sentence that conveyed much: "I had never seen him, but I held him fast: now I see him not, but I can no longer hold him."[39]

A second voyage

The profound impression made by Emerson on young Alexander Ireland during his visit to Edinburgh in 1833 deepened over the years. In the fall of 1846, Ireland – now a resident of Manchester and active in the movement for adult education in northern England and Scotland – pencilled a hasty invitation (followed by letters) urging Emerson to visit England again, this time as a public lecturer. Emerson was tempted. "I should like to see your solid England," he wrote to Carlyle, after referring to the lecture invitation. "The map of England is good reading to me," he added. To Ireland, he made it clear that "literary propagandism in England" had no appeal for him – and that it seemed doubtful that there were a sufficient number of British men and women outside London "to whom my name was favorably known." (Ireland had given assurances – and would repeat them with added details – that a "Union" of Mechanics' Institutes and other organizations devoted to part-time adult education would provide ample opportunities for Emerson to give a series of lectures as well as individual lectures in numerous towns and cities throughout northern England and Scotland.) Carlyle, a month later, wrote of an encounter with Ireland – a man "full of energy, and broad sagacity and practicality." And he offered still another assurance and incentive: a London audience "of really

Aristocratic Persons" – suggesting that such an experience would do Emerson good because his American friend was himself an aristocrat.[40]

There was another important reason for him to accept the challenge of England. Emerson was at a static point in his life and career and an English audience, he speculated in his journal, might provide "that stimulation which my capricious, languid, and languescent study needs. The Americans are too easily pleased. We get our education ended a little too quick in this country."[41] A letter from James William Hudson, representing the Yorkshire Union of Mechanics' Institutes, seems to have provided Emerson with the decisive impetus (". . . we should hail with delight the great transatlantic Essayist and our Lecture Halls would be crowded with men who have already learned to love and now only wait to *see* the American poet"). Emerson thanked Hudson for his invitation and for "the animating field of literary labor which it opens for me in England"; he had written to Alexander Ireland, he informed Hudson, of his decision to accept. On October 5, 1847, Emerson sailed from Boston on the packet ship *Washington Irving*. The voyage was stormy and swift and by October 21 the coast of Ireland was visible ("We could see towns, towers, churches, harvests; but the curse of eight hundred years we could not discern").[42]

The *Washington Irving* reached Liverpool on October 22. After a brief sojourn in London, where he stayed with the Carlyles, Emerson settled down to an arduous schedule of lectures in northern England and Scotland. For one of the first, he chose Montaigne as his subject, and used the occasion to pay a public tribute to his dead friend John Sterling – recalling to his audience their common love of the French essayist. Many of Emerson's lectures elicited praise, but it may have been the depth of his feeling for Sterling that moved a reporter for *The Manchester Examiner* to describe this lecture as probably "the most interesting ever, till then, delivered within the walls of the Athenaeum."[43]

Emerson's reluctance to accept Ireland's invitation may have stemmed from the doubt expressed by Sterling early in their correspondence that "there are in Britain, except in London, a hundred persons to be found" capable of understanding and appreciating his message. In Sterling's view, the reason for this was a repressive element in England not present in America – the powerful social authority of the orthodox Church.[44] In late 1847, Emerson had no difficulty finding audiences eager to see and listen to him; but he soon came into direct collision with Church orthodoxy.

In his lecture on Swedenborg delivered in the Manchester Athenaeum on November 4, 1847, Emerson included a sentence that aroused a storm: "Man, wheresoever thou seest him, in brothels, gaols, or on gibbets, is on his way upward to all that is good and true." Also troublesome to many listeners was Emerson's sharp criticism of Swedenborg's view of evil: "That pure malignity should exist, is an absurd proposition; it is atheism."[45] The Reverend Mr George Gil-fillan, then widely known for his liberal views and initially friendly toward Emerson, sharply objected to the sentence about man's upward progress, even in brothels ("Who has anointed his eyes," asked Gilfillan, so that he could look calmly "upon the loathsome shapes of human depravity?")[46] A correspondent to *The Nottinghamshire Guardian* urged the cancellation of Emerson's lectures because the American struck at "the foundation of those principles of Christian faith and practice which are founded on eternal truth . . ."; and there were unsuccessful attempts within the Mechanics' Institutes of Nottingham and Derby to prevent Emerson from speaking. In Scotland, there were similar attempts and an invective even more vehement ("monstrous untruths, forming altogether the rarest melange of philosophy and folly ever presented . . .").[47]

These storms were similar to those aroused among orthodox Churchmen in America – most notably after Emerson's Divinity School address. And, just as in America, there were also approval and applause from the newspaper press, the audiences he addressed, the new friends he found wherever he went. A commentator for *The Leeds Times* conveys the excitement and enthusiasm that Emerson elicited from many, if not most, of his listeners: "Crowded and delighted audiences hung upon the eloquence of the lecturer each evening; and we cannot think that man or woman there present left . . . without experiencing that elevation of thoughts and aspirations which is inseparable from communion with the master mind, the genius, the original thinker."[48] To his wife, Emerson wrote of the warmth of feeling he had encountered in the towns he had thus far visited (Nottingham, Derby, Leicester, Preston, Chesterfield, Birmingham) and informed her that "My admiration & my love of the English rise day by day."[49]

In London, Carlyle was expressing doubt about Emerson's success as a lecturer in the north ("his doctrines are too *airy* and thin for the solid practical heads of the Lancashire region"); a strain had developed during Emerson's visit when the American showed insufficient enthusiasm for Carlyle's hero Cromwell. When Emerson returned to London in the spring of 1848, Carlyle signed a petition (along with Dickens and other notables) urging the American to agree to a course of lectures before the Literary and Scientific Institution at Portman Square. (Emerson agreed to these lectures and to another series, at popular prices, in Exeter Hall.) Emerson's first course of lectures was attended largely by the literary and social aristocracy of London; his Exeter Hall series, a correspondent for *The Examiner* suggested, was more enthusiastically received by some of the young men among "the poets, critics, philosophers, historians, scholars, and other divine paupers" who could pay a shilling for admission. (Thirty-four years later, an obituary notice in *The Manchester Guardian* recalled these Exeter Hall lectures as "wonderfully stimulative to the young and fresh intellects to whom they were perhaps mainly addressed.")[50] But Carlyle, who attended all of the lectures, was unenthusiastic.

Shortly after Emerson's departure from England, Carlyle wrote about his American friend and his lectures to his sister. He described Emerson as complacent and amiable, "sincere of heart" but "rather *moonshiny*" and impractical in his speculations. The lectures he summed up as "pleasant moonshiny discourses" of less than compelling interest. Emerson, in turn, was displeased by Carlyle's wide-ranging "sneers and scoffs" and told him (he recorded in his journal): "What a fine fellow you are to bespatter the world with this oil of vitriol." And he summed up in language verging on the vitriolic his view of Carlyle's social philosophy: "Carlyle is no idealist in opinions, but a protectionist in political economy, aristocrat in politics, epicure in diet, goes for murder, money, punishment by death, slavery, and all the pretty abominations, tempering them with epigrams."[51]

Despite this deep division and these acerbities, the two men came together during the last days of Emerson's stay in England for an excursion to Stonehenge that muted their differences and strengthened the old bond between them. On the train trip to Salisbury, Carlyle referred to the superiority of English culture and how much an American could learn in London if he made an earnest effort to overcome his antipathy toward Englishmen. Emerson did not disagree with Carlyle but expressed the feeling, inspired by the geography of America, "that we play the game with immense advantage; that there and not here is the seat and centre of the British race . . . and that England, an old and exhausted island, must one day be contented, like other parents, to be strong only in her children." But as the two friends walked together within the ancient temple at Stonehenge, "The old sphinx put our petty differences of nationality out of sight" and to the Druidical stones these two pilgrims were as one.[52]

An uneasy friendship

Several years before his second visit to England, Emerson opened a letter to Carlyle with an expression of pleasure at putting his friend's name once more at the head of a sheet of paper – an act that "signifies how much gladness, how much wealth of being, that the good, wise, man-cheering, man-helping friend, though unseen, lives there yonder, just out of sight." This was an ardent note never again sounded in the lifelong but uneasy friendship that followed Emerson's second visit. "You must always thank me for silence, be it never so long & must put on it the most generous interpretations," Emerson wrote at the opening of a letter in July 1851 – followed, to be sure, by a comment on the good understanding and feeling that exists between them.[53] But their correspondence, in the decades after 1848, was marked by longer silences and deeper divisions.

Carlyle's criticism of *Representative Men* (1850) in response to

a copy of the British edition sent to him by the publisher at
Emerson's request (a standing request for all his books), contained qualified praise for the work as a whole and dissatisfaction with the way Emerson concluded each one of his chapter–
essays on great men.[54] What Carlyle overlooked (or chose to
overlook) is that Emerson's approach to his representative
men, set forth in the introductory "Uses of Great Men" – an
approach at odds with Carlyle's view of heroes and hero-
worship – prepares us for chapter endings that emphasize the
shortcomings and incompleteness of any and every man.
Great men, Emerson observes, "answer questions which I
have not skill to put." We can best understand and benefit
from the greatest genius if we see him not as an original force
but "as an exponent of a vaster mind and will" – a vaster mind
to which every man is linked. Great men exist, says Emerson,
"that there may be greater men" – and his purpose in *Representative Men*, as in all of his writings – was to bolster the self-
reliance of each reader, to remind us of the God dimly per-
ceived but present in each of us. In its appeal to youth and the
future, Emerson's book strikes a distinctively American note
on the last page of his last chapter ("Goethe; or The Writer"):
"The world is young: the former great men call to us affectionately. We too must write Bibles, to unite again the heavens
and the earthly world."[55] Carlyle's earlier lectures *On Heroes*
foreshadow – perhaps influence – Emerson's visions of eternal
spirit and cosmic law. His great men are sometimes overwhelmed by the dark forces of this material world, but they
are never Emerson's "former great men" affectionately calling
to us. Mahomet is likened to "lightning out of Heaven; the
rest of men waited for him like fuel, and then they too would
flame."[56] Emerson's lesser men have a different and closer
kinship to the great men who inspire them than Carlyle's
followers and the great men they do well to worship ("In all
epochs of the world's history [writes Carlyle] we shall find the
Great Man to have been the indispensable saviour of his
epoch").[57] For Emerson, great men were no less – and no
more – than inspired and inspiring reminders to every man
that he was his own indispensable savior.

Emerson's *Essays*, first and second series, his *Poems*, his
lecture tour had an enormous impact on Britain – especially

so on young people groping for larger meaning in what seemed an increasingly meaningless society dominated by soulless commerce and sterile Church orthodoxy. To young Matthew Arnold, there came a voice from across the Atlantic "– a clear and pure voice . . . as new, and moving, and unforgettable as [the voices] of Newman, or Carlyle, or Goethe."[58] In response to Emerson's success and widening fame, there was a formidable reaction in the conservative press. Shortly after Emerson's return to America, the *English Review* featured a lengthy article, "The Emerson Mania," denouncing this dangerous "paradox-master" and his subversive teachings. A lengthy review in the *Critic* (of a one-volume edition of Emerson's complete works) suggested that "the rapt, simple, dreaming enthusiast" Britain had looked for on the basis of his writings turned out to be, in the flesh in late 1847, "a calm, cold-faced" Yankee whose eye, at times, "shot out a basilisk glance which reminded you of some serpent lurking and looking down from amid the thick summer of a forest tree."[59]

Emerson was accustomed to hostility at home and abroad but his sensitivity to British opinion in 1850 is reflected in a journal entry shortly after the appearance, in London, of *Representative Men*: "The English journals snub my new book; as indeed they have all its foregoers. Only now they say, that this has less vigour & originality than the others. Where then was the degree of merit that entitled my books to their notice? They have never admitted the claims of either of them."[60] Such attentiveness to unfavorable criticisms (in the *Athenaeum* and *Eclectic Review*)[61] was uncharacteristic and may reflect his increasing sense of alienation from Carlyle, his increasing conviction – expressed so vividly to Carlyle at Stonehenge – that the future of England was to be looked for on the continent of America. To understand America better, he was getting ready to write a book about England.

His sense of separation from Carlyle must have been intensified by Carlyle's biography of John Sterling, published in late 1851. At the time of Sterling's death, Carlyle (in accordance with his dying friend's instruction) returned to Emerson a large parcel containing the American's letters to Sterling. News of the forthcoming biography trickled out and three months before its appearance a troublesome paragraph appeared in a New York magazine: "Among Sterling's most intimate correspondents was Ralph Waldo Emerson, and even Carlyle cannot write his life, we suspect, without having access to the extraordinary series of letters the poet sent to his American friend."[62]

Emerson called it, in a letter to Carlyle, "a foolish paragraph" and said he could not recall anything in Sterling's letters that would be of value to Sterling's biographer. His comment to Carlyle on *The Life of John Sterling* was brief and favorable ("I rejoiced with the rest of mankind"); to his journal he was more confiding and revealing. He praised the author for having replaced "the vicious conventions of writing" with a flexible and direct style. But having said this, Emerson then said what he found to be missing in Carlyle's book about Sterling: "But he does not, for all that very much uncover his secret mind."[63] A modern biographer of Sterling has asserted that Carlyle has not represented adequately or accurately Sterling's changing religious views;[64] this may be the shortcoming Emerson is referring to. Carlyle admirably demonstrated his sacred sense of duty as friend and historian in describing clearly and fairly Sterling's many points of disagreement with his biographer–friend. But Sterling's letters to Emerson might well have provided Carlyle with valuable new insights into Sterling's religious views. And an even graver omission is the absence in *The Life of John Sterling* of a reference of any kind to Ralph Waldo Emerson – after Carlyle, the man Sterling loved most dearly.

During this period, Emerson was gathering his impressions of England – through travel diaries of his two visits, new lectures on England on the Lyceum circuit, old and recent memories now newly focused – for a personal and American book that would reveal almost as much about its author and his native land as it does about its subject. *English Traits*, when it made its appearance in the summer of 1856, struck the poet Arthur Hugh Clough as somewhat too mild ("I think you praise us too highly – I was anxious for more rebuke"). The fiery Carlyle, who thought highly of his friend Clough, had a very different view of *English Traits*. It is, he said in a burst of unqualified enthusiasm, an extraordinary book "by a real *man*, with eyes in his head; nobleness, wisdom, humour and many other things in the heart of him."[65]

Behind Emerson's genuine feeling for that which he admired in British character (pluck, uncompromising honesty, energy, stability, endurance) is a tough-minded wit that never permits the praise to cloy – a wit that is equally quick to plant barbs (perhaps) seldom painful because administered with such good will and (almost) affection. The "absolute homage" paid to wealth is summed up thus: "An Englishman who has lost his fortune is said to have died of a broken heart"; British reserve thus: "It is almost an affront to look a man in the face without being introduced"; the sterility of modern scholarship and literature thus: "I seem to walk on a marble floor, where nothing will grow."[66]

Emerson was fascinated by old families ("this cleaving through ages to the same spot of ground, captivates the imagination") and by the old names of old places ("what stores of primitive and savage observation it infolds!"):

Cambridge is the bridge of the Cam . . . Exmouth, Dartmouth, Sidmouth, Teignmouth, the mouths of the Ex, Dart, Sid and Teign rivers. Waltham is strong town; Radcliffe is red cliff; and so on: – a sincerity and use in naming very striking to an American, whose country is whitewashed all over by unmeaning names, the cast-off clothes of the country from which its emigrants came; or named at a pinch from a psalm-tune.[67]

These families and names did not, however, compensate for something vital that was missing in this island "anchored at the side of Europe, and right in the heart of the modern world." Nature ("the great mother") was a sleeping but potent force in America – a force no longer felt in modern England: "There, in that great sloven continent, in high Alleghany pastures, in the sea-wide sky-skirted prairie, still sleeps and murmurs and hides the great mother, long since driven away from the trim hedge-rows and over-cultivated garden of England."[68] In a letter to Carlyle written while *English Traits* was in the making, Emerson had told of a visit to St Louis and evoked a picture of the powerful Mississippi and a sprawling "incomplete" America, capable thus far of "nothing higher" than physical work ("Room for us all, since it has not ended, nor given sign of ending, in bard or hero"). Carlyle was struck by Emerson's description of the mighty forces at work on the great continent ("Your glimpses . . . have here and there something of the *epic* in them").[69] The bard Emerson referred to as not yet arrived in his 1853 letter to Carlyle made his stunning appearance in the summer of 1855; *Leaves of Grass* may have contributed to Emerson's striking pictures of the great American continent in *English Traits*.

Emerson had hailed Whitman's book as "the most extraordinary piece of wit and wisdom that America has yet contributed" – and addressed its obscure author with a deference and respect that mark him as the great poet that America had been waiting for – that he himself had called for in "The Poet" and "Merlin." To Carlyle, Emerson wrote of *Leaves of Grass* with respect ("a nondescript monster which yet has terrible eyes & buffalo strength, & was indisputably American") and regret (the book has been dismissed by his American friends as immoral); he would send a copy so that Carlyle could judge for himself.[70]

Carlyle's silence seems to have been his response; another British friend, Clough, was unenthusiastic ("remarkable but is it not rather a waste of power & observation").[71] In the meanwhile, Emerson's enthusiastic letter (widely publicized by Whitman) drew fire from British reviewers. A commentator for the *Saturday Review* was agreeably surprised by the praise in *English Traits* – but disinclined "to share Mr. Emerson's eulogiums with the last 'rowdy' New York writer," whose expressions of "sensuality and lawlessness" received Mr Emerson's blessing as "an entirely original and genuine manifestation of the 'Oversoul.'" Several years later, a critical notice (in the same journal) of the 1860 edition of *Leaves of Grass* adds Carlyle to the reviewer's disdainful picture: "It is curious to observe the effect of the secondary Carlylism of Emerson on a thorough American rowdy."[72]

Emerson's sympathies for abolitionism had been intensified by the passage, in 1851, of "the abomination of our Fugitive Slave-Bill" – as he described it in a letter to Carlyle.[73] Carlyle's views on slavery (that an "engagement for life" on just terms between master and servant is better than one from day to day) had been expressed to John Sterling in 1834 at their very

first meeting; Sterling (who had seen the institution at first
hand in the West Indies) had responded, "with a kindly jeer,"
that he would have the Negroes consulted about their views
on the matter.[74] Carlyle's position was elaborated in his
Occasional Discourse on the Nigger Question, published in *Fraser's
Magazine* in 1849 and widely distributed as a pamphlet in 1853.
The war widened the differences between the two friends:
Emerson saw it as "the battle for Humanity," Carlyle – in a
letter to his brother – as "profoundly foolish-looking." From
a former disciple, D. A. Wasson, there was an outraged
"Letter to Thomas Carlyle" in the *Atlantic Monthly* of October
1863 ("You are great, but not towards us Americans. Towards
us you are little and insignificant and superfluous"). Emerson's
reactions were milder. Carlyle's attitude was "unfortunate" but
predictable in a writer who habitually exaggerated to startle
his readers. In his journal, in 1864, he wrote: "Each of the
masters has some puerility, as Carlyle his pro-slavery whim."[75]
In January 1866, Emerson wrote to convey his admiration for
Carlyle's recently-completed monumental *Frederick the Great*
(and to transmit Ellery Channing's praise: "I have read these
[volumes], & they have made it impossible for me to read
any other books but his"). Five months later, Emerson wrote
again – this time a long letter of tender condolence on learning
of the sudden death of Carlyle's wife. Carlyle, after a long
interval, responded warmly and gratefully (Emerson's had
been "almost the only truly *human* speech I have heard from
anybody living; – and still my stony silence cd not be broken").[76] Then followed a silence of almost three years. That
it was not a "stony silence" is made clear by a letter from
Carlyle to Emerson – dated November 18, 1869 – that broke
the long silence with words that made clear his deep feeling
for Emerson and America.

A gift

It was, for Carlyle, a dusky and lonely world and, though his
correspondence with his friend was all but extinct, "my love
and brotherhood to you remain alive and will while I myself
do." There was time for this last letter and for one more reply
from Emerson before "the final silence." He had long wanted

to demonstrate his gratitude to New England ("New England, acting mainly through one of her sons called Waldo Emerson") by presenting to it the books he had purchased and used in writing his *Cromwell* and *Frederick the Great* – about 325 volumes ("The extreme insignificance of the Gift – this and nothing else, always gave me pause"). He had talked over the bequest during a meeting with Emerson's friend Charles Eliot Norton and would await their consultation and instructions. (In a later letter to Norton, Carlyle described the gift as "a proof of my grateful, loving, and hopeful feelings . . . to the great *New English Nation* named America.") Norton suggested that Carlyle's wishes would be best carried out if the books were bestowed upon the Library of Harvard College – and he called the gift "a pledge of confidence [that] is no slight bond between the people of the two Englands." Emerson wrote to Carlyle about his gift: "It has every charm of surprise & nobleness & large affection."[77]

The correspondence between the two friends did not stop with the satisfactory and satisfying completion of the details needed to carry out the bequest. There was a lengthy and vivid description by Emerson of his trips to California; and Carlyle's extraordinary response – his last letter, dated April 2, 1872 – an apocalyptic vision of "that wild Western world of yours" and of the consoling prospect, in the distant future, that there will be more than "a hundred million men and women on this Planet who can all read Shakespeare and the English Bible and the (also for a long time biblical and noble) history of their Mother Country." Carlyle closed: "Write to me, or even do not write, *and* I will surely write again."[78] He was in error; he never wrote again. But seven months later the two friends sat face to face once more in Carlyle's study in Chelsea.

A last visit

In the early morning of July 24, 1872, Emerson's house burned and was extensively damaged. No one was hurt and the neighbors rallied to save most of Emerson's books and manuscripts. And there was a rallying among friends and neighbors soon after for a subscription fund (soon met) to restore the house and, during its reconstruction, to enable Emerson to visit England once more – and to see Egypt and its ancient splendors. His daughter Ellen would accompany him.[79]

Emerson spent two or three hours in lively conversation with his old friend. To his wife, he wrote about the heartiness and warmth of Carlyle's manner, but little concerning the substance of their talk. After ten leisurely days in England – and several more meetings with Carlyle – Emerson and his daughter departed for their tour of Europe and Egypt. On their return, he declined all speaking engagements, but was persuaded by his friend Thomas Hughes to speak briefly and informally at the Working Men's College. (Two of the workers sent him two sovereigns to help pay for the restoration of his house.)[80]

There were several more meetings between the two friends that elicited from Carlyle some of his long-standing exasperation with Emerson's perennial placidity ("It's a verra strikin' and curious spectacle [he wrote to Norton] to behold a man so confidently cheerful as Emerson in these days"). On what he thought was the day of Emerson's departure from London, Carlyle walked along with William Allingham to bid their American friend goodbye, speaking of Emerson as "A mild, pure, gentle spirit" who had "made golden sentences, diamond sentences, sentences to be always grateful for." (They were delayed and reached their omnibus stop too late for their visit – unaware that Emerson had already left London the day before.)[81]

Emerson had refused an invitation to lecture before the students of Oxford University but – two weeks before he left England for America – he visited Oxford to hear lectures by Max Muller and Ruskin. ("No other man in England that I meet," wrote Carlyle to Emerson in his last letter, "has in him the divine rage against iniquity, falsity and baseness that Ruskin has and that every man ought to have.") In their conversation after his lecture, Emerson found Ruskin's views as gloomy as Carlyle's, and worse – for they were not punctuated or relieved by Carlylean laughter.[82]

A legacy

Among Emerson's books, Carlyle most valued *Conduct of Life* ("You have grown older, more pungent, piercing") – and it was the concluding "Illusions" that he singled out for special praise. In this extraordinary essay, Emerson pictured man engulfed by "pillows of illusion" (as thick "as flakes in a snow-storm"), groping from childhood to old age through an elaborate, lifelong masquerade in which all (or almost all) participate as masquers and dupes ("The intellectual man requires a fine bait; the sots are easily amused"). But in the midst of this "snow-storm of illusions," there were the gods still sitting around each one on their thrones – there waiting for him who "fixes his fortune in absolute Nature."[83]

This is a vision of a world of appearances and deception (and self-deception) akin to Melville's dark evocation in *The Confidence-Man*. (In 1856, at about the same time Melville was writing his novel, Emerson wrote in his journal: "Men had rather be deceived than not; witness the secure road to riches of Barnum and the quacks.")[84] It is akin, too, to Hawthorne's characters struggling for truth in a world of shadows ("To the untrue man [says the narrator of *The Scarlet Letter*], the whole universe is false, – it is impalpable, – it shrinks to nothing within his grasp"); and, perhaps most strikingly, it parallels the extraordinary confrontation (just before the narrative permanently breaks off) in Poe's *Arthur Gordon Pym*: amidst the milky mist that engulfs the boat there opens a chasm in which appears a gigantic shrouded godlike figure ("And the hue of the skin of the figure was the perfect whiteness of the snow").[85] (The British edition, published several months after the American, omits the white god and closes with Pym's preceding journal entry telling of "a limitless cataract" and glimpses of "a chaos of flitting and indistinct images"; Poe may have deleted the white god for a more shadowy conclusion – one less suggestive of transcendental salvation.)

With some reservations, Melville praised *Conduct of Life* and singled out a sentence in "Illusions" ("This reality [of simple virtues] is the foundation of friendship, religion, poetry and art") for enthusiastic marginal comment: "True & admirable! Bravo!" His Carlylean strictures had always been accompanied by Carlylean admiration – with a nautical flavor ("I love all men who *dive*") and Emerson was one of the soul-divers he valued.[86] In a similar vein, Hawthorne – through his narrator-observer in "The Hall of Fantasy" – also offered qualified

praise to Emerson in words and sentiments that sound much
like Carlyle's: "No more earnest seeker after the truth than
he, and few more successful finders of it; although, sometimes, the truth assumes a mystic unreality and shadowyness
in his grasp."[87]

There is in Emerson's soul-diving a tough-mindedness and
intrepidity that help explain his importance to Melville and
Hawthorne. Saul Bellow, while defining Dostoevsky's power,
also (I suggest) defines Emerson's. The novel of ideas stops
being merely didactic and becomes art, Bellow says, "when
the views most opposite to the author's own are allowed to
exist in full strength."[88] Before writing Father Zossima's
refutation of Ivan's rejection of God, Dostoevsky informed a
correspondent that he had, through Ivan's arguments, almost
completely devastated his own position. Emerson similarly all
but devastated his own position in the profound and moving
tribute he paid to Montaigne and his skeptical views – before
refuting those views.

Emerson had as little patience for the strategies of storytelling as he did for Carlyle's Teufelsdröckhian rhetoric – but
his kind of tough-minded truth-seeking was at the heart of
the narrative art of Poe, Melville and Hawthorne (impatient
though they were with the "shadowyness" of *his* rhetoric).
Emerson believed that "Truth and goodness, and beauty, are
but different faces of the same All"; that "The eye is the best
of artists"; that "Nature is the vehicle of thought"; that
"Words are signs of natural facts." Seeing and saying were
sacred acts, integrally and intimately related; there was a
"radical correspondence between visible things and human
thoughts" and the ability to link a thought to its proper
symbol was rooted in one's "simplicity of character" and love
of truth. Such a person, such a lover of truth, would "fasten
words again to visible things" – in contrast to him whose
character had become fraudulent and whose language was
imitative and corrupt.[89] In this scheme of things, the poet was
not an adornment but was central: "He stands among partial
men for the complete man, and apprises us not of his wealth,
but of the common wealth." The true poet was no mere
craftsman but one who had opened himself to the divine aura
and liberated himself and others in the celebrations of some

new fact and thought: "He unlocks our chains and admits us to a new scene."[90]

Only men who relish life were able to create meaningful art; Emerson deplored those superficial artists who "reject life as prosaic, and create a death which they call poetic." The true creator did not look to the old arts for inspiration; he found it, instead, in his own world – in the everyday objects that surround him. It is the instinct of the creative genius "to find beauty and holiness in new and necessary facts, in the field and roadside, in the shop and mill."[91]

Emerson looked (as yet in vain) for the American poet who would understand and celebrate "the value of our incomparable materials":

Our log-rolling, our stumps and their politics, our fisheries, our Negroes and Indians, our boats and our repudiations, the wrath of rogues and the pusillanimity of honest men, the southern planting, the western clearing, Oregon and Texas, are yet unsung. Yet America is a poem in our eyes; its ample geography dazzles the imagination, and it will not wait long for metres.

This, from "The Poet" (1844), was a clear call (stamped with the cataloging and rhythmic sprawl that would be the signature of the one reader who would and could respond to that call) for an American bard who would match, or surpass in new forms, the eloquence of Homer, Chaucer and Shakespeare. (This was a call not for good or great poets but for *the* poet, an American Bard–Messiah whose genius would be inexhaustible: "All the creatures by pairs and by tribes [will] pour into his mind as into a Noah's ark, to come forth again to people a new world.")[92]

Emerson's legacy of essays and poems is a magnificent and imperishable one – but his *Representative Men* (1850) cannot be placed alongside other productions of the extraordinary half-decade in which it appeared: *The Scarlet Letter*, *Moby-Dick*, *Uncle Tom's Cabin*, *Walden*, *Leaves of Grass*; none of Emerson's books is on a level with these. But – except for Mrs Stowe's novel – his presence is pervasive in each one of them; Thoreau and Whitman were disciples who overshadowed their master.

Emerson is central to the rise of American literature and he speaks to us not only through his own voice but through the voices he encouraged and helped shape – voices that speak to us with undiminished vitality in our time. And in this century, one of America's greatest poets has gratefully acknowledged Emerson's central place in his education as a writer: "Some of my first thinking about my own language," wrote Robert Frost toward the end of his life, "was certainly Emersonian." Frost goes on to quote a famous Emerson sentence ("Cut these sentences and they bleed") and a passage from "Monadnoc" about American speech that he especially values.[93]

Frost is recalling, somewhat inaccurately, a sentence from "Montaigne, or, the Skeptic" that deserves to be reproduced in full – along with the sentences in praise of Montaigne's style that precede it: "The sincerity and marrow of the man reaches to his sentences. I know not anywhere the book that seems less written. It is the language of conversation transferred to a book. Cut these words, and they would bleed; they are vascular and alive."[94] It is the words and not the sentences that would bleed if cut – but both are living extensions of a living man. Emerson compared Montaigne's style to "the necessary utterances of men about their work" and contrasted the spontaneous eloquence of blacksmiths and teamsters to the self-conscious refinement of Harvard College men. In the passage from "Monadnoc" cited by Frost, the poet would dispense with the learned discourse of preachers and teachers for "that hardy English root" – still living and eloquent among the "Rude poets of the tavern hearth." (Here Emerson reflects the view pervasive in nineteenth-century America that the American vernacular preserves the uncorrupted language of old England – a view echoed in *Moby-Dick*[95] and vividly expressed by Bronson Alcott as he reports his shock of recognition on first reading the great English seventeenth-century writers:

I remember hearing the same words, and was indeed accustomed to use them, in my boyhood and native village, into which the refinements of the brisk town had not found the way. It lay so remote and secluded there on the mountains; neither was there a scholar to modify the homely speech of the people. They spoke the speech of Shakespeare and Beaumont and Ben Jonson.[96]

Early in his career, Robert Frost wrote about the same

passage from "Monadnoc" on the flyleaf of a presentation copy of *North of Boston*: "All writing, I dont care how exalted, how lyrical, or how seemingly far removed from the dramatic, must be as colloquial as this passage from 'Monadnoc' comes to." And Frost adds a sentence that clarifies his own strength as a poet – and Emerson's importance to him and to us: "I am as sure that the colloquial is the root of every good poem as I am that the national is the root of all thought and art."[97] Emerson's lifelong involvement with England (and with his British counterpart, Carlyle) helped him to discover the American continent as a place and America as a poem – to discover "the value of our incomparable materials" and the central importance to the American writer of an American voice.

A Brother's house:
Thoreau's resurrection ode

I do not propose to write an ode to dejection.

WALDEN: Where I Lived, And What I Lived For

Who does not feel his faith in a resurrection and immortality strengthened by hearing of this?

WALDEN: Conclusion

"A Byron in Concord"

The evidence is unclear whether young Henry Thoreau loved the lovely Ellen Sewall but did not reveal his feeling out of loyalty to his brother John who wooed and was, for a time, engaged to her; and whether Ellen broke off her engagement because of her feeling for Henry – only to break off *their* friendship at the insistence of her father.[1] What is unmistakably clear is that there was an intensely close and loving relationship between the two brothers. John, two years older than Henry, had an open and sunny disposition – and an eye for the girls that was less (or more) than transcendental. A blithe and gossipy letter from nineteen-year-old John Thoreau to his friend George Stearns cautions against indiscreet kissing and complains about his own dull lot in Concord: "For my part I am exempt from all such temptations; as there is naught here save a few antiquated spinsters, or December virgins, if you will; and well may I sing, 'What's this dull town to me? no girls are here.'"[2] The two brothers were clever with their hands and their mechanical skills contributed to the rising prosperity of their father's pencil-manufacturing business; they went on numerous hunting and camping trips together; it was John's elaborate ornithological notebook that spurred Henry to a systematic study of the birds of Concord; both were equally fascinated by Indian life and lore; both were gifted teachers, and the Thoreau school they began in 1838, shortly after Henry graduated from Harvard (Henry in charge of the classics courses, John of English Literature), emphasized nature studies in the field as much as books.[3]

The school was closed in early 1841 because of John's illness (the beginnings of tuberculosis). But John's death, on January 11, 1842, was unrelated to his pulmonary disease; it was a sudden and terrible death that almost ended the life of his grief-stricken brother. John cut his hand and lockjaw set in soon after; he died in a delirium with Henry at his side.[4]

Emerson told of the tragedy in the Thoreau family in a letter to his brother a few days after John's death. But on January 24, Emerson wrote again to convey concern and some consternation at an unexpected development:

My pleasure at getting home on Saturday night . . . was somewhat checked by finding the Henry Thoreau who has been at his fathers since the death of his brother was ill & threatened with *lockjaw!* his brothers disease. It is strange – unaccountable – yet the symptoms seemed precise & on the increase. You may judge we were all alarmed & I not the least who have the highest hopes of this youth.

That morning, Henry's symptoms had diminished somewhat – but further news of Thoreau's strange illness and recovery was broken off by the sudden death, of scarlet fever, of little Waldo Emerson. (Five-year-old Waldo fell ill the day before Emerson wrote to his brother about Henry Thoreau – and the grief-stricken father wrote again three days later, a few hours after the boy's death.)[5]

On March 11, two months after his brother's death, Thoreau was sufficiently recovered to send Emerson an elegiac letter on nature's eternal cycle of death and life ("Every blade in the field – every leaf in the forest – lays down its life in its season as beautifully as it was taken up"). To his friend Isaiah Williams he wrote about his brother's death and his own "sympathetic lockjaw" with similar transcendent tranquility. Before John's death, Williams had reflected sadly – in a letter to Thoreau – on the fact that his youthful idealism was gradually giving way to a greater contentment with things as they are in this practical world; Thoreau responded to these sentiments by quoting a passage from Byron's *Don Juan* and adding some comments that reveal much about his own state of mind:

> No more, no more! Oh never more on me
>   The freshness of the heart can fall like dew
> Which out of all the lovely things we see,
>   Extracts emotions beautiful and new,
> Hived in our bosoms like the bag o' the bee,
>   Think'st thou the honey with these objects grew
> Alas! 'Twas not in them, but in thy power,
>   To double even the sweetness of a flower.
>
> No more, no more! Oh! never more, my heart!
>   Cans't thou be my sole world, my universe
> Once all in all, but now a thing apart,
>   Thou canst not be my blessing, or my curse;
> The illusion's gone forever –

Thoreau suggests to his friend that "Earth sends no sweeter strain to Heaven than this plaint." Our very grief discourages "time's encroachments" and "All our sin too shall be welcome for such is the material of Wisdom, and through her is our redemption to come."[6]

The passage from *Don Juan* (Canto I, ccxiv, ccxv) quoted by Thoreau eloquently reinforces Williams' melancholy complaint about his vanishing dreams – but omits Don Juan's concluding ironic lines (lines known well by Thoreau):

> The illusion's gone forever, and thou art
>   Insensible, I trust, but none the worse,
> And in thy stead I've got a deal of judgement,
>   Though heaven knows how it ever found a lodgement.

Thoreau's counsel to Williams offers in place of Don Juan's wry acceptance of the head for the heart the possibility of renewal and redemption ("Though I am weak, I am strong too"). His attunement to Byron is demonstrated by his grasp of the fusion, in *Don Juan*, of deep feeling and racy wit. The importance of that attunement can be measured by the fact that Thoreau reached out to Byron while he was recovering from the gravest crisis of his life.

Byron's significance for Thoreau was clearly revealed five years earlier in a college essay on moral excellence. Most men, Thoreau observes, are religious by habit – with no meaningful grasp of what they profess to believe. "However paradoxical it may seem," he asserts, it appears to me that to reject *Religion* is the first step towards moral excellence; at least, no man ever attained to the highest degree of the latter by any other road. Byron's character is a favorite argument with those who maintain the opposite opinion; a better for my own purpose I could not have desired. He advanced just far enough on the road to excellence to depart from the religion of the vulgar, nay further, twelve lines . . . of his poetry, contain more true religion than was ever possessed by any or all of his calumniators.[7]

A year and a half later, in December 1838, Thoreau entered in his journal an observation on the British poet that takes his college essay a step further in celebrating Byron's adherence to his own nature, despite the rejection and repudiation of his countrymen:

BYRON

Nothing in nature is sneaking or chapfallen . . . but each is satisfied with its being, and so is as lavender and balm. If skunk-cabbage is offensive to the nostrils of men, still has it not dropped in consequence, but trustfully unfolded its leaf of two hands' breadth. What was it to Lord Byron whether England owned or disowned him, whether he smelled sour and was skunk-cabbage to the English nostril or violet-like, the pride of the land and ornament of every lady's boudoir? Let not the oyster grieve that he has lost the race; he has gained as an oyster.[8]

It is important to recognize that the lowly and generally despised skunk-cabbage was, to Thoreau, an admirable and heroic production of nature – an emblem of courage and eternal life. It is praised in *Walden* for its persistent and perennial verdure in the midst of winter – and, in Thoreau's journal, we are invited to learn from nature and this lowly plant about death and resurrection:

If you are afflicted with melancholy at this season [fall], go to the swamp and see the brave spears of skunk-cabbage buds already advance toward a new year. Their gravestones are not bespoken yet. Who shall be sexton to them? . . . Its withered leaves fall and are transfixed by a rising bud. Winter and death are ignored; the circle of life is complete.[9]

That Byron "was skunk-cabbage to the English nostril" was praise for Byron and less than praise for the England he refused to conciliate. He was courageous and closer to nature (and enduring life) than those he offended.

In its own wisdom, Thoreau's body had acted for him after his brother's death struggle. He did not choose to do so, but some central core of his being chose for him and he too underwent a death struggle, to live on as a writer dedicated to the proposition that Don Juan's lost-lamented "freshness of the heart" need never die. "*I* am my destiny," Thoreau informed Isaiah Williams after quoting the passage from *Don Juan*; "My destiny is now arrived – is now arriving."[10] His destiny was to transact some private business at Walden Pond (the writing of a book, *A Week on the Concord and Merrimack Rivers*, that would memorialize John), to discover new truths about his life, other lives, eternal life – to become the author of *Walden*.

In *Walden* there is a passage that stands apart in its passionate urgency (an urgency rarely to be found in the prose of his master, Emerson):

Let us settle ourselves, and work and wedge our feet downward through the mud and slush of opinion, and prejudice, and tradition, and delusion, and appearance, that alluvion which covers the globe . . . till we come to a hard bottom and rocks in place, which we can call *reality*, and say, This is, and no mistake . . . Be it life or death, we crave only reality. If we are really dying, let us hear the rattle in our throats and feel cold in the extremities; if we are alive, let us go about our business.[11]

He had heard the rattle in his brother's throat, felt it in his own, and was ready to live and go about his business. The dark time was past and he was now ready to become, in Perry Miller's phrase, "a Byron in Concord." He would soon be ready "to transact some private business with the fewest obstacles" at Walden Pond.[12]

"Rugged" Carlyle: Raleigh and resurrection

Emerson was of central importance and, after Thoreau's graduation from Harvard College and return to Concord, a living presence; but Carlyle was, from his college days on, a more compelling presence. "He had no favorite among modern writers save Carlyle," observed Ellery Channing – a close friend of Emerson and Thoreau and an ardent admirer of

Carlyle.[13] One of Emerson's earliest journal entries about his young disciple saw him as a budding Carlyle: "Everything that boy says makes merry with society, though nothing can be graver than his meaning. I told him he should write out the history of his college life, as Carlyle has his tutoring."[14]

Emerson is referring to the account of Teufelsdröckh's education in *Sartor Resartus* (book II, chap. 3) – an account acknowledged by Carlyle to parallel his own school experience.[15] Thoreau valued *Sartor* highest among Carlyle's works and stressed its special status as a personal record ("Sartor Resartus is, perhaps, the sunniest and most philosophical, as it is the most autobiographical of his works, in which he drew most largely on the experience of his youth").[16] Thoreau's own writings are almost invariably centered in his own experience: "I should not talk so much about myself," the narrator announces in the opening pages of *Walden*, "if there were anybody else whom I knew as well."[17] Except for some animadversions on college professors and the observation that his cabin on Walden Pond was more favorable to serious reading than a university, Thoreau did not pursue Emerson's suggestion that he write a history of his college days. But Teufelsdröckh's "Clothes philosophy" does find its way into *Walden*. Asks Teufelsdröckh: "Lives the man that can figure a naked Duke of Windlestraw addressing a naked House of Lords?" And the narrator of *Walden* reflects: "It is an interesting question how far men would retain their relative rank if they were divested of their clothes."[18]

A key to Carlyle's appeal to Thoreau is contained in a sentence of praise in an essay (written at Walden Pond), "Thomas Carlyle and His Works": "We are every where impressed by the rugged, unwearied, and rich sincerity of the man."[19] All but one word ("rugged") could apply equally to Emerson – but it is a crucial word that measures the distance between Carlyle and Emerson, between Thoreau and Emerson. There was, however, a serious reservation that Thoreau felt (one he shared with Emerson) about Carlyle's genius. His humor, though "vigorous and titanic" (and "always subordinate to a serious purpose") defeats its own purpose by its failure to provide the simplicity and frankness that is required in looking back at a work. Carlyle's writing, Thoreau noted in his journal,

could be called "essentially dramatic, excellent acting, entertaining especially to those who see rather than those who hear,
not to be repeated more than a joke."[20]

It was in another, older English master that Thoreau found
the richest inspiration and greatest impetus for *Walden* (and
its first version, *A Week on the Concord and Merrimack Rivers*):
Sir Walter Raleigh. He finds no better representative of the
heroic character in the history of England. Among his impressive qualities (a natural leader of men in war and peace,
a prodigy of wit and wisdom), not least to Thoreau is Raleigh's
genuineness and lack of pretense ("notwithstanding his so
great mastership in style, and his conversation with the learned-
est and politest persons, yet he spoke broad Devonshire to his
dying day").[21]

Thoreau's essay on Raleigh (written in 1843–4) dwells on
the Englishman's extraordinary courage and vision during his
thirteen-year imprisonment in the Tower of London. His
history of the old world completed, "he began to dream of
actions which would supply materials to the future historian of
the new." The prisoner, Thoreau observes, was preparing for
voyages beyond "the comfort or ambition of his freest contemporaries." His release for an expedition to Guiana followed,
and Thoreau quotes at length from Raleigh's descriptions of the
unspoiled wilderness of South America that he traversed; and
it was no small matter to Thoreau that – though an unrelenting
enemy to the Spaniards – "the Indians experienced in him a
humane and gentle defender" and, on his return to Guiana,
"remembered his name and welcomed him with enthusiasm."[22]

Thoreau dwells on Raleigh the writer, a remarkable stylist
"even in the midst of so many masters." The writers of that
age possess a vigor and naturalness rare in modern times and
a quotation from one of them in the work of a modern author
was a refreshing and invigorating experience ("It is as if a green
bough were laid across the page"). As a prisoner in the Tower,
Raleigh was forced to substitute words for deeds; the truest
writer will be – out of necessity – "some captive knight
after all."[23]

That Thoreau is writing as much about himself as about
Raleigh is made evident by the curious digression that follows
these observations. He devotes a lengthy paragraph to the

salutary effects of physical labor on the writer's style ("The scholar may be sure he writes the tougher truth by the calluses on his palms"). Raleigh's healthy sentences – we eventually learn – have this quality ("In whichever hand is the pen we are sure there is a sword in the other").[24]

Thoreau praises Raleigh as a poet and gives several examples of "his unmatched sweetness and vigor"; his poems tell us more about Raleigh's character than official records or traition, for they reveal to us the secret of his inner life without distortion or deception. It was fitting that Raleigh should have written poems the night before his execution, and Thoreau quotes one that may have been intended for an epitaph for himself:

> Even such is time, that takes on trust
> Our youth, our joys, our all we have,
> And pays us but with age and dust;
> Who in the dark and silent grave,
> When we have wandered all our ways,
> Shuts up the story of our days!
> But from this earth, this grave, this dust,
> The Lord shall raise me up, I trust.

And, after describing Raleigh's serene courage on the day of his execution, Thoreau concludes the portion of his essay dealing with Raleigh's death and his writings on death with a sentence from his *History of the World*: "O eloquent, just and mighty Death! Whom none could advise, thou hast persuaded, what none has dared, thou hast done . . . thou hast drawn together all the far-stretched greatness, all the pride, cruelty, and ambition of man, and covered it all over with these two narrow words, – Hic Iacet!"[25]

Raleigh's God is not Thoreau's God but both (each in his own way) have an unswerving faith in resurrection. In *A Week* (Thoreau's epitaph for his dead brother), Thoreau meditates about the tombstones in an old graveyard overlooking the Merrimac River (and provides us with a startling gloss on Raleigh's "Hic Iacet" passage): "Why should the monument be so much more enduring than the fame which it is designed to perpetuate, – a stone to a bone? 'Here lies,' – 'Here lies:' – why do they not sometimes write, There rises? Is it a monument to the body only that is intended?"[26] Raleigh's presence is variously felt in *This Week*; his style is praised and a passage is quoted from his *History of the World*. But Thoreau's most extended gloss on resurrection and "these two narrow words, – Hic Iacet" is *Walden*.

Walking westward: a resurrection ode

In the early 1850s *Walden* was being shaped and – during intervals in its numerous revisions – Thoreau was writing in his journal and lecturing about walking westward, about wildness. "I must walk toward Oregon and not toward Europe," he wrote; eastward is history, westward is the future and adventure. "Columbus felt the westward tendency more strongly than any before"; he responded to it and discovered a new world. Thoreau tells of seeing a panoramic pictorial display of the Rhine that evoked a sense of a vanished heroic age and an atmosphere of chivalry; soon after, he saw a panorama of the Mississippi – "and felt that *this was the heroic age itself,* though we know it not, for the hero is commonly the simplest and obscurest of men."[27]

The west is another name for the wild; in wildness is the preservation of the world. "In literature," Thoreau asserts, "it is only the wild that attracts us." Tameness and dullness are interchangeable words. It is the untamed and wild thinking in *Hamlet* that pulls us to it; since the days of the minstrels, English literature has been "an essentially tame and civilized literature, reflecting Greece and Rome." No literature has yet emerged which adequately expresses nature and our deep yearning for the wild. The poets of the world may some day be inspired by fables of the west, by an American mythology. In the meanwhile, Thoreau regretfully sees Americans trading off their wild, natural heritage for a cultural refinement comparable to that of an English gentility:

Here is this vast, savage, howling mother of ours, Nature, lying all around, with such beauty, and such affection for her children, as the leopard; and yet we are so early weaned from her breast to society, to that culture which is exclusively an interaction of man on man, – a sort of breeding in and in, which produces at most a merely English nobility, a civilization destined to have a speedy limit.[28]

(In his journal, Thoreau comments on the paucity of footpaths in the vicinity of large English towns because of the encroachments of the landowners; the inhabitants, as a result, are restricted to parks and highways – a confinement, Thoreau reports, that would be the death of him.)[29]

"Walking" closes with passages that celebrate, for those attuned to nature, the glorious present and the promise of a brighter future. "He is blessed over all mortals who loses no moment of the passing life in remembering the past," asserts Thoreau, and reminds us of the crowing cock expressing nature in its health and soundness, arousing in us "a pure morning joy." The concluding passage tells of a November walk at sunset through a remote meadow ("We walked in so pure and bright a light, gilding the withered grass and leaves, so softly and serenely bright, I thought I had never bathed in such a golden flood, without a ripple or murmur to it"). There is the promise, in this sunset, of a brighter sun that will one day "shine into our minds and hearts with a great awakening light."[30]

For two years (from the early summer of 1845 to the late summer of 1847), Thoreau lived alone at Walden Pond and wrote drafts of two books: *A Week on the Concord and Merimack Rivers* and *Walden*. *A Week* opens with four lines addressed to John Thoreau:

> Where'er thou sail'st who sailed with me,
> Though now thou climbest loftier mounts,
> And fairer rivers dost ascend,
> Be thou my Muse, my Brother –.[31]

The memorial that Thoreau constructed for his brother is the chronicle of a two-week vacation voyage taken by the brothers in the spring of 1839; at Walden Pond, Thoreau transformed his diary notes into a prose-poem encompassing a slender narrative and a series of poetic meditations – the fortnight reduced to a week to allow for a cyclical (or circular) structure – each of the seven sections of the book centered on a single day in the life of the voyagers. *A Week* opens with a serio-comic introductory section paying tribute to the Concord River and promising the reader extraordinary sights and encounters with extraordinary men ("You shall see men you never heard of before . . . rude and sturdy, experienced and wise men . . . greater men than Homer, or Chaucer, or Shakespeare, only they never got time to say so; they never took to the way of writing").[32] The tone is lighthearted and the mood exultant; the organization is lighthearted and casual: it meanders like the rivers the voyagers are traversing. One of the high points in *A Week* (literally and poetically) is Thoreau's digressive account of an excursion to the top of Saddle-back Mountain; from the summit, he sees, far below, "the windings of a water-course, some unimagined Amazon or Orinoko" – and he finds himself above the mist and clouds, closer to "the region of eternal day."[33] Here and elsewhere (as in the description I have quoted earlier of an old graveyard overlooking the Merrimac River) there are intimations of eternal life and resurrection. The book closes with a sentence that reminds us, in late summer, of the previous spring (and of the springs to come): the voyagers maneuver their boat to shore and fasten it to the wild appletree, "whose stem still bore the mark which its chain had worn in the chafing of the spring freshets."[34] There will be other spring freshets.

A draft of *A Week* completed, Thoreau used his second year at the Pond to write the first version of his masterpiece. For *Walden*, he finds an organization that admirably serves his resurrection ode: the passage of the seasons. (The two years and two months of his residence at the Pond are shortened, he informs the reader, to a single cycle of the seasons: "Thus was my first year's life in the woods completed; and the second was similar to it.")[35] *Robinson Crusoe* is mentioned in *A Week* (a boy with his head full of that marvelous book and a thirst for adventure visits their craft with great curiosity and long-ing)[36] and Defoe's magical account of self-reliant survival hovers over the early chapters of *Walden*. But the atmosphere of the seasons (starting with summer and closing with spring) soon pervades the book and provides structural unity and rich imagery for the poetic meditations on death and resurrection that are at its core.

The *Walden* that finally emerged after several years of inter-mittent revisions is a great leap forward from *A Week* in another way: it is a more aggressive, more astringent book. The opening chapter, "Economy," announces its intention to satisfy the curiosity of his townsmen about his life in the woods – and then proceeds to reprimand them and the world with a withering wit that, on occasion, makes his master Carlyle seem almost kindly and genial ("as for the Pyramids, there is nothing to wonder at in them so much as the fact that so many men could be found degraded enough to spend their lives constructing a tomb for some ambitious booby, whom it would have been wiser and manlier to have drowned in the Nile, and then given his body to the dogs").[37] But his devastating complaint about the mean and hopeless lives his neighbors lead is set in sharp contrast to the sweet reasonableness with which he sets forth his "faith and experience" concerning a simpler and wiser way of life:

I would not have any one adopt *my* mode of living on any account; for, beside that before he has fairly learned it I may have found out another for myself. I desire there may be as many different persons in the world as possible; but I would have each one be very careful to find out and pursue *his own* way, and not his father's or his mother's or his neighbor's instead.[38]

This alternation of savage thrust and openhearted reasonableness functions with force, because the two voices are one voice conveying with urgency and eloquence man's desperate condition – and infinite capacity for change. Emerson's complaint to Carlyle ("All writing is necessitated to be exoteric, & written to a human *should*, instead of to the terrible *is*")[39] is best answered by Thoreau's presentation, in *Walden*, of *his own* observation of "the terrible *is*" among his townsmen; *his own* experience of "a human *should*" then and now, in the present, at Walden Pond. Like Whitman (and almost simultaneously with Whitman), Thoreau celebrates himself and informs his neighbors and the world that "what I assume you shall assume, / For every atom belonging to me as good belongs to you."

In *A Week*, Thoreau pays numerous tributes to the vanishing Indian tribes and conveys his deep feeling for the importance of wildness and the wilderness ("There is in my nature, methinks, a singular yearning toward all wildness").[40] In *Walden*, native Indian wisdom in the conduct of life in the

woods is more integrally linked to Thoreau's descriptions of
his own life there; but Indian legends also figure importantly
in contributing to the mythic aura that envelops Concord and
its surroundings: Walden Pond is named after an old squaw
named Walden who alone escaped from a geological dis-
turbance brought on by the wrath of some deity during a pow-
wow on a hill; the hill sank and stones rolled down its side
and became the shore of the pond. (But Thoreau suggests
other possible origins: it may be named after an English town,
Saffron Walden.)[41] And the idea of wildness is much more
centrally emphasized – with England serving to represent the
cultivation and tameness that, to Thoreau, represent man's
spiritual death.

Walking home through the woods at evening, Thoreau was
tempted by the sight of a woodchuck crossing his path "to
seize and devour him raw; not that I was hungry then, except
for that wildness which he represented." He came while living
at the side of the pond, to "love the wild not less than the
good." He contrasted the primitive and solitary American
amusements of hunting and fishing with the English proclivity
for games. "Almost every New England boy among my contemporaries shouldered a fowling-piece between the ages of
ten and fourteen; and his hunting- and fishing-grounds were
not limited, like the preserves of an English nobleman, but
were more boundless even than those of a savage."[42]

In *Walden*, Thoreau creates a great American mythology to
set alongside *Moby-Dick* and *Leaves of Grass*. When Walden
Pond is invaded by a hundred ice "harvesters" in the winter of
1846–7, Thoreau describes the busy "husbandmen" with great
precision – and takes satisfaction in knowing "that the swelter-
ing inhabitants of Charleston and New Orleans, of Madras and
Bombay and Calcutta, drink at my well."[43] And the coming of
spring is presented not as a gradual onset but an apocalyptic
revelation. The music of melting ice mingles with the sounds
and sights of new life: "Walden was dead and is alive again."
All is transformed ("Suddenly an influx of light filled my house,
though the evening was at hand") and the witness of these
miracles is transformed ("I heard a robin in the distance, the
first I had heard for many a thousand years, methought, whose
note I shall not forget for many a thousand more"). In the

morning of a first spring day, the woods are bathed "in so pure and bright a light as would have waked the dead, if they had been slumbering in their graves, as some suppose." Without the unexplored forests and meadows surrounding it, the life of the village would stagnate. Wildness is essential; we must explore all things – but require "that all things be mysterious and unexplorable." In this world of nature, death plays its part ("I love to see Nature so rife with life that myriads can afford to be sacrificed"). There is no need for pity or tenderness: "The impression made on a wise man is that of universal innocence."[44]

Walden closes with reflections on England and America ("It is said that the British Empire is very large and respectable, and that the United States are a first-rate power") and a fable of resurrection and eternal life. The two great nations are powerful but a man has within him a tide that rises and falls – a tide "which can float the British Empire like a chip, if he should ever harbor it in his mind." The fable, a story familiar to New England, has to do with "a strong and beautiful bug" that came out of the dry leaf of an old table of appletree wood. The egg, deposited in the living tree many years before, seems to have been hatched by the heat of an urn – and the bug gnawed its way out. Thoreau asks: "Who does not feel his faith in a resurrection and immortality strengthened by this?" And the lesson is clear: Who knows what beautiful life, whose egg has been buried "in the dead dry life of society," may unexpectedly emerge from the midst of society's most fashionable furniture, "to enjoy its perfect summer life at last!"

The last sentences in the book return to England and America – to John Bull and Brother Jonathan – to the mass of men leading lives of quiet desperation on both sides of the Atlantic. Can they learn the lesson of the appletree table? Time will not tell; only they can tell:

I do not say that John or Jonathan will realize all this; but such is the character of that morrow which mere lapse of time can never make to dawn. The light which puts out our eyes is darkness to us. Only that day dawns to which we are awake. There is more day to dawn. The sun is but a morning star.[45]

A gift from Cholmondeley: a gift for Cholmondeley

"'Welcome, Englishmen! welcome, Englishmen!' for I had had communication with that race," announces Thoreau at the close of his chapter "Visitors" in *Walden*.[46] A procession of Englishmen came to Concord, attracted by the presence there of Emerson and Bronson Alcott. It is unclear which English visitors came to Walden Pond during Thoreau's stay there – but the Englishman who meant most to him arrived in Concord in September 1854, just about a month after the publication of *Walden*. A graduate of Oriel College, Oxford, Thomas Cholmondeley came with a letter of introduction to Emerson from his friend Arthur Hugh Clough – who had visited Emerson and met Thoreau a year earlier. Cholmondeley (as Thoreau explained in a letter to a friend, "pronounced Chumly") had come out of admiration for Emerson's writings; but he soon found a kindred spirit and a more compelling influence in the younger man – in whose house he stayed for several weeks as a paying guest. The Englishman had also a recently published book, *Ultima Thule; or, Thoughts suggested by a Residence in New Zealand* – an account based on the personal experience of a year in the colony (and setting forth a program for the emergence in New Zealand of a "brighter Britain"). While very much involved with problems of community and Church polity in his book, Cholmondeley had expressed ideas about law in a struggling new nation that help explain his pull toward America and Emerson (the law, he says in *Ultima Thule*, is made for man – not man for the law; whenever laws become separated from man's "living will," they "soon corrupt, or simply lapse and melt away").[47]

Soon Cholmondeley was Thoreau's traveling companion on walks throughout the countryside and, accompanied by Harrison Blake, for a climb up Wachusett Mountain where, on October 20, they watched a sunrise. (In his journal, Thoreau wrote: "This is the time to look westward. All the villages, steeples, and houses on that side were revealed; but on the east all the landscape was a misty and gilded obscurity.")[48] When Cholmondeley left Concord for a six-week stay in Boston before returning to England, Thoreau wrote letters of introduction on his behalf, identifying his new friend as "an

English country gentleman of simple habits and truly liberal mind." To an American friend touring Europe, Emerson wrote about Cholmondeley: "He has lived in Concord & now lives in Boston & threatens to carry Henry Thoreau to England."[49]

In a letter from Hodnet, Shropshire, written shortly after coming home, Cholmondeley tells of accepting the offer of a captaincy in the Shropshire militia and the likelihood that he will soon be seeing action in the Crimea. And he reminds Thoreau of his promise "to come over sometime to England, which you will find a very snug & hospitable country – though perhaps decaying & not on such a huge scale as America." Thoreau's opening sentence, in his reply, suggests that the idea of a visit to England is not implausible: "I *am* glad that you have arrived safely at Hodnet, and that there is a solid piece of ground of that name which can support a man better than a floating plank in that to me as yet purely historical England."[50]

While readying himself to go to war, Cholmondeley also busied himself in another way. In October 1855, shortly before he left for the Crimea, the Englishman wrote a note to accompany a gift he was sending to his American friend. Through the London bookseller John Chapman, he had collected and was sending "a nest of Indian Books for you" – twenty-one rare works (in forty-four volumes) almost exclusively related to ancient Hindu literature. Cholmondeley hoped Thoreau "will accept this trifle from one who has received so much from you & one who is anxious to become your friend & to induce you to visit England." Thoreau wrote at length to thank his friend for this "magnificent" and "princely" gift. When word came from the bookseller of the treasure that was on its way, Thoreau fashioned a case to hold them out of driftwood – and he described to Cholmondeley how he had unwrapped the parcel when it came ("wading knee deep in Indian philosophy and poetry"), sorting out the books from a heap of papers marked with evidence "of having come from that fabulous region the 'Strand,' not far this side Colchis toward which you are gone." He placed the books in their case and, on waking the following morning, was not convinced it was reality "until I peeped out and saw their bright backs."[51]

In October of 1856, Thoreau wrote again to thank his benefactor – and in the hope that, the war now over, Cholmondeley might be back in England. In a rare confiding, Thoreau informed his friend of his poor health – but "it has not touched my spirits however, for they are as indifferently tough . . . as a dried fungus." He dwells "as much aloof from society as ever," is still immersed in nature and prizes as "infinitely far and grand and wild" the great west and northwest. He is pleased to think of Cholmondeley "*in* that England, where we all seem to have originated, or at least sojourned which Emerson values so much, but which I know so little about." Thoreau conveyed the concern of his family for their English friend's safety – and the pleasure they would have in seeing him in America again.[52]

To this letter, Cholmondeley wrote a lengthy reply from Rome. After providing colorful descriptions and anecdotes of his travels, he addressed himself to his American friend and offered some friendly advice. Thoreau was too much alone; he should "be a member of some society not yet formed." He asked his friend to "Forgive my English plainness of speech" – and inquired whether there were no clubs in Boston he might join. But if there were good reasons for this "quasi" retirement – it need not be so lonely a retirement: "Take up every man as you would a leaf, and look attentively at him." Thoreau's meditations on higher laws as they revealed themselves in common things may lead to a great work – but "this kind of study may become too desultory." Why not write a history of Massachusetts or, still better, of Concord? Cholmondeley then discoursed at considerable length on literature – with great praise for Emerson's *Essays* (and less praise for his *English Traits*); commented on the fragments he had seen "by a certain W. Whitman" ("But why write fragments?"); offered praise and less than praise for Carlyle ("A good preacher, but after all a creaking, bumping, tortuous, involved, and visionary author"). Cholmondeley asked Thoreau to send him a copy of Emerson's *Poems* – a book he had been unable to find – and asked also for a catalog of local histories and some reliable guides to Canadian or Louisiana research (he was currently working at an essay on America).[53]

Thoreau does not seem to have written a reply to this

extraordinary communication; no further letters from the American to Cholmondeley have come to light. But he did respond to his English friend's request for Emerson's *Poems* by sending a gift of four books: the Emerson volume, his own *Walden*, the first edition of Whitman's *Leaves of Grass*, a book by F. L. Olmstead on the southern states (a region Cholmondeley was especially interested in).[54]

In November 1856, Thoreau, accompanied by Bronson Alcott, had visited Whitman at his home in Brooklyn; Thoreau presented Whitman with a copy of *A Week on the Concord and Merrimack Rivers* – and received in return the recently-published second edition of *Leaves of Grass*. After reading it, Thoreau informed Harrison Blake that "it has done me more good than any reading for a long time" and "We ought to rejoice greatly in him." But Thoreau was also disturbed by the "disagreeable" and "sensual" portions of the book ("It is as if the beasts spoke");[55] his passion for the wild and the untamed had no place in it for the gratification of passionate sexual desire. "Chastity is the flowering of man," he announces in *Walden*, after discoursing on the uncleanness of "the generative energy" when we do not assert control over it, its invigorating and inspiring influence "when we are continent."[56] Though deeply troubled by *Leaves of Grass*, he found Walt Whitman "the most interesting fact to me at present" and his book "very brave and American, after whatever deduction"[57] – and it is not surprising that he should send it to Cholmondeley in his parcel of American books.

Cholmondeley, in reply, devoted a comparatively small portion of his long, rambling letter to Thoreau's gift of books. He praised Emerson's poems as "beautiful and glorious," passed over *Walden* for later comment (that does not seem ever to have been conveyed), expressed total bafflement toward *Leaves of Grass* – and found Whitman's views on sexuality "absurdly false": "I believe that rudeness & excitement in the act of generation are injurious to the issue. The man appears to me not to know how to behave himself. I find the gentleman altogether left out of the book! . . . His is a tongue 'not understanded' of the English people."[58] (When Cholmondeley tried to read aloud from Whitman in the Hodnet Rectory, his stepfather the Reverend Mr Zachary Macaulay put an abrupt halt to the proceedings by threatening to throw the book into the fire.)[59] Cholmondeley's unenthusiastic response to *Walden* and *Leaves of Grass* – coming as it did after his "English plainness of speech" about Thoreau's solitary way of life – seems to have cooled the American's enthusiasm for his English friend. In June 1857, Cholmondeley added a postscript to a letter to F. B. Sanborn: "I should be glad if Thoreau would write to me that long letter he owes."[60] In December 1858, Cholmondeley came again to Concord and accompanied Thoreau on a visit to his friend Daniel Ricketson in New Bedford – and a tour of that whaling town. Two months later, Thoreau informed Ricketson of another visit to Concord by Cholmondeley ("He is a good soul, and I am afraid that I did not sufficiently recognize him").[61] Cholmondeley wrote again two years later – but Thoreau did not respond.

Cholmondeley was Thoreau's closest English friend and their relationship tells us much about both men. In a letter to Harrison Blake in 1848, Thoreau referred to "the man of common sense" as "the Englishman of the world" – and suggested that the solid foundation on which this solid citizen stood ("our respectable daily life") was actually "the veriest illusion."[62] Cholmondeley was an uncommon Englishman who had embarked on a pilgrimage to remote New Zealand to work toward a more meaningful and self-reliant England; his visits to America and Concord were a manifestation of the same questing spirit. Despite Cholmondeley's shortcomings as a literary critic and his blindness to the worth of *Walden* and *Leaves of Grass*, he was astute in his concern that Thoreau's isolated observations of nature might lead to desultoriness. (Thoreau's journal came increasingly to be his central concern; *Walden* was his last large structure.) In 1841, he tells his friend Lucy Brown how he went to a hill each evening to watch the sun set, and added: "But I forgot that you think more of this human nature than of this nature I praise. Why won't you believe that mine is more human than any single man or woman could be?"[63] Cholmondeley's concern about Thoreau's lack of involvement with human nature was shared by others – Emerson among them. And it was, on occasion, also a concern of Thoreau. Shortly before receiving Cholmondeley's letter advising him to "Take up every man as you take up a leaf,"

Thoreau wrote in his journal: "It would be sweet to deal with men more, I can imagine, but where dwell they? Not in the fields which I treasure."[64]

Cholmondeley and Thoreau shared a characteristic that makes their correspondence an enlightening one: a total and uncompromising candor and lack of pretense. An indication of Cholmondeley's importance to Thoreau is that the American – a lifelong advocate of looking away from England, of looking and walking westward, of doing away with poverty by limiting his needs – was moved to tell his English friend: "If I am ever rich enough I shall think seriously of going to England and finding you out in your cottage on the south shore."[65] That they eventually parted is less significant than the fact that they came together as closely as they did.

A Brother's house

Thomas Cholmondeley was the oldest son of the Reverend Mr Charles Cowper Cholmondeley, rector of Overleigh, Cheshire. His mother's brother was Reginald Heber; when Bishop Heber left for India in 1823, the Reverend Mr Cholmondeley succeeded his brother-in-law as rector at Hodnet, Shropshire.

Thomas Cholmondeley was born in 1823 and brought up in Hodnet; after the death of his father, his mother married the Reverend Mr Zachary Macaulay, the new rector at Hodnet.[66]

"You will be glad to hear that I am safe at my Mothers home in Salop [Shropshire] after a most disagreeable passage to England in the steamer America," wrote Cholmondeley to Thoreau from Hodnet after his first visit to America – and his extended stay in the Thoreau household. In his reply, Thoreau expressed pleasure in learning of Cholmondeley's safe return to Hodnet – and to know that there was such a place. There follows a paragraph of unusual eloquence and feeling – a revealing paragraph:

But have I not seen you with my own eyes, a piece of England herself? And has not your letter come out to me thence? I have now reason to believe that Salop is as real a place as Concord, with, at least, as good an underpinning of granite floating in liquid fire. I congratulate you on having arrived safely at that floating islet, after your disagreeable passage in the steamer America. So are we not all making a passage, agreeable or disagreeable in the steamer Earth, trusting to arrive at last at some less undulating Salop and Brother's house?[67]

In the first draft of *Walden*, Thoreau had included a reference to Melville's *Typee*;[68] he may also have read *White-Jacket* – and its closing scene in which a man-of-war is likened to "this old-fashioned world of ours afloat." But the passage in his letter to Cholmondeley – with its images of "granite floating in liquid fire," a "floating isle," "some less undulating Salop" – also recalls Thoreau's passionate cry for reality in *Walden*: the passage (quoted earlier in this chapter) calling for us to "wedge our feet downward . . . till we come to a hard bottom" that is truly reality. The reality, for Thoreau, is our final arrival in the steamer Earth "at some less undulating Salop and Brother's house." (Melville's "never-sinking world-frigate" makes its voyage with sealed orders, its destination unknown – "though our Lord High Admiral will yet make all wrongs right, for 'Life is a voyage that's homeward bound!'")[69]

Cholmondeley had written that he was "safe at my Mothers home in Salop"; through what seems to have been an inadvertent misreading (understandable because Cholmondeley's handwriting is not clear) – perhaps a trick of the eye akin to the trick his body had played after his brother's death – Thoreau substituted a "Brother's" for a "Mothers" house.[70] At Walden Pond, he had built a house in which "to transact some private business"; and in that house he had fashioned an imperishable book for his brother – for all his brothers. (In *Walden*, he refers to the million Irishmen who built the railroads as "brothers of mine" who could have spent their time better "than digging in this dirt.")[71] In his own lifelong voyage, Thoreau never faltered in his trust that he would "arrive at last at some less undulating Salop and Brother's house."

"Leaves of Grass":
England and the outsetting bard

English roots: an English Master

When Emerson received and read the tall thin book in July
of 1855, he was moved to convey his deep conviction that
this was a masterpiece in a letter that greets his unknown
benefactor "at the beginning of a great career, which yet
must have had a long foreground somewhere, for such a start."
Emerson, of course, figured importantly in that foreground.
Whitman told a friend: "I was simmering, simmering, simmering; Emerson brought me to a boil."[1] But who had brought
this not-so-young Brooklyn journalist (and author of occasional
unremarkable poems and stories) to a simmer?

As a boy he had absorbed the sonorities and splendors of
the King James Bible and returned to them – and to commentaries on biblical poetry – while the first versions of *Leaves
of Grass* were being sketched.[2] Ossian was also an important
influence – linked, in his mind, to the Hebrew poets. ("Is it
not," he wrote about 1846, "Isaiah, Job, the Psalms and so
forth, transferred to the Scotch Highlands?")[3] Shakespeare
was, in Whitman's view, England's only "first-class genius"
– exceptional among a vast number of writers marked by an
"artificial beauty" derived from the classics. (And even Shakespeare was primarily a painter of British feudalism in its heyday;
his mighty poems are viewed as "poisonous to the idea of the
pride and dignity of the common people, the lifeblood of
democracy.")[4]

Shortly after he became editor of the Brooklyn *Daily Eagle*
in March 1846, Whitman called for American writers who
would rival the "glorious gods of intellect" of the past (Homer,
Shakespeare, Goethe) – and for an American people ready to
support these writers.[5] His nationalistic fervor did not, however, prevent Whitman from expressing grudging admiration

(that gave way, on occasion, to enthusiasm) for several British writers, most notably Coleridge and Carlyle.

In a notice of *Biographia Literaria*, Whitman praised Coleridge as a writer who combined unaffected artlessness with fascinating subtleties; in some respects, Whitman observed, "we think this man stands above all poets: he was passionate without being morbid – he was like Adam in Paradise, and almost as free from artificiality."[6] His deepest feeling, however, was reserved for Thomas Carlyle.

Whitman reviewed *Heroes and Hero-Worship*, *Sartor Resartus*, *The French Revolution* and *Past and Present* in late 1846 – shortly before he began making notes for *Leaves of Grass*.[7] These reviews and later writings suggest that Carlyle may well have served as the catalyst transforming a Brooklyn newspaper editor into a national bard. It was Carlyle who brought Whitman to a simmer – and perhaps to a boil. In 1856, Whitman addressed Emerson as his "Master";[8] Carlyle seems to have been his English Master.

Whitman is drawn reluctantly, but inexorably, into Carlyle's spell. He finds, in his review of *Heroes*, a "rapt, weird, (grotesque?) style" almost obscuring the "many noble thoughts." Carlyle's deep feeling for the downtrodden and his anger at those in power are applauded – but Whitman wishes those feelings were conveyed in a plainer style. *Sartor Resartus* is, in the same review, the occasion for a single sentence – but it is a sentence that suggests the puzzling problem (and compelling influence) that Carlyle was beginning to be: "This has all of Mr Carlyle's strange wild way; and all his fiery-breath and profundity of meaning – when you delve them out."[9]

Five weeks later, Whitman conveys the fact (in his notice of *Past and Present*) that Carlyle has exerted his spell:

One likes Mr. Carlyle, the more he communes with him; there is a sort of fascination about the man. His weird, wild way – his phrases, welded together as it were, with strange twistings of the terminatives of words – his startling suggestions – his taking up, fish-hook like, certain matters of abuse – make an *original* kind of composition, that gets, after a little usage, to be strangely agreeable![10]

Sartor Resartus seems to have made the strongest impression. An undated manuscript notebook entry (that belongs to the period in which the first edition of *Leaves of Grass* was being drafted) sounds like a response to *Sartor*, especially the chapters titled "The World out of Clothes" and "Adamatism": "One grand faculty we want, – and that is the power to pierce fine clothing and thick-coated shams, and settle for sure what the reality of the thing clothed and disguised is, and what it weighs stark naked; the power of slipping like an eel through all blandishments and graspings of convention." "Another newspaper piece, "Life of a Dandy," is strikingly reminiscent of "The Dandiacal Body" in *Sartor*; and Whitman's columns in the New Orleans *Daily Crescent* are liberally sprinkled with echoes of *Sartor* and *Past and Present*. In the satirical sketch "John J. Jinglebrain" (suggestive of "Sir Jabesh Windbag," among others, in *Past and Present*), Whitman proclaims: "Man is an eating animal, aye, a drinking one too . . . a clothes-wearing animal" (suggestive of "Man is a Tool-using Animal . . . a Laughing Animal . . . the Cooking Animal," in *Sartor*).[12]

An extended passage from *Sartor* (describing Teufelsdröckh's view from his attic quarters high above the town) set alongside Whitman's "I Sit and Look Out" (1860) may serve to illustrate the indebtedness of *Leaves of Grass* to Carlyle.

Teufelsdröckh speaks:

I look down . . . The joyful and sorrowful are there; men are dying there, men are being born . . . Wretchedness cowers into truckle-beds, or shivers hunger-stricken into its lair of straw . . . while Councillors of State sit plotting, and playing their high chess-game, whereof the pawns are Men. The Lover whispers his mistress that the coach is ready; and she, full of hope and fear, glides down, to fly with him over the borders . . . the Mother, with streaming hair, kneels over her pallid dying infant . . . All these heaped and huddled together . . . But I . . . sit above it all; I am alone with the Stars.[13]

From Whitman's "I Sit and Look Out":

I sit and look out upon all the sorrows of the world,
    and look upon all oppression and shame,
. . . .

I see in low life the mother misused by her children, dying,
    neglected, gaunt, desperate,
I see the wife misused by her husband, I see the treacherous
    seducer of young women,
. . . .

> I observe the slights and degradations cast by arrogant persons
>   upon laborers, the poor, and upon negroes, and the like;
> All these – all the meanness and agony without end I sitting
>   look out upon,
> See, hear, and am silent.[14]

These excerpts from Teufelsdröckh's meditation as he sits and looks out give us (literally) a panoramic view of the human condition – of joys and suffering, of the powerlessness of the people and the indifference of the powerful and, finally, of Teufelsdröckhs's compassion and powerlessness in the presence of these human and eternal mysteries. He is simultaneously the anguished and triumphant seer – triumphant in his ability to penetrate the veils that hide and disguise personal suffering; anguished in his role as sympathetic and helpless witness.[15] While "I Sit and Look Out" parallels in the outlines of its vision the excerpt from *Sartor*, it tends toward a diffuseness and abstraction ("sorrows of the world"; "oppression and shame") uncharacteristic of Whitman at his best. "Song of Myself" (1855) has numerous passages that convey with greater concreteness Teufelsdröckh's attic-window vision of the human condition; one of them, the picture of "the twenty-ninth bather" (later numbered section 11) – the young woman who "owns the fine house by the rise of the bank" – provides not only concrete imagery of extraordinary vividness but a narrative framework (not present in "I Sit and Look Out") that is a counterpart, transformed and transmuted, of Carlyle's in *Sartor*.

Omitted from the Teufelsdröckh passage quoted above is Carlyle's central *persona*, the young English editor of Teufelsdröckh's book (proclaims the Editor: "Teufelsdröckh is our friend, Truth is our divinity").[16] It is the Editor who serves as our guide and mediator as we enter the mind and heart of Teufelsdröckh. At the close of Teufelsdröckh's extraordinary account of the world as seen from his watchtower, the Editor looks into the Professor's face for some evidence of feeling – "but with the light we had, which indeed was only a single tallow-light, and far enough from the window, nothing save that old calmness and fixedness was visible."[17] The woman who hides behind the blinds of the window to watch the young men bathing in a stream far below is hidden from them – but not

from the poet–prophet (who sees all from his invisible watchtower):

Where are you off to, lady? for I see you,
You splash in the water there, yet stay stock still in your room.[18]

Whitman's poet–prophet alternates between Teufelsdröckh's
visions and pronouncements and the Editor's explanations and
pleadings to his readers. At the close of *Sartor*, the Editor
speaks to his readers and reminds those who have been disturbed and irritated by the Professor that he bears them no ill
will, that "with outstretched arms and open heart" he bids all
"a kind of farewell."[19] Whitman's seer is both human ("It is
you talking just as much as myself, I act as the tongue of you")[20]
and superhuman ("I depart as air, I shake my white locks at the
runaway sun");[21] but like the Editor in *Sartor* he too asks for
patience from his readers ("Missing me one place search
another, / I stop somewhere waiting for you").[22] The persuasive appeal of "Song of Myself" – and other poems in the
early editions of *Leaves of Grass* – is by no means identical
with the rhetorical framework of *Sartor*; but it is as if Emerson's
Orphic poet is given a passionate and ironic voice – a whirling
voice alternating between oracular Teufelsdröckhian pronouncements and an Editor's questioning of these pronouncements ("Speech is the twin of my vision [announces the prophet-
seer in "Song of Myself"], it is unequal to measure itself, / It
provokes me forever, it says sarcastically, / *Walt you contain
enough, why don't you let it out then?*").[23]

Although the presence of *Sartor* is most clearly visible in
Leaves of Grass, Heroes and Hero-Worship may have also served
as a decisive influence on Whitman's poet–prophet–bard – and
on his "Chants Democratic." In his lecture on "The Hero as
Poet," Carlyle reminds us that

all passionate language does of itself become musical, – with a finer
music than the mere accent; the speech of a man even in zealous
anger becomes a chant, a song. All deep things are Song; as if all
the rest were but wrappages and hulls! The primal element of us;
of us, and of all things.[24]

In *Heroes* Carlyle celebrates Burns as "the most gifted British
soul we had in all that century of his" and pays tribute to his
humble origins and rustic dialect – to "the rugged downright-

ness, penetration . . . manfulness that was in him."[25] These
and numerous other Carlylean passages could – and in a sense
did – serve as a preface to *Leaves of Grass*.

In 1867, Whitman's anger was aroused by Carlyle's attack on
American democracy in his article "Shooting Niagara and
After?" and he responded with "Democracy," an essay directed
at the criticisms of "an eminent and venerable person abroad"
and vehemently defending the power of the American people
to correct the evils described by Carlyle.[26] Several years later,
Whitman experienced a change of heart and, in *Democratic
Vistas* (1871), explained that his anger at Carlyle's criticisms
had given way, on further study and reflection, to respect "as
coming from an earnest soul, and as contributing certain sharp-
cutting metallic grains, which, if not gold or silver, may be
good hard, honest iron."[27] Though he eventually sets forth a
hopeful prospect for the future of America, Whitman – in the
opening section of *Democratic Vistas* – presents a grim view of
its failures and shortcomings, a view that seems Carlylean in its
dark urgency:

I say we had best look our times and lands searchingly in the face,
like a physician diagnosing some deep disease. . . . What penetrating
eye does not everywhere see through the mask? The spectacle is
appaling [*sic*]. We live in an atmosphere of hypocrisy throughout.
The men believe not in the women, nor the women in the men . . .
The great cities reek with respectable as much as non-respectable
robbery and scoundrelism. In fashionable life, flippancy, tepid
amours, weak infidelism, small aims, or no aims at all, only to kill
time.[28]

This grim spectacle does not represent post-Civil War dis-
illusionment; there are corrosive Carlylean pictures in the
first edition of *Leaves of Grass* ("They who piddle and patter
here in collars and tailed coats . . . I am aware who they are
. . . and that they are not worms and fleas").[29] Carlyle, early
and late, was a pervasive presence for Whitman and *Leaves of
Grass*.

And when Carlyle died, Whitman wrote an obituary tribute
characterized by a biting eloquence worthy of his English
master:

It is time the English-speaking people had some true idea about the
verteber of genius, namely power . . . How he shakes our comfort-

able reading circles with a touch of the old Hebraic anger and prophecy . . . How he splashes like leviathan in the seas of modern literature and politics! Doubtless . . . one needs first to realize from actual observation, the squalor, vice and doggedness ingrain'd in the bulk-population of the British Islands, with the red tape, the fatuity, the flunkeyism everywhere, to understand the last meaning in his pages.[30]

English "Leaves": "An Englishwoman's Estimate"

The tall thin quarto that Emerson hailed with enthusiasm in July 1855 was greeted – almost without exception on both sides of the Atlantic – by silence or hostility. But a few critics recognized the importance of *Leaves of Grass*; one of the earliest was an anonymous reviewer, in mid-March 1856, for the London *Weekly Dispatch*. The English critic is impressed by Emerson's praise ("What Emerson has pronounced to be good must not be lightly treated") but has found for himself – after an initial feeling of a strangeness and audacity in this volume verging upon absurdity – that

his poems in time will become a pregnant text-book, out of which quotations as sterling as the minted gold will be taken and applied to every form and phrase of the "inner" or the "outer" life; and we express our pleasure in making the acquaintance of Walt Whitman, hoping to know more of him in time to come.[31]

Emerson and Thoreau were not successful in spreading the word about *Leaves of Grass* among their English friends; and the praise of the reviewer for the London *Weekly Dispatch* seems to have attracted little attention. But Walt Whitman's reputation in England was vastly advanced through a chain of circumstances that led, in February 1868, to the publication of the first English version of *Leaves of Grass* – a volume titled *Poems by Walt Whitman*, selected and edited by William Michael Rossetti, published in London by J. C. Hotten.

James Grindrod, a peddler–bookseller, came to Sunderland with a stock of American books (unwanted books at bargain prices) and it was through Grindrod that several copies of *Leaves of Grass* were acquired by Thomas Dixon, a laboring man with a curiosity about unconventional books. Dixon turned over a copy to his friend, the poet and sculptor William Bell

Scott – who in turn passed on a copy of the strange American book as a Christmas gift to his close friend Rossetti. Rossetti was deeply stirred by the book – but waited for more than ten years to publish an appraisal. His article on *Leaves of Grass* – in the London *Chronicle*, July 6, 1867 – made it clear that his long delay in committing himself to print had by no means diminished his great enthusiasm for the American bard; in it he announced that *Leaves of Grass* was "incomparably the largest poetic work of our period" – that Whitman's poetry "may be expected to stand in a relation to future poetic efforts hardly less typical and monumental than the Homeric poems toward Grecian and epic work, or those of Shakespeare toward English and dramatic."[32]

William Rossetti's voice was an influential and eloquent one – and the *Chronicle* article had a widespread effect. Soon after, Rossetti was negotiating with John Camden Hotten for the publication of a volume of poems selected from the 1867 edition of *Leaves of Grass*. (An earlier conference seems to have resulted in the decision that a complete edition could not be brought out in England without "legal prosecution on any publisher.")[33] Rossetti proceeded to compile his selection, guided – he informed Whitman in a letter dated December 8, 1867 – by two rules: "to omit *entirely* every poem which contains passages or words which modern squeamishness can raise an objection to"; to include, from the remaining poems, "those which I most entirely and intensely admire." Rossetti emphatically denied that the resultant volume was a bowdlerization ("If any blockhead chooses to call my Selection 'an expurgated edition,' that lie shall be on his own head, not mine").[34] Although *Poems by Walt Whitman* omitted "Song of Myself," a poem of central importance; the "Children of Adam" poems; and the powerful and haunting "The Sleepers," the four-hundred-page volume contained much that was characteristic and valuable. It was especially appropriate that Rossetti should introduce his anthology with several epigraphs – one of them from Carlyle: "Yes, truly, it is a great thing for a nation that it get an articulate voice – that it produce a man who will speak forth melodiously what the heart of it means."[35]

Rossetti's edition was, in an important way, a turning-point in Whitman's struggle for recognition; he summed up his feelings in a letter to Moncure D. Conway, his representative in London during the negotiations about the book:

Indeed, my dear friend, I may here confess to you that to be accepted by those young men of England, & so treated with highest courtesy & even honor, touches one deeply. In my own country, so far, from the organs, the press, & from authoritative sources, I have received but one long tirade of shallow impudence, mockery, & scurrilous jeers. Only since the English recognition have the skies here lighted up a little.[36]

Among "those young men of England" who were honoring Whitman was the poet Swinburne, who had come upon *Leaves of Grass* and was mightily impressed; in August 1862 he informed his friend Richard Monckton Milnes that the poem "A Word Out of the Sea" (later titled "Out of the Cradle Endlessly Rocking") "is the most lovely and wonderful thing I have read for years and years. I could rhapsodize about it for ten more pages, for there is such beautiful skill and subtle power in every word of it, but I spare you."[37] Soon after, Swinburne reviewed Alexander Gilchrist's biography of William Blake – a work left unfinished at the author's sudden death and completed by his widow Anne Gilchrist (with the counsel and assistance of William Michael and Dante Gabriel Rossetti). Swinburne was struck by the resemblances he found between Whitman and Blake, and his own book about Blake – published in 1868 – closes with a rhapsodic comparison of the two poets; Blake's mind, Swinburne observes, so closely resembles Walt Whitman's that we are persuaded to take somewhat seriously the beliefs of those "who preach the transition of souls or transfusion of spirits."[38]

A transfusion of spirits of another kind took place in June 1869; Anne Gilchrist informed William Rossetti that a friend had put into her hands, a fortnight earlier, a copy of Rossetti's edition of Walt Whitman's poems – and she can now read no other book ("it holds me entirely spell-bound, and I go through it again and again with deepening delight and wonder"). Rossetti responded with "keen pleasure." "That glorious man Whitman," he wrote to Mrs Gilchrist, "will one day be known as one of the greatest sons of earth, a few steps below Shakespeare on the throne of immortality." He would hasten to send a copy of his edition – and offered to let her see a copy of the complete *Leaves of Grass*, an unbound copy containing Whitman's own final corrections ("Anybody who values Whitman as you do ought to read the whole of him").[39]

The outcome of this correspondence was "An Englishwoman's Estimate of Walt Whitman" – an eloquent and penetrating appreciation based on Mrs Gilchrist's letters to Rossetti; Rossetti arranged for its anonymous publication in the Boston *Radical* for May 1870, with an explanatory footnote by himself and some prefatory excerpts from the letters he had exchanged with his unnamed friend. After reading the essay, Whitman wrote to inform Rossetti how "deeply touched" he was "by the sympathies and convictions, coming from a woman and from England"; he was especially gratified by the praise "of a true wife and mother" – one whose poetic sense "must also move through and satisfy science as much as the esthetic . . ." He had, Whitman said, "hitherto received no eulogium so magnificent."[40]

In her essay, Mrs Gilchrist had identified "*the* great source" of Whitman's power as his grasp upon the present, "the fearless and comprehensive dealing with reality." Until Whitman's voice was heard, "the leaders of thought have (except in science) been men with their faces resolutely turned backwards." This poet restored the possibility of greatness and power in the present and future ("The present is great enough for him, because he is great enough for it") – and she suggested that Whitman had joined forces with the scientist in liberating man from constricting views of materialism and extinction:

Science knows that whenever a thing passes from a solid to a subtle air, power is set free to a wider scope of action. The poet knows it too, and is dazzled as he turns his eyes toward "the superb vistas of death." He knows that "perpetual transfers and promotions" and "the amplitude of time" are for a man as well as for the earth.

Earlier in the essay, Mrs Gilchrist had praised Whitman for the poems that celebrate the body – poems that liberate us from the voices that say to us: "Motherhood is beautiful, fatherhood is beautiful; but the dawn of fatherhood and motherhood is not beautiful." Woman, she said, cannot be harmed by these poems, for how can it be a part of the scheme of creation that – in a true union of man and woman – "what is natural and happy for the one should be baneful to the other?"[41]

Along with his expressions of gratification on reading "An Englishwoman's Estimate," Whitman enclosed two recent photographs of himself – one for Rossetti, the other "for the lady (if I may be permitted to send it to her)." Rossetti transmitted to Mrs Gilchrist both the photograph and (at the poet's suggestion) Whitman's letter.[42] In the year following the publication of Mrs Gilchrist's article, the American poet was a frequent subject of discussion in her correspondence with Rossetti; Rossetti was somewhat taken aback but agreed with Mrs Gilchrist's likening of Whitman to Christ ("broadly considered"). In the fall of 1870, she informed Rossetti about a serious illness and they exchanged views on literary and political matters during her convalescence.[43] In the summer of 1871, a communication from Whitman to Rossetti precipitated a crisis in the life of the Englishwoman who was his most fervent admirer.

Whitman sent copies of his latest edition of *Leaves of Grass* – with a request that Rossetti convey "to *the lady* the set enclosed for her." Rossetti did not reply until early October; he had been absent from England – but "the copy of your work transmitted for 'the lady'" had been forwarded to her. And, Rossetti added, "to judge from a letter of acknowledgment she wrote me, you have probably by this time heard from her direct."[44] Whitman had indeed heard from "the lady"; in a lengthy letter written on September 3, 1871, Anne Gilchrist opened her heart to Walt Whitman to tell the story of her life – to tell of her overpowering love for him.

A pilgrimage of love

Whitman's beloved books had reached her – but her heart was so full of anguish, her eyes so blinded, that she could not read. Anne Gilchrist told the story of her marriage – an early marriage never truly consummated for her because she could not feel the love a wife should feel for her husband; she felt "as if my nature were poor & barren beside his. But it was not so, it was only slumbering – undeveloped." Children came and brought them closer together; in an atmosphere of poverty and affection she learned the lessons of frugality and household management. Tragedy visited them, in 1861, when her husband succumbed to scarlet fever. She mourned him – but "To the last my soul dwelt apart & unmated & his soul dwelt apart unmated."

She did not believe her dead husband would be grieved with her now. The strenuous work of bringing up her children had brought her much tranquil happiness. But now she sought not happiness, but "the very life of my Soul":

In May 1869 came the voice over the Atlantic to me. O the voice of my Mate: it must be so – my love rises up out of the very depths of the grief & tramples upon despair. I can wait – any time, a lifetime, many lifetimes – . . . but nothing in life or death can tear out of my heart the passionate belief that one day I shall hear that voice say to me "My Mate. The one I so much want. Bride, Wife, indissoluble eternal!"

Her opportunity to speak out came at last through Rossetti – and it was only at Rossetti's suggestion that her name was withheld from her article. She had fed her heart "with sweet hopes: strengthened it with looking into the eyes of thy picture." Now she would wait no longer. Just a year ago, when she seemed to be dying, she had told her children of her love – and bidden them, after her death, to "go fearlessly to America, as I should have planted them down there – Land of Promise, my Canaan."[45]

Impatient at his failure to respond, Mrs Gilchrist sent a second fervent letter to Whitman on October 23; before it arrived – two months after her passionate outcry of September 3 – the poet wrote a short tactful reply. He was not insensible to her love; he too sent his love. His book was his best letter. He understood "the loving & womanly letter it has evoked. Enough that there exists between us so beautiful & delicate a relation, accepted by both of us with joy."[46]

Though that word "enough" was like a blow on the breast to her, wrote Anne Gilchrist in reply, she asked only "leave and security to write freely to you"; she did not ask him to write to her unless he was "inwardly impelled & desirous of doing so." She meditated at length on what their relationship

could be. It would be three years in May "since I first read the
book, first knew what the word love meant" – and she could
joyfully wait many more years and face the sternest probation
if at last he would say "this is the woman I have waited for . . .
the one I so much want."⁴⁷

A month later, in a calmer mood, Mrs Gilchrist wrote to
enclose photographs of herself and two of her children, to express the wish that he would come to her in London ("to come
& see if you feel happy beside me"), to tell about her modest
but comfortable home. To this less intense letter, Whitman
responded promptly – enclosing a newspaper copy of his new
poem "The Mystic Trumpeter" – with friendly comment about
the Gilchrist children and a reference to the letters he had
received from Tennyson cordially inviting the American poet
to visit him ("Sometimes I dream of journeying to old England,
on such a visit – & then of seeing you & your children – but
it is a dream only"). He refered to the sunny cheerfulness of
her letters and mentioned a long letter he had recently sent to
Rossetti. ("Nothing in my life . . . has more spiritually soothed
me" – he had written to Rossetti – than Mrs Gilchrist's "warm
appreciation and friendship.")⁴⁸

Mrs Gilchrist apparently replied (in a letter that has not
survived) too fervently, for the poet warned her, in his response, not to create an imaginary ideal figure "and so de-
votedly invest your love in it." But Mrs Gilchrist, in her
answer, asked him not to "warn" her anymore ("it hurts so,
as seemingly to distrust my love"). In April 1872, she asked
him – if it is troublesome to write – to post a newspaper as a
token of his well-being – but, after receiving several newspapers
in June, she pleads again for a letter ("And if you say 'Read my
books, & be content – you have me in them' – I say, it is
because I read them so that I am not content"). In July she
rejoiced at receiving his gift of *As a Strong Bird on Pinions Free* –
but in late January she wrote sadly about his long silence
("Shall you never find it in your heart to say a kind word to
me again? or a word of some sort?").⁴⁹

Even as she wrote, Whitman lay stricken with a paralytic
stroke – suffered on January 23, 1873 – that immobilized his
left side. His friends rallied round him and he seemed to be
making a gradual recovery. But he was subjected to two other

blows – the second, the most shattering. A month after his stroke, his sister-in-law Martha (whom he regarded as a beloved sister) died after a long illness; and on May 23 his mother died.[50]

For his mother's funeral about thirty relatives and friends gathered in the house where she died (at 322 Stevens Street in Camden) and one of them, Helen E. Price, noticed – as she took her seat among the mourners –

a curious thumping at intervals that made the floor vibrate beneath my feet. I was so absorbed in my own grief that at first I was hardly conscious of it. I finally left my chair, and going to the back of the room where we were sitting, I noticed a half opened door leading to another room. Glancing in, I saw the poet all alone by the side of his mother's coffin. He was bent over his cane, both hands clasped upon it, and from time to time he would lift it and bring it down with a heavy thud on the floor. His sister-in-law [Louisa Whitman] told me he had sat there all through the previous night.[51]

To his closest friend, John Burroughs, Whitman wrote, a few days later, that he was living in the rooms in which his mother died, "waiting for time to restore my health . . . but I feel that the blank in life & heart left by the death of my mother is what will never to me be filled – ."[52]

Alarmed by newspaper reports of the seriousness of his illness, Mrs Gilchrist wrote at length to tell of her great concern and to convey – once more – her undying love.[53] But before her letter could reach him, Whitman wrote to her – on August 17, 1873 – with news about his paralysis and double bereavement; his letter conveyed a tenderness never before as openly expressed – and there was an enclosure that told Mrs Gilchrist she had not waited in vain.

He had lost "a dear sister" and, in May, "my inexpressibly beloved mother died in Camden." The progress of his recovery had been erratic; he was able to move about with difficulty – and he thought "the probabilities are quite strong yet that I shall get well, (though I may not)." He had often thought of her and her children, had been rereading her letters and looking at the pictures she sent in January 1872; and he asked that she "not think hard of me for not writing oftener, especially the last seven months – If you could look into my spirit & emotions you would be entirely satisfied & at peace." The letter closed with a sentence that was, for Anne Gilchrist, an unmistakable pronouncement: "The enclosed ring I have just taken from my finger & send you with my love."[54] (It may have been – though we cannot know for certain – his mother's wedding ring.)

Mrs Gilchrist responded with alarm and ecstasy – her joy prevailing ("because its portion is eternal"). The ring that pressed his flesh "now will press mine so long as I draw breath." She longed to comfort and help him – but could now endure his silence with understanding.[55] But, except for mailing intermittent newspapers and magazines containing copies of his poems, Whitman now became very silent. Despite numerous letters from her (one of them asking that he underline the words "London" or "England" as a code response to questions about his health when he mailed newspapers to her),[56] Whitman stopped writing for almost two years. (He sent forty communications to his young comrade–companion Peter Doyle during this same period.) When he finally did write, it was a short letter – friendly and noncommittal.[57]

His letter came when she needed it most, Mrs Gilchrist replied a month later – while she was tending her dying mother. The death of her mother apparently freed the daughter to think about and plan a move to America – and she acted with decisiveness. In January 1876, she announced that she had their tickets for an August voyage to Philadelphia ("Soon, very soon, I come, my darling," she wrote in February).[58] Whitman responded promptly, conveying strong disapproval of her "American trans-settlement" ("Don't do any thing toward such a move . . . without further advice from me"); his health is improved, he reported, and "If I should get well enough to voyage, we will talk about it yet in London – ." But Anne Gilchrist was not to be dissuaded; "I have waited patiently – 7 years – patiently," she wrote in reply, ". . . – I cannot wait any longer."[59]

On August 30, 1876, Mrs Gilchrist set sail for America with three of her children and a quantity of furniture. On September 13, Whitman crossed the river that separated Camden and Philadelphia to visit Mrs Gilchrist at the Montgomery House shortly after her arrival.[60] There is no surviving record of this first face-to-face meeting but there seems to have occurred an almost immediate understanding by Anne Gilchrist – and acceptance of the painful fact – that the ring Whitman had sent to her would never be *her* wedding ring. They became warm and affectionate friends, but passionate urgency (and references to marriage) disappeared from her letters when she resumed correspondence with him after leaving Philadelphia in the spring of 1878.

During her two-year stay, she established her family in living-quarters with a room set aside for Whitman – a frequent visitor, sometimes for a week at a time.[61] In a letter to Rossetti, Mrs Gilchrist told of the delightful evenings they were having and how she wished "you could make one in the circle round our tea table where sits on my right hand every evening but Sunday Walt Whitman." There was lively conversation on a variety of topics – literature, religion, science, politics. Whitman was full of reminiscences and anecdotes, one a little at Emerson's expense and the strict Sabbatarianism prevalent in Boston some years back. During a visit to Emerson's house, the Swedish writer Frederika Bremer wanted to illustrate a characteristic of her country's music and went to the piano – only to be told by Emerson himself, "No, Miss Bremer, this is Sunday evening, I would rather not – ." Whitman talked about Thoreau with approval, but felt that "he was morbid" – that it was less a love of woods and streams that made him live in the country than "a morbid dislike of humanity." He recalled Thoreau saying, while they walked together in Brooklyn – "What is there in the people? Pshaw! what do you (a man who sees as well as anybody) see in all this cheating political corruption?" Whitman did not at all like to hear his Brooklyn spoken of in this way.[62]

After leaving Philadelphia, Mrs Gilchrist and her children stayed for a time in New England – and she wrote to both Whitman and Rossetti about her meetings with Emerson. ("His conversation," she informed Rossetti, "reverted continually to Carlyle and their early intercourse.") There followed a stay of several months in New York City before the Gilchrists set sail for "dear old England" on June 7, 1879. The day before they left, Whitman came to see them. "I need not tell you," Anne Gilchrist wrote to Rossetti shortly after her return, "we felt the parting from him very much as he did, I think from us."[63]

Anne Gilchrist settled in Keats Corner, Hampstead, and re-

sumed her correspondence with Whitman until her death in
1885. During the years that remained to her, she busied herself
with several literary enterprises – a new edition of her husband's
Life of Blake, a life of Mary Lamb (in the series entitled *Eminent
Women*) and several essays. "A Confession of Faith," a new
and final appreciation of Walt Whitman, appeared in *To-Day*
five months before her death. Even more than in "An Englishwoman's Estimate," Mrs Gilchrist emphasized the connection
between the man of science and the poet as crucial to the progress of mankind. She quoted from Whitman's "Miracles"
("Why! who makes much of a miracle? / As to me, I know of
nothing else but miracles") and followed these lines with a
significant passage that links Carlyle to Whitman in her defi-
nition of the poet's function in the modern world:

The natural *is* the supernatural, says Carlyle. It is the message that
comes to our time from all quarters alike; from poetry, from science,
from the deep brooding of the student of human history. Science
materialistic? Rather it is the current theology that is materialistic
in comparison. Science may truly be said to have annihilated our
gross and brutish conceptions of matter and to have revealed it to
us as subtle, spiritual, energetic beyond our powers of realization.
It is for the Poet to increase these powers of realization. He it is
who must awaken us to a perception of a new heaven and a new
earth here where we stand on this old earth. He it is who must, in
Walt Whitman's words, indicate the path between reality and the
soul.[64]

Anne Gilchrist was one of the few critics on either side of
the Atlantic to emphasize Whitman's involvement with
science.[65] For her, it was a long-standing subject of compelling
interest. "Is it not remarkable," she wrote to a friend in 1865
(four years before Whitman entered her life), "how the latest
views of science corroborate Blake and the mystics in regarding
everything as Force Power!"[66] Two years after her death,
Whitman's poetic tribute "Going Somewhere" (a phrase taken
from "A Confession of Faith") identifies her as "My science-
friend, my noblest woman-friend / (Now buried in an English
grave – and this a memory-leaf for her dear sake)."[67] Whitman
had many perceptive and devoted English admirers – but there
were few more perceptive and none more devoted than Anne
Gilchrist.

Other pilgrims

In "A Confession of Faith," Mrs Gilchrist cites Carlyle's view that "there is no grand poem but is at bottom a biography" as having special applicability to *Leaves of Grass* and Whitman:

It is no vain boast when he exclaims,
> "Camerado! this is no book;
> Who touches this touches a man."

He has infused himself into words in a way that had not before seemed possible; and he causes each reader to feel that he himself or herself has an actual relationship to him . . . to those who comprehend him he stands "higher than the highest."[68]

To few other readers did he seem to stand as close as to Anne Gilchrist – but many who were moved by the poem were also moved to reach out to the man. "I wish to see my benefactor," wrote the renowned Emerson to the unknown Whitman soon after reading *Leaves of Grass* for the first time, "and have felt much like striking my tasks, and visiting New York to pay you my respects." Emerson did indeed strike his tasks not long after and made a pilgrimage to Whitman's house in Brooklyn; years later, Whitman described "the taste of lovableness he left behind when he was gone" – and said, further, that he could easily understand Carlyle's likening of Emerson's appearance at his house in Craigenputtock "to the apparition of an angel."[69] Thoreau, Alcott – and many others – made similar pilgrimages.

In England, another early enthusiastic reader – independent of the Rossetti circle – was Richard Monckton Milnes (later Lord Houghton). Soon after encountering the 1855 edition of *Leaves of Grass*, Milnes wrote to his friend Hawthorne (then American Consul at Liverpool) to ask for information about Walt Whitman, to express admiration ("it is a most notable and true book") – and to tell Hawthorne that he saw a connection between Whitman and Thoreau ("It is of the same family as those delightful books of Thoreau's which you introduced me to, and which are so little known and valued here"). When Lord Houghton came to America in 1875 – shortly before Anne Gilchrist's pilgrimage – he visited Whitman at Camden, despite the fact that the poet was *persona non grata* (Emerson excepted) in the genteel literary circles of Boston and Concord.

Lord Houghton told the poet about attempts to dissuade him from calling – and the two men settled down to some lively and congenial talk over a dish of baked apples (all that Whitman could offer).[70]

In July 1877, Anne Gilchrist wrote from Philadelphia to Rossetti to introduce the friend who would convey her letter, a recent English pilgrim to Camden. He was Edward Carpenter, who had resigned a fellowship at Trinity College, Cambridge to spread Whitman's gospel of love and brotherhood among working-class men and women. Carpenter had discovered Whitman through the Rossetti *Selection* – a discovery that transformed his life. From Trinity Hall he had written ardent letters and on a day in May 1877, called on Whitman in Camden. When he returned to England it was with the feeling that he had encountered an authentic prophet – that the poet in the flesh "seemed to fill out *Leaves of Grass* and form an interpretation of it."[71]

Rossetti was favorably impressed by Carpenter and by the account he gave of his days with Whitman. He was, he informed Mrs Gilchrist, "particularly pleased that on Carpenter – as a University Man imbued with all those highstrung traditions of culture so characteristic of University Men –" Whitman had produced as powerful an impression as he was used to finding in "men of a somewhat different stamp."[72] Whitman himself was struck by the understanding and enthusiasm he received from highly-cultivated Englishmen – while their American counterparts reacted with uniform hostility.[73] (Among those who made pilgrimages to Whitman's garret in Washington or to his Camden residence – in addition to Lord Houghton and Carpenter – were Edmund Gosse, Ernest Rhys, John Morley, Justin McCarthy, Oscar Wilde, Sir Edwin Arnold.) But Whitman's warmest response was reserved for a group of Lancashire men – nicknamed by one of them "Bolton College" – who established and maintained an affectionate relationship with the poet during the last six years of his life.

"Our number," wrote J. W. Wallace, "included a doctor, a clergyman, two lawyer's clerks, two bank clerks, a cotton-waste dealer, a hosiery manufacturer, another assistant architect, a newspaper editor, an accountant, and one or two artisans."[74] Wallace, an assistant architect, lived with his father in a small house in Boston. The "little company of men" who gathered each Monday evening in his house had widely different characteristics and ideas, "were united only in a common friendship." They gathered weekly for sociability and the "perfectly free interchange of ideas."[75] Several of them were admirers of Whitman and he was often the subject of readings and discussion. In 1887, a correspondence was initiated with the poet that culminated, in 1890 and 1891, in visits to Camden by Dr John Johnston and Wallace. Dr Johnston had instructions from the group to keep a detailed record of his impressions; his *Notes of Visits to Walt Whitman and Friends in 1890* is a simple and eloquent account of his meetings with the poet and his visit to Whitman's birthplace at West Hills. Among the poet's last written messages during his final illness was a note scrawled to Dr Johnston to tell of his condition ("deadly weak yet, but the spark seems to glimmer yet") and to extend thanks to his "cheery British friends"; on the next day (February 7, 1892), he added a postscript – his last message to "Bolton College" before his death: "Same cond'n cont'd – More & more it comes to the fore that the only theory worthy our modern times for g't literature politics and sociology must combine all the bulk-people of all lands, the women not forgetting. But the mustard plaster on my side is stinging & I must stop – Good–bye to all!"[76] It was "the bulk-people" of England that Whitman valued most. (When Herbert Gilchrist – who settled in America after his mother's death – expressed surprise at the poet's deep involvement with his Bolton admirers ["they're not famous in England at all"], Whitman responded with considerable warmth: "Thank God, they're just nobody at all, like all the people who are worth while.")[77] As early as 1860, George S. Phillips (an English journalist residing in New York) had predicted that the sentences of *Leaves of Grass* would "one day . . . be woven into the common speech of the people of America."[78] But Phillips – who found in the 1860 edition "The genius of this continent and of this wonderful civilization" – was himself educated at Trinity College, Cambridge, and Whitman's sentences, though they have profoundly moved people of all kinds, have been woven not into the common speech of the American people,

but into the uncommon writings of scholar–critics and poets
– many (if not most) of them Englishmen.

Other estimates: "Ave America!"

Two essays half a century apart (one written in 1869 and
printed, after some discouraging rejections, in 1871; the second
written in 1918 and printed, after similar discouragements, in
1921) deserve special mention among numerous noteworthy
British critical estimates of Whitman. Poet–scholar Edward
Dowden provided the most eloquent and searching commentary during Whitman's lifetime; poet–novelist D. H. Lawrence
has done the same (in a very different way) in this century.

In September 1869, the young professor of English literature at Trinity College, Dublin, wrote to his brother: "Do you
know Walt Whitman? If not you must. I have just got his
'Leaves of Grass' and am likely some time to have a short
(eight or ten pp.) paper in *Macmillan* on 'The Poetry of Democracy – Walt Whitman.'"[79] But Whitman was an explosive
subject and Dowden's essay was published only after much
trouble and delay; *Macmillan's Magazine* rejected it and *The
Contemporary Review*, after the article was accepted and set up
in type, returned it because it might offend contributors. Dowden's essay, considerably expanded, finally came out in *The
Westminster Review* in July 1871.[80] Though his tone is apolo-
getic, Dowden's comment about his article – in the letter to
Whitman that accompanied a copy sent to the poet – explains
much about its persuasive appeal: "... I wrote more coolly than
I feel because I wanted those, who being ignorant of your
writings are perhaps prejudiced against them, to say: 'Here is
a cool judicious impartial critic who finds a great deal in
Whitman – perhaps after all we are mistaken.'"[81] Whitman's
opponents tended to be strident and abusive, his admirers
rhapsodic and reverential; Dowden's article is, in contrast,
refreshingly restrained and lucid – and persuasive.

The New World, he argues, calls for a new art – an art that
has heretofore not made its appearance. ("Irving might have
walked arm-in-arm with Addison"; though prairie and forest
occupy Bryant's canvas, there is not a true communion or kinship with these influences.) In Emerson a true advance emerged

("We tasted in him the flavour of strange sap, and knew the ripening of another sun and other winds"). Now an hour's acquaintance with Walt Whitman and *Leaves of Grass* makes it clear that we are in the presence of "a man not shaped out of old-world clay, not cast in any old-world mould, and hard to name by any old-world name." He demands to be accepted or rejected; he cannot be ignored.[82]

Drawing on Tocqueville's distinction between the literature of an aristocracy and that of a democracy, Dowden carefully and convincingly set forth his picture of Whitman as "Bard of America, the Bard of democracy" – as one who valued science and democracy as the great and beneficent twin powers in the modern world ("after the chemist, geologist, ethnologist, finally shall come the Poet worthy that name"). As the poet of democracy (and at the same time a mystic), Whitman saw the visible realities of this earth "as symbols of the impalpable and spiritual" – but all he beheld may also be seen by other men. His was no isolated idiosyncratic vision but a vision of men and women *en masse* ("the people itself, in its undiminished totality, marches through his poems making its greatness and variety felt"). Whitman's self-celebration, Dowden reminds us, is a celebration of all that is distinctively American – and all the versions of his hero come to us (beyond the "poignant feeling of personality" that pervades every line), finally, as "Brother Jonathan." The American people, in turn, are not set apart or above other peoples but are, rather, the promise "of all that is most powerful and promising for the progress of mankind."[83]

Dowden is a sophisticated critic attuned to Whitman's creation of a complex identity of himself ("the hardest of all facts and the only entrance to all facts") – a *persona* that is both self and not self; he quotes a passage from "As I Ebbed with the Ocean of Life" to illustrate Whitman's sense of a double-self, a sense of the real *Me*, which stands "untouched, untold, altogether unreached":

> Withdrawn far, mocking me with mock-congratulatory signs and bows,
> With peals of ironical laughter at every work I have written,
>
> ....

Now I perceive I have not understood anything
– not a single object; and that no man ever can.
I perceive Nature, here in sight of the sea, is
    taking advantage of me, to dart upon me, and sting me,
Because I have dared to open my mouth to sing at all.

And – after quoting an extended dark passage from *Democratic Vistas* – Dowden suggests that Whitman's picture of America is ugly enough to satisfy Carlyle; there is no despair in Whitman: "He takes account of the evil anxiously, accurately; and can still rejoice."[84]

Dowden closes his study with a response to what has been called by some critics Whitman's "materialism" as expressed in the poems that celebrate the body and bodily desire. These, Dowden points out, are the poet's answer to medieval ascetic teachings ("As to thy body, thou art viler than muck"). In the life of a nation, a great advance in material benefits is admirable – but only as it contributes to "a great spiritual civilization"; similarly, "in the life of the individual all that is external, material, sensuous, is estimated by the worth of what it can give to the soul." Even in death – perhaps especially in death – there is, in Whitman's vision, a "delicious tenderness and mystery not without some element of sensuousness curiously blended with it." Whitman does not solve the mystery but arouses in his readers a palpable awareness of its urgency; his pupil, observes Dowden, "must part from him as soon as possible, and go upon his own way."[85]

What Dowden touches on, D. H. Lawrence dwells on in the first of a series of twelve essays he wrote on American literature in Cornwall in 1917–18. Dowden complained that Bryant had not truly absorbed the American landscape into his poems ("The mountains are not his sponsors; there are not the unconscious ties between him and them which indicate kinship").[86] In "The Spirit of Place," Lawrence argues that Englishmen have not taken sufficient account, in American literature, of an "alien quality [that] belongs to the American continent itself."[87] In that alien quality, Lawrence saw a promise of new spiritual life beyond the present stage of sterile and repressive materialism. The new Americans took Europe and a "lust of anti-life" with them to their new continent ("The New Englanders, wielding the sword of the spirit backwards, struck down the primal impulsive being in every man, leaving only a mechanical, automatic unit"). [88] But every great locality had its own great life force – and one awaits the inevitable quickening of the American soul ("So will the machine-parts open like buds and the great machines break into leaf"). [89]

"The Spirit of Place" served as an introduction to the essays on Franklin, Crevecoeur, Cooper, Poe, Hawthorne, Dana and Melville that followed. The concluding and culminating essay, on Whitman, sets forth in terms of passionate praise (and some discerning qualifications of that praise) Whitman's lofty place among American writers and his supreme contribution to the promise of America. (The strident and derisive criticism of Whitman added at a later date when the essay was rewritten for *Studies in Classic American Literature* [1923] is not evident in the version that appeared in *The Nation and the Athenaeum* for July 23, 1921.) [90]

Lawrence opens his essay with seven arresting words: "Whitman is the greatest of the Americans." He is also: "One of the greatest poets of the world" – but there is, at the same time, a troublesome "element of falsity" that Lawrence must define before proceeding to take the measure of his greatness. There is something "overdone" and "self-conscious" in Whitman – as in all the American writers who are laying open "the secrets which the Christian epoch has taken two thousand years to close up." Here (as did Dowden) Lawrence referred to the Christian attempt "to annihilate the sensual being in man." In their reaction to this repressiveness, Whitman (and the other pioneers of American literature) was guilty of premeditated provocations of the physical self – with a resultant spuriousness and self-awareness that borders on madness. [91]

Having voiced this objection, Lawrence pays tribute to Whitman as one who has penetrated further into life-knowledge than any man – beyond Dostoevsky, who "has burrowed underground into the decomposing psyche." It is Whitman who, by exploring "the *deepest centres* of the lower self," achieved an awareness of the higher self "greater, perhaps, than any man in the modern world." With this awareness comes an all-embracing expansiveness ("At last all is one, all is love, even hate is love, even flesh is spirit"). And here Lawrence voiced his second objection: Whitman's way to "Allness" was through

endless sympathy, endless merging – a process that violates a
basic need to move back toward self as well as forward toward
the "Other"; the direction must be twofold. Individuals are
endlessly different and Whitman's "One Identity is a prison of
horror, once realized."[92]

Lawrence closes his essay with observations on the new mode
of existence that Whitman has opened up for modern man. In
this new fulfillment, woman plays a subordinate role ("Function
of sex, function of birth"); comradeship, manly love, is to be
"the final cohering principle of the new world, the new Democracy." In this final state of the soul's responsibility, death is a
necessary and ever-hovering presence to "link up the mystic
circuit" of creative life. Lawrence quotes the great lines from
"Out of the Cradle Endlessly Rocking":

> Whereto answering, the sea
> Delaying not, hurrying not,
> Whispered me through the night, and very plainly before
>   daybreak,
> Lisp'd to me the low and delicious word death,
> And again death, death, death, death,
> Hissing melodious, neither like the bird nor like my aroused
>   child's heart,
> But edging near as privately for me rustling at my feet,
> Creeping thence steadily up to my ears and laving me
>   softly all over,
> Death, death, death, death, death –

Whitman finds himself on the shore of the last sea – the last
barrier removed ("The extreme of life: so near to death"). He
leads us into a new epoch in which there are "perfect circuits
of vital flow between human beings: simple sexless friendships; powerful sexual attachments between man and woman
culminating in marriage; the love between comrades ("the
final progression from marriage . . . the last seedless flower of
pure beauty, beyond purpose").[93]

Whitman has set us on the truth path. He is "The greatest
modern poet" – at his best, both spontaneous and controlled,
setting forth "the whole being," sensual and spiritual (unlike
Swinburne, who is an exaggeration of one side of us):

It is perfect and whole. The whole soul speaks at once, and is too
pure for mechanical assistance of rhyme and measure. The perfect

utterance of a concentrated spontaneous soul. The unforgettable loveliness of Whitman's lines!

> "Out of the cradle endlessly rocking."

Ave America![94]

In New Mexico, several years later, Lawrence drastically revised his paean to Whitman and America for the essay that concludes *Studies in Classic American Literature*; shrill ridicule and great praise are set side by side with little or no attempt to explain their coexistence.[95] His hope for America seems to have dimmed as he wrote to an American friend – from a ship bringing him across the Atlantic back to England in September 1925 – about the plight of the creative artist in the New World: "Hawthorne and Melville and Whitman reached a point of imaginative or visionary adjustment to America which, it seems to me, is again entirely lost, abandoned: because you can't adjust yourself vitally, inwardly, to a rather scaring world, and at the same time, get ahead."[96]

In 1929, the dying Lawrence wrote the extended essay, *Apocalypse*, his last book. In his introduction to this "splendid valediction" – posthumously published – Richard Aldington says of Lawrence and all his books that "He could have echoed Whitman truly, for who touches Lawrence's books touches a man."[97] The last pages of Lawrence's last book demonstrate his close kinship with the American poet – eloquently convey the spirit of Whitman as Lawrence understood and experienced it; an extended passage may serve here as a fitting close:

What man most passionately wants is his living wholeness and his living unison, not his own isolate salvation of his "soul." Man wants his physical fulfilment first and foremost since now, once and once only, he is in the flesh and potent. For man, the vast marvel is to be alive. For man, as for flower and beast and bird, the supreme triumph is to be most vividly, most perfectly alive. Whatever the unborn and the dead may know, they cannot know the beauty, the marvel of being alive in the flesh. The dead may look after the afterwards. But the magnificent here and now of life in the flesh is ours, and ours alone, and ours only for a time. We ought to dance with rapture that we should be alive and in the flesh, and part of the living, incarnate cosmos. I am part of the sun as my eye is part of me. That I am part of the earth my feet know perfectly, and my blood is part of the sea. My soul knows that I am part of the human race, my soul is an organic part of the great human soul, as my spirit is part of my nation.[98]

Afterword: Ave Mark Twain!

In his essay "Walking," Thoreau speculates on what fables the West will be able to add to those of the East. "The valleys of the Ganges, the Nile, and the Rhine having yielded their crop," he observes, "it remains to be seen what the valleys of the Amazon . . . and the Mississippi will produce." At some future age, it is possible that "the poets of the world will be inspired by American mythology."[1] Even as he wrote a great fable of the West was being shaped in the mind and heart of a writer born and raised in a Mississippi valley town – and it was somehow fitting (though prompted by international copyright concerns) that *Adventures of Huckleberry Finn* should first appear (on December 10, 1884) in London.

The book at first fared only moderately well in England and Mark Twain suggested to his publisher Andrew Chatto that "it must be because the English people do not understand that dialect . . ."[2] But the English people came to understand that dialect surpassingly well; by 1909, *Huckleberry Finn* had outsold all the other books by Mark Twain issued by Chatto and Windus,[3] and though the book was never as popular in England as in America, it was the English critics who led the way in recognizing Twain as an "authentic man of genius" and *Huckleberry Finn* as a masterpiece belonging "among the greatest books of the world."[4] In the *Pall Mall Magazine*, in 1899, William Archer wrote that "if a work of incontestable genius has been issued in the English language during the past quarter of a century, it is that brilliant romance of the great rivers, *The Adventures of Huckleberry Finn*."[5] Similar tributes had been expressed by other British critics (most notably Andrew Lang and Sir Walter Besant); American critics were much slower to recognize the greatness of this new fable of the West.

It was fitting that, on May 3, 1907, Mark Twain should

receive a cablegram inviting him to come to Oxford to receive an honorary Doctor of Letters degree. He had received similar honors from Yale and Missouri – but "an Oxford decoration," he wrote at the time, "is a loftier distinction than is conferrable by any other university on either side of the ocean and is worth twenty-five of any other, whether foreign or domestic."[6] He had been involved, since his first visit in 1872, in a love affair with England (marked by the occasional stormy misunderstandings that accompany such deep attachments); "I would like to stay here about fifteen or seventy-five years," he wrote to James Redpath from London during his first visit.[7] He returned the following year for a lecture tour and there were numerous other visits, some for extended periods of time.

After a lecture tour around the world in 1895–6 (accompanied by his wife and daughter Clara), Mark Twain took a house in Guildford for another extended stay in England; two other daughters, Suzy and Jean, would be arriving from America in a week. Instead there came a letter explaining that Suzy was slightly ill. Cablegrams followed with reassuring, but ambiguous, messages. Twain's wife took alarm and sailed for home with Clara. Three days later – while his wife and daughter were in mid-Atlantic – Twain received the fateful cablegram: "Suzy was peacefully released to-day." She had been suddenly and fatally stricken by spinal meningitis.[8]

His wife returned to England from the house of death in Hartford (a house Mark Twain never entered again); to secure greater seclusion, the family moved from Guildford to Tedworth Square, Chelsea.[9] The 24-year-old Suzy was the light of Mark Twain's life; he was shattered and buried himself (as best he could) in work. To his closest friend Howells, he wrote: "Will healing ever come or life have value again?" And he provides a bitter answer to a bitter question: "And shall we see Suzy? Without doubt! without *shadow* of doubt, if it can furnish opportunity to break our hearts again."[10]

The week of the Oxford University conferral ceremony was filled with public appearances and speech-making. On June 25, 1907, about 250 guests gathered at the Savoy Hotel, London, for the Society of Pilgrims luncheon honoring Mark Twain. (Featured on the menu were Saumon du Mississippi, Asperge

Sauce Hannibal, and Savoury Hannibal.)[11] The guest of honor was in excellent form and told several delightful stories at his own expense in his own inimitable way. But at the close of an anecdote about an earlier visit, Mark Twain suddenly (and with a confiding openness that was unprecedented and never to be repeated) talked to his audience about "an incident which will always connect me with England in a pathetic way" – talked at length about the death of his daughter ("She was twenty-four years of age and in the bloom of young womanhood, and we were unsuspecting"). He asks forgiveness for telling about this heartbreaking bereavement. He must sometimes "lay the cap and bells aside, and recognize that I am of the human race like the rest, and must have my cares and griefs." And he closes on a note of gladness and gratitude for the hundreds of letters he has received this week "from all conditions of people in England – men, women, and children –" letters that convey something far more precious than compliment and praise; there is in them an affection that represents the ultimate reward. "All these letters," Mark Twain said finally, "make me feel that here in England – as in America – when I stand under the English flag, I am not a stranger. I am not an alien, but at home."[12]

On the following day at Oxford, Lord Curzon presented the degree, intoning (in Latin) the ceremonious language of praise and conferral: "Most jocund, pleasant and humorous man, who shakes the sides of all the circuit of the earth with your native joyousness, I, by my authority and that of the entire university, admit you to the honorary degree of Doctor of Letters."[13] Among those also honored were Rudyard Kipling, Auguste Rodin, Camille Saint-Saëns, Sidney Colvin, Sidney Lee. But the warm applause of the audience for each of the recipients swelled to a roar when Mark Twain stepped forward. Kipling would vividly recall, almost three decades later, how "even those dignified old Oxford dons stood up and yelled."[14]

Notes

1: "*Who reads an American book?*"

1 Frank Luther Mott, *A History of American Magazines, 1741–1850* (Cambridge, Mass.: Harvard Univ. Press, 1939), p. 188.

2 H. C. Allen, *The Anglo-American Relationship Since 1783* (London: Adams & Charles Black, 1959), p. 132.

3 Quoted in William B. Cairns, *British Criticisms of American Writings, 1783–1815*, Univ. of Wisconsin Studies in Language and Literature, no. 1 (Madison, 1918), p. 11.

4 *The Diverting History of John Bull and Brother Jonathan*, New Edition (New York: Harper & Brothers, 1835), p. 172.

5 Quoted in John J. McCloskey, "The Campaign of Periodicals after the War of 1812 for a National American Literature," *PMLA*, 50 (Mar. 1935), 264.

6 *Ibid.*, pp. 269–70; the concluding quotation is from McCloskey's summary of the review.

7 Quoted in John Bach McMaster, *A History of the People of the United States from the Revolution to the Civil War*, 8 vols. (New York: D. Appleton and Company, 1888–1937), V, 314.

8 Cairns, *British Criticisms of American Writings, 1815–1833*, Univ. of Wisconsin Studies in Language and Literature, no. 14 (Madison, 1922), p. 11.

9 For a valuable account of the founding, see John Clive, *Scotch Reviewers: The Edinburgh Review, 1802–1815* (Cambridge, Mass.: Harvard Univ. Press, 1957), pp. 186–97.

10 Letter dated October 25, 1791, reproduced in Henry Thomas, Lord Cockburn, *Life of Lord Jeffrey with a Selection from His Correspondence* (Edinburgh: Adam and Charles Black, 1852), II, 4–5.

11 Letter of November 2, 1791, *ibid.*, 5–6.

12 *Ibid.*, I, 100.

13 *Ibid.*, 73.

14 *Memoirs, Journal, and Correspondence of Thomas Moore* (London: Longman, Brown, Green & Longmans, 1853), I, 199–213; the duel, such as it was, took place at Chalk Farm, London, on the morning of August 11, 1806.

15 Cockburn, *Life of Lord Jeffrey*, I, 34.

16 Letter to Murray dated December 14, 1829, *The Letters of Sydney Smith*, ed. Nowell C. Smith (Oxford: Clarendon Press, 1953), II, 511.

17 Letter dated January 10, 1809, *ibid.*, I, 152.

18 Cockburn, *Life of Lord Jeffrey*, I, 215. Charlotte Wilkes, Jeffrey's fiancée, was the daughter of Charles Wilkes (1764–1833), a solid citizen of America since 1780 "in every sense except the legal, for he never became an American." William Charvat, "Francis Jeffrey in America," *New England Quarterly*, 14 (June 1941), 310–11.

19 Charvat, "Francis Jeffrey," pp. 311–12.

20 Clive, *Scotch Reviewers*, p. 169.

21 Quoted in Hesketh Pearson, *The Smith of Smiths: Being the Life, Wit and Humour of Sydney Smith* (London: H. Hamilton, 1934), p. 35.

22 Letter dated August 17, 1819, *Letters of Sydney Smith*, ed. Nowell C. Smith, I, 331.

23 Quoted in Clive, *Scotch Reviewers*, p. 38.

24 Letter dated November 23, 1818, *Letters of Sydney Smith*, ed. Nowell C. Smith, I, 305.

25 Review of four travel books about America, *Edinburgh Review*, 31 (Dec. 1818), 139, 144.

26 Review of Adam Seybert's *Statistical Annals of the United States of America*, *Edinburgh Review*, 33 (Jan. 1820), 79.

27 "The Verdict of Sydney Smith," in *The Third Dimension: Studies in Literary History* (New York: The Macmillan Company, 1965), pp. 41, 50–1.

28 *Letters of Sydney Smith*, ed. Nowell C. Smith, I, 386. The review (of a volume by "Miss Wright") was not printed.

29 Review of three travel books about America, *Edinburgh Review*, 40 (July 1824), 427–42; the quoted passages are on pp. 430, 432–3.

30 Cooper to Charles Wilkes, January 6, 1830, *The Letters and Journals of of James Fenimore Cooper*, ed. James F. Beard (Cambridge, Mass.: The Belknap Press of Harvard Univ. Press, 1960), I, 400. The review, a joint critique of Cooper and Basil Hall's *Travels in North America*, is in the *Edinburgh Review*, 49 (June 1829), 473–525. The reviewer is identified as William Empson in *The Wellesley Index to Victorian Periodicals, 1824–1900*, ed. Walter E. Houghton (Toronto: Univ. of Toronto Press, 1966), I, 471.

31 *Letters on American Debts* (London: Longman, Brown, Green, & Longmans, 1843), p. 16.

32 *Life, Letters and Journals of George Ticknor* (Boston: James R. Osgood and Company, 1876), II, 214–16.

33 Review of Sydney Smith's *Works*, *North American Review*, 59 (July 1844), 104–28.

34 *Wit and Wisdom of the Rev. Sydney Smith*, ed. Evert A. Duyckinck (New York: A. C. Armstrong & Son, 1882); the quoted statements by Duyckinck are on pp. 69 and 188. American interest in Sydney Smith was strong enough to occasion repeated reprintings of this collection.

35 "Hawthorne and His Mosses," *The Literary World*, August 17 and 24, 1850; in *Moby-Dick*, ed. Harrison Hayford and Hershel Parker (New York: W. W. Norton & Company, 1967), p. 543.

36 *The Raven and the Whale: the War of Words and Wits in the Era of Poe and Melville* (New York: Harcourt, Brace and Company, 1956), pp. 285–6.

37 Review of *Lady Holland's Memoir of Rev. Sydney Smith, North American Review*, 82 (Jan. 1856), 107.

38 "Nil Nisi Bonum," *Roundabout Papers* (New York: Harper & Brothers, 1863), p. 282.

2: *Washington Irving: uneasy ambassador*

1 *The Sketch Book of Geoffrey Crayon, Gent.*, 3rd edn, 2 vols. (London: John Murray, 1820), I, v.

2 Irving to Murray, October 31, 1820, in *Washington Irving and the House of Murray: Geoffrey Crayon Charms the British, 1817–1856*, ed. Ben Harris McClary (Knoxville: Univ. of Tennessee Press, 1969), p. 31.

3 William L. Hedges, *Washington Irving: An American Study, 1802–1832* (Baltimore: The Johns Hopkins Press, 1965), p. 128.

4 *The Sketch Book of Geoffrey Crayon, Gent.* (New York: C. S. Van Winkle, 1819), p. 119. This first printing of "English Writers on America" differs from the British edition in a number of minor details; the argument and tone in the American and British editions are, however, essentially the same.

5 Quoted in Benjamin T. Spencer, *The Quest for Nationality: An American Literary Campaign* (Syracuse, N. Y.: Univ. of Syracuse Press, 1957), p. 27.

6 Quoted in Pierre M. Irving, *The Life and Letters of Washington Irving* (New York: G. P. Putnam, 1862), I, 310–11.

7 *Ibid.*, 311–12.

8 *Ibid.*, 312–18.

9 Quoted in Stanley T. Williams, *The Life of Washington Irving* (New York: Oxford Univ. Press, 1935), I, 143.

10 See Amos L. Herold, *James Kirke Paulding: Versatile American* (New York: Columbia Univ. Press, 1926), p. 7.

11 Hedges, *Washington Irving*, pp. 47, 52–3.

12 Paulding to Irving, September 5, 1812, *The Letters of James Kirke Paulding*, ed. Ralph M. Aderman (Madison: Univ. of Wisconsin Press, 1962), p. 32.

13 *The Analectic Magazine*, 2 (Sept. 1813), 223–4: for Irving's authorship of this review, see Irving, *Life and Letters*, I, 299.

14 An excerpt from Brevoort's letter is quoted in Irving, *Life and Letters*, I, 300; Scott's letter to Brevoort (dated from Abbotsford April 23, 1813) is *ibid.*, p. 240.

15 Here and in what follows in the paragraph I have drawn on R. B. Van Wart, "Washington Irving and Scotland," *Blackwood's Magazine*, 266 (July–Dec. 1949), 257–63; Scott is quoted on p. 261.

16 Irving to Murray, October 26, 1820, in *Washington Irving and the House of Murray*, ed. McClary, pp. 28–30.

17 Paulding to Irving, March 20, 1824, *The Letters of James Kirke Paulding*, ed. Aderman, p. 69.

18 Paulding to Irving, November 11, 1840, *ibid.*, p. 288.

19 The paragraph was inserted into the second edition (also published

in 1820), II, 402–3. See Jacob Blanck, *Bibliography of American Literature* (New Haven and London: Yale Univ. Press, 1969), V, 19.

20 In the following account, I have drawn on Ben Harris McClary, "Mr. Irving of the Shakespeare Committee: A Bit of Anglo-American Jealousy," *American Literature*, 41 (1969), 92–5; and my "*John Bull* versus Washington Irving: more on the Shakespeare Committee Controversy," *English Language Notes*, 9 (June 1972), 272–7.

21 *John Bull*, 2 (July 7, 1822), 653. Irving's version of Murray's publication of *The Sketch Book* is very different: "It was not until Murray found the work was making its own way with the public that he became a purchaser of it." Irving to Colonel Thomas Aspinwall, April 4, 1829; quoted in Williams, *Life of Washington Irving*, I, 175.

22 "Irvine" is a variant spelling of the family name.

23 McClary, "Mr. Irving of the Shakespeare Committee," p. 95.

24 French Journal, entry of March 27, 1824, *The Complete Works of Washington Irving* (Madison: Univ. of Wisconsin Press, 1969–): *Journals and Notebooks, 1819–1827*, ed. Walter A. Reichart (1970), III, 310.

25 "Traits of America," *John Bull*, 4 (July 18, 1824), 237; the references are to Thomas Campbell and Felix M'Donogh's *The Hermit in London*, 5 vols. (London: Colburn, 1819–20).

26 *The Sketch Book*, 3rd edn, I, 3–4.

27 Henry James, *Hawthorne* (1879), rpt. in Edmund Wilson, *The Shock of Recognition: The Development of Literature in the United States Recorded by the Men Who Made It* (New York: Farrar, Strauss and Cudahy, 1955), p. 521.

28 McClary, "Mr. Irving of the Shakespeare Committee," p. 93; in 1828, Sir Walter Scott used "Stratford-on-Avon" as a source of information during a visit to Stratford: see *The Journal of Sir Walter Scott* (Edinburgh: David Douglas, 1890), II, 155.

29 Review of *The Sketch Book*, *Edinburgh Review*, 34 (August 1820), 160.

30 *American Writers: A Series of Papers Contributed to Blackwood's Magazine (1824–1825)*, ed. F. L. Pattee (Durham, N. C.: Duke Univ. Press, 1937), pp. 129, 135.

31 "Letters of Timothy Tickler," no. 18, *Blackwood's Magazine*, 16 (1824), 296.

32 *The Literature of the United States* (Baltimore: Penguin Books, 1954; 1964), pp. 55–6.

33 *The Works of Washington Irving*, new edn, rev., *Knickerbocker's New-York* (New York: George P. Putnam, 1848), I, 284.

34 *Ibid.*, pp. 333–4.

35 Williams, *Life of Washington Irving*, I, 276, 278.

36 *Ibid.*, pp. 284, 295–6.

37 *Journals and Notebooks, 1819–1827*, ed. Reichart, p. 563.

38 Hedges, *Washington Irving*, p. 250.

39 *Ibid.*, pp. 253, 263.

40 *The Letters of Washington Irving to Henry Brevoort*, ed. George S. Hellman (New York: G. P. Putnam's Sons, 1915), II, 196.

41 Irving to Peter Irving, April 9, 1829, printed in Coleman O. Parsons, "Washington Irving Writes from Granada," *American Literature*, 6 (1934–5), 441.

42 Williams, *Life of Washington Irving*, II, 4–6.

43 Bryant to Irving, December 29, 1831, in Irving, *Life and Letters*, II, 472–3.

44 Bryant to Irving, April 24, 1832, *ibid.*, pp. 477–8.

45 Williams, *Life of Washington Irving*, II, 33.

46 "The Irving Dinner," *The New-York Mirror*, 9 (June 9, 1832), 386.

47 *North American Magazine* (Nov. 1833), p. 66; quoted in Williams, *Life of Washington Irving*, I, 337 n. 56.

48 *New-York Mirror* (March 29, 1834); quoted in Williams, *Life of Washington Irving*, II, 337 n. 54.

49 *The Literary Remains of the Late Willis Gaylord Clark*, ed. Lewis Gaylord Clark (New York: Burgess, Stringer & Co., 1844), pp. 278–9; Clark is summarizing the observations of an unnamed critic in the *American Review*.

50 See Williams, *Life of Washington Irving*, II, 338 n. 76.

51 "The Irving Dinner," p. 390; the quotation that follows (from Chancellor Kent's address) is on p. 386.

52 Williams, *Life of Washington Irving*, II, 36.

53 *Ibid.*, p. 74.

54 *Ibid.*, p. 73; the third volume of Spanish materials was omitted from the revised edition of 1848.

55 *A Tour on the Prairies* (Philadelphia: Carey, Lea, & Blanchard, 1835), pp. vii–xv.

56 *The Diary of Philip Hone, 1828–1851*, ed. Bayard Tuckerman (New York; Dodd, Mead and Company, 1889), I, 138.

57 Review of *A Tour on the Prairies*, *American Ladies' Magazine*, 8 (June 1835), 359.

58 Review of *A Tour on the Prairies*, *North American Review*, 88 (July 1835), I, 14.

59 Review of *Miscellanies* (and other travel books on America), *The Quarterly Review*, 54 (Sept. 1835), 412; review of "Washington Irving's Miscellanies," *Fraser's Magazine*, 12 (Oct. 1835), 409–12.

60 *Washington Irving's Works*, Hudson edn, *The Crayon Miscellany* (New York: G. P. Putnam's Sons, 1865), IX, 48–9.

61 Review of *Astoria*, *Southern Literary Journal*, N.S., I (Mar. 1837), 30–41; quoted in Ruth Hudson, "A Literary 'Area of Freedom' between Irving and Twain," *The Western Humanities Review*, 13 (Winter 1959), 48.

62 See Wayne R. Kime, "Washington Irving and Frontier Speech," *American Speech*, 42 (Feb. 1967), 5–18.

63 See Edgeley W. Todd, "Washington Irving Discovers the Frontier," *The Western Humanities Review*, 11 (Winter 1957), 37.

64 Williams, *Life of Washington Irving*, II, 46–7.

65 Cooper to Carey and Lea, April 20–May 3?, 1833, in *Letters and Journals of James Fenimore Cooper*, ed. James F. Beard (Cambridge, Mass.: 1960), VI, 320.

66 *The Plaindealer*, 1 (Jan. 14, 1837), 102.

67 *Ibid.* (Jan. 14, Jan. 28, Feb. 18, 1837), 102, 130–1, 186–7.

68 William Cullen Bryant, *A Discourse on the Life, Character and Genius of Washington Irving* (New York: G. P. Putnam, 1860), pp. 33–4. Williams and other biographers mention only the first of the two alterations.

69 Quoted in Spencer, *The Quest for Nationality*, pp. 85–6.

70 Dickens to Irving, April 21, 1841, *The Letters of Charles Dickens*, ed. Madeline House and Graham Storey (Oxford: Clarendon Press, 1969), II, 267–8.

71 W. C. Desmond Pacey, "Washington Irving and Charles Dickens," *American Literature*, 16 (1945), 332.

72 Dickens to John Forster, February 28, 1842, *Letters of Charles Dickens*, ed. House and Storey, III, 96.

73 Diary entry dated December 1, 1859; quoted in Pacey, "Washington Irving and Charles Dickens," p. 337.

74 See William Charvat, *The Profession of Authorship in America, 1800–1870*, ed. Matthew J. Bruccoli (Columbus: Ohio State Univ. Press, 1968), esp. pp. 73–4.

75 Longfellow to G. W. Greene, July 23, 1839; quoted in Williams, *Life of Washington Irving*, II, 107.

76 Williams, *ibid.*, pp. 111–13, 199.

77 *A Book of the Hudson* (New York: G. P. Putnam, 1849), p. vii.

78 Williams, *Life of Washington Irving*, II, 228–31; Irving's quoted comment is taken by Williams from "Leaves from the Journal of Frederick C. Cozzens," *Lippincott's Monthly Magazine* (May 1890), pp. 741–2.

79 Hawthorne to Irving, July 16, 1852; quoted in Williams, *Life of Washington Irving*, II, 205–6.

3 : Homeward Bound: the two voices of Fenimore Cooper

1 Cooper to Griswold, August 7, 1842, *The Letters and Journals of James Fenimore Cooper*, ed, J. F. Beard, IV, 305–7; Griswold's letter is quoted in n. 4, p. 307.

2 Cooper to Carey and Lea, April 20–May 3 ? 1833, *ibid.*, VI, 320.

3 Review of *Bracebridge Hall*, *The Literary and Scientific Repository* for May 1822; in *Early Critical Essays (1820–1822) by James Fenimore Cooper*, ed. James F. Beard (Gainesville, Fla.: Scholars' Facsimiles and Reprints, 1955), p. 137.

4 *Ibid.*, pp. 97, 98, 100.

5 See George E. Hastings, "How Cooper Became a Novelist, "*American Literature*, 12 (1940), 20–51; according to Hastings, p. 39, *Precaution* "repeats almost every detail of situation, setting, characterization and plot used by Jane Austen."

6 Quoted in W. B. Cairns, *British Criticisms of American Writings, 1815–1833*, p. 113.

7 Quoted in Marcel Clavel, *Fenimore Cooper and his Critics* (Aix-en-Provence: Universitaire de Provence, 1938), p. 68.

8 Review of Lockhart's *Life of Scott*, p. 364; the quotations that follow are on pp. 363–4.

9 See Robin Mayhead, *Walter Scott* (Cambridge: Cambridge Univ. Press, 1973), esp. pp. 25–6; the quoted passage is on p. 26.

10 D. H. Lawrence, *Studies in Classic American Literature* (London: Martin Secker, 1924), p. 66.

11 *Home as Found* (New York: W. A. Townsend, 1860), p. 372.

12 Quoted in Spencer, *The Quest for Nationality*, p. 78.

13 *Gleanings in Europe; England*, ed. Robert E. Spiller (New York: Oxford Univ. Press, 1930), p. 262.

14 Cooper to Samuel Carter Hall, May 21, 1831, *Letters and Journals*, ed. Beard, II, 84.

15 Cooper, *Notions of the Americans*, ed. Robert E. Spiller (New York: Frederick Ungar, 1963), II, 106–7.

16 Charvat, *The Profession of Authorship in America, 1800–1870*, ed. Bruccoli, pp. 68–9.

17 Cooper, *Notions of the Americans*, ed. Spiller, II, 108.

18 *Ibid.*, I, 254.

19 Quoted in Orm Överland, *The Making and Meaning of an American Classic: James Fenimore Cooper's "The Prairie"* (New York: Humanities Press, 1973), p. 30.

20 Notice of a new edition of *The Spy*, *The Pioneers* and *Wyandotte* in *The Critic* (London), July 23, 1859, p. 86.

21 Cooper, *The Chainbearer* (1845), quoted in A. N. Kaul, *The American Vision: Actual and Ideal Society in Nineteenth-Century Fiction* (New Haven: Yale Univ. Press, 1963), pp. 117–18.

22 *The Prairie: A Tale* (New York: Holt, Rinehart and Winston, 1966), pp. 80–1.

23 Introduction to *The Prairie*, pp. xvi–xviii; the quoted phrase in the sentence following is on p. xvi.

24 Review of *The Pathfinder* (1840), quoted in *Fenimore Cooper: The Critical Heritage*, ed. George Dekker and John P. McWilliams (London and Boston: Routledge & Kegan Paul, 1973), p. 197; Balzac's tribute is directed not only to *The Pathfinder* but to "those that preceded it."

25 *The Pioneers* (New York: Holt, Rinehart and Winston, 1965), p. 236; the quotation that follows is on p. 237.

26 *The Deerslayer* (New York: Washington Square Press, 1961), p. 21. In *Cooper's Landscapes: An Essay on the Picturesque Vision* (Berkeley: Univ. of California Press, 1976), Blake Nevius has argued convincingly that Cooper's scenic landscapes are transformed, in *The Deerslayer* and other late novels, from an involvement with the sublime to the picturesque – a shift that took place because of Cooper's response to European landscape painting and theories of landscape gardening. I do not, however, agree that this shift necessarily made for a more vivid and forceful pictorialism: the scenic grandeur of *The Pioneers* is not limited to "prospects" and is not surpassed in any of the later works.

27 *The Pioneers*, p. 383.

28 *Love and Death in the American Novel* (Cleveland: World, 1960), p. 153.

29 See Nicolaus Mills, *American and English Fiction in the Nineteenth Century* (Bloomington: Indiana Univ. Press, 1973), pp. 34–49.
30 Cooper, *Notions of the Americans*, ed. Spiller, II, 100–1.
31 See John P. McWilliams, *Political Justice in a Republic: James Fenimore Cooper's America* (Berkeley: Univ. of California Press, 1972), p. 19.
32 *England: With Sketches of Society in the Metropolis* (Paris: Baudry's European Library, 1837), pp. 260, 268.
33 *Ibid.*, pp. 78–9; the emphasis is Cooper's.
34 *Ibid.*, pp. 144–5; the pencilled markings in the Newberry Library copy are on p. 145; a marginal annotation on p. 70 of *Recollections of Europe*, also published in Paris in 1837, is dated October 14, 1837. These books were published elsewhere with the title *Gleanings in Europe*.
35 *The American Democrat* (New York: Knopf, 1931), p. 115.
36 See "Cooper's Notes on Language," *American Speech*, 4 (1928–9), 294.
37 Conrad's essay (1898) is quoted in *Fenimore Cooper: The Critical Heritage*, ed. Dekker and McWilliams, pp. 287–8.
38 "Fenimore Cooper's Literary Offenses," *ibid.*, pp. 277–8, 285; "Fenimore Cooper's Further Literary Offenses," ed. Bernard De Voto, *The New England Quarterly*, 19 (1946), 293–7.
39 *The Pioneers*, pp. 100–1.
40 *Mark Twain's Autobiography* (New York and London: Harper & Brothers, 1929), I, 97.
41 *The Colloquial Style in America* (New York: Oxford Univ. Press, 1966), p. 22.
42 *The British Magazine*, 1 (April 1823), 65; quoted in Cairns, *British Criticisms of American Writings, 1815–33*, p. 123.
43 *The Pioneers*, p. 51.
44 This and the quotations that follow are from *The Pioneers*, pp. 167–75.
45 "Jim Baker's Blue Jay Yarn," in *The Portable Mark Twain*, ed. Bernard De Voto (New York: Viking Press, 1946), p. 44.
46 Percival's letters are quoted in Lounsbury, *James Fenimore Cooper*, p. 61: Mark Twain's epigraph is a composite quotation (put together without indications of ellipses) from *ibid.*, pp. 239, 240.
47 *The Pioneers*, p. 174.
48 Quoted in *Fenimore Cooper: The Critical Heritage*, ed. Dekker and McWilliams, p. 249.

4: *Yankee invasion: John Neal's campaign*

1 Neal to Carey and Lea, February 26, 1822; quoted in Benjamin Lease, *That Wild Fellow John Neal and the American Literary Revolution* (Chicago and London: Univ. of Chicago Press, 1972), p. 40.
2 *The Magazine of Foreign Literature*, 1 (1823), 102; Cairns, *British Criticisms of American Writings, 1815–33*, p. 208.
3 See McCloskey, "The Campaign of Periodicals after the War of 1812," *PMLA*, 50 (Mar. 1935), p. 264.
4 *The Portico*, I (April 1816), 351; quoted in Mott, *A History of American Magazines*, p. 296.

5 *The Rise of the American Novel* (New York: American Book Company, 1948), p. 167.

6 "Yankee Notions," *The London Magazine*, N.S., 4 (April 1826), 448.

7 *Wandering Recollections of a Somewhat Busy Life* (Boston: Roberts Brothers, 1869), p. 224.

8 A brief letter from Neal to Cooper dated October 18, 1822, Yale University Library, refers to an earlier letter accompanying the manuscript of "Walpole" (*Randolph*) and *Logan*.

9 See Cairns, *British Criticisms of American Writings, 1815–33*, pp. 118, 115.

10 *Seventy-Six* (London: Whittaker, 1823), I, 1–11.

11 Quoted in Cairns, *British Criticisms of American Writings, 1815–33*, p. 210.

12 "Seventy-Six," unidentified clipping in John Neal's scrapbook, Houghton Library, Harvard University.

13 *Seventy-Six*, II, 11.

14 *Ibid.*, III, 320.

15 The quoted words (not directed specifically to *Seventy-Six*) are from Bridgman, *The Colloquial Style in America*, p. 22.

16 *Randolph* ([Philadelphia], 1823), II, 206.

17 *Logan*, II, 134–5.

18 See Lease, *That Wild Fellow John Neal*, pp. 31–7.

19 Rachel Neal to John Neal, October 19–22 (the letter was written in installments), 1823; collection of Mrs Sherwood Picking.

20 Neal, "Yankee Nations," pp. 446–7.

21 Neal, *Wandering Recollections*, p. 239.

22 For a detailed account of Neal's association with Blackwood and *Blackwood's* see Lease, *That Wild Fellow John Neal*, pp. 47–64.

23 "N. B. from C. N.," *Blackwood's*, on an unnumbered page facing Neal's article; "A Summary View of America" is on pp. 617–52.

24 Neal, *American Writers*, ed. F. L. Pattee, pp. 29–44.

25 Quoted *ibid.*, p. 213; the punctuation follows Neal's emendation in his scrapbook of contributions to *Blackwood's* and other British magazines, The Houghton Library, Harvard University.

26 *Ibid.*, p. 204.

27 Neal to Blackwood, June 26 and 30, Blackwood Papers, National Library of Scotland; Neal, "William Blackwood," *Atlantic Monthly*, 16 (December 1865), 670.

28 This description is from a review of the novel (attributed to "F. J." and "rejected from the Edinburgh Review") in P. G. Patmore, ed., *Rejected Articles* (London: Henry Colburn, 1826), p. 274.

29 Moir's critique was enclosed (unsigned) in Blackwood's letter to "Holmes," November 8, 1824; William Blackwood and Sons Limited archives.

30 *British Critic*, 2 (July 1826), 406; quoted in Cairns, *British Criticisms of American Writings, 1815–33*, p. 213.

31 *Literary Chronicle and Weekly Review*, 7 (July 16, 1825), 449; quoted in Cairns, *British Criticisms of American Writings, 1815–33*, p. 210.

32 P. G. Patmore, ed., *Rejected Articles*, p. 265.
33 Quoted in *Fenimore Cooper: The Critical Heritage*, ed. Dekker and McWilliams, pp. 157–9.
34 Editor's footnote to Neal's poem, "The Birth of a Poet," *The Edinburgh Literary Journal*, 1 (May 16, 1829), 386.
35 Lease, *That Wild Fellow John Neal*, pp. 60–3.
36 *London Magazine*, N.S., 16 (May 1826); quoted in *Fenimore Cooper: The Critical Heritage*, ed. Dekker and McWilliams, p. 83.
37 Neal, *Wandering Recollections*, p. 275; for further details concerning the Neal–Bowring quarrel, see Lease, "John Neal's Quarrel with the *Westminster Review*," *American Literature*, 26 (1954), 86–8.
38 John Bowring, ed., *The Works of Jeremy Bentham* (Edinburgh: William Tait, 1843), x, 555–6.
39 *Authorship* (Boston: Gray and Bowen, 1830), pp. 3–5; for Mark Twain's account of his visit to Westminster Abbey, see Howard G. Baetzhold, *Mark Twain and John Bull: The British Connection* (Bloomington: Indiana Univ. Press, 1973), p. 20.
40 Neal, *Wandering Recollections*, pp. 251–2.
41 *Our Country* (Portland: S. Colman, 1830), pp. 25–36; the quoted sentence is on pp. 27–8.
42 This paragraph draws on Lease, "John Neal and Edgar Allan Poe," *Poe Studies*, 7 (1974), 38–41.
43 Review of W. G. Simms' *Views and Reviews in American History*, *The Salem Advertiser*, May 2, 1846; reprinted in Randall Stewart, "Hawthorne's Contributions to *The Salem Advertiser*," *American Literature*, V (1933–4), 331–2.
44 *American Writers*, ed. F. L. Pattee, p. 197. Neal is commenting on Harriet Vaughan Cheney's *A Peep at the Pilgrims in 1636* (Boston, 1825).
45 "Unpublished Preface," *Rachel Dyer: A North American Story* (Portland, Shirley and Hyde, 1828), pp. ix–xvi.
46 Review of J. G. Whittier's *The Supernaturalism of New England*, *The Literary World*, 1 (Apr. 17, 1847), 247–8.
47 Neal, *Wandering Recollections*, pp. 11–22.
48 "Rachel Dyer," *The Yankee and Boston Literary Gazette* (1829), 39.
49 "Unpublished Preface," *Rachel Dyer*, p. xv.
50 *Rachel Dyer*, pp. 79–80.
51 For a representative sampling of Neal's best work, see *The Genius of John Neal: Selections from His Writings*, ed. Lease and Hans-Joachim Lang (Frankfurt and Bern: Peter Lang, 1978).
52 *The Complete Works of Edgar Allan Poe*, ed. James A. Harrison (New York: Thomas Y. Crowell, 1902), xvi, 152, and xii, 154.
53 "Edgar A. Poe," *Portland Advertiser Weekly*, April 30, 1850.
54 Neal, Preface to *The Down-Easters* (New York: Harper & Brothers, 1833), I, iv.

5 : *Poe's England and the divided self*

1 See Margaret Alterton, *The Origins of Poe's Critical Theory*, University of Iowa Humanistic Studies, 11, no. 3 (Iowa City: Univ. of Iowa, 1925), 7–45.
2 Quoted in Alterton, *Poe's Critical Theory*, p. 12 n.27.
3 Blackwood to Neal, February 19, 1825, Blackwood Letter Books, Edinburgh.
4 Alterton, *Poe's Critical Theory*, p. 13.
5 *Ibid.*, pp. 15–17.
6 William Charvat, *The Origins of American Critical Thought, 1810–1835* (New York: A. S. Barnes, 1961), p. 57; Alterton, *Poe's Critical Theory*, p. 34.
7 Michael Allen, *Poe and the British Magazine Tradition* (New York: Oxford Univ. Press, 1969), pp. 29–33; for an extensive list of studies linking Poe's writings to *Blackwood's* and other British magazines, see *ibid.*, p. 209 n.2.
8 Poe to T. W. White, April 30, 1835, *The Letters of Edgar Allan Poe*, ed. John Ward Ostrom (New York: Gordian Press, 1966), 1, 57–8.
9 "The Iron Shroud," *Blackwood's Edinburgh Magazine*, 28 (August 1830), 364–71; for Mudford's authorship, see Alterton, *Poe's Critical Theory*, p. 27 n.62.
10 Volume and page numbers in parentheses refer to *The Complete Works of Edgar Allan Poe*, ed. James A. Harrison (New York: Thomas Y. Crowell, 1902). For other possible sources of this tale, see Arthur Hobson Quinn, *Edgar Allan Poe: A Critical Biography* (New York and London: D. Appleton-Century, 1941), pp. 359–60.
11 See G. R. Thompson, *Poe's Fiction: Romantic Irony in the Gothic Tales* (Madison: Univ. of Wisconsin Press, 1973), pp. 171–2, 192–3.
12 Herman Melville, *Moby-Dick*, ed. Harrison Hayford and Hershel Parker (New York: W. W. Norton, 1967), p. 169.
13 See Allen, *Poe and the British Magazine Tradition*, pp. 126–8.
14 See Terence Martin, "The Imagination at Play: Edgar Allan Poe," *Kenyon Review*, 28 (1966), 200–1.
15 W. H. Auden has linked these tales; see Introduction to *Edgar Allan Poe: Selected Prose and Poetry*, in *The Recognition of Edgar Allan Poe*, ed. Eric W. Carlson (Ann Arbor: Univ. of Michigan Press, 1966), p. 223.
16 Thompson, *Poe's Fiction*, p. 7.
17 Quinn, *Edgar Allan Poe*, p. 65; the details and quotations that follow are *ibid.*, pp. 65–80.
18 See, for example, Floyd Stovall, *Edgar Poe the Poet* (Charlottesville: Univ. Press of Virginia, 1969), p. 260.
19 Preface to *The Short Novels of Dostoevsky* (New York: Dial Press, 1945), pp. ix, xvii.
20 E. T. A. Hoffmann, *The Devil's Elexir*, 2 vols. (Edinburgh and London: William Blackwood and T. Cadell, 1824). Lockhart's review, "The Devil's Elexir," appeared in *Blackwood's Magazine*, 16 (July 1824),

55–67; Palmer Cobb, *The Influence of E. T. A. Hoffmann on The Tales of Edgar Allan Poe* (Chapel Hill, N.C.: The Univ. Press, 1908), pp. 31–48.

21 *The Gift for 1836* (Philadelphia: E. L. Carey & A. Hart, [1835]), pp. 166–71; *The Gift* was published in early September of 1835.

22 See Horace E. Thorner, "Hawthorne, Poe, and a Literary Ghost," *New England Quarterly*, 7 (1934), 152. On October 12, 1839, Poe sent Irving a copy of "William Wilson" – with an acknowledgment of its debt to Irving's piece on Byron; see Poe, *Letters*, II, 689.

23 "Hawthorne and His Mosses," in *Moby-Dick*, ed. Hayford and Parker, pp. 541–2.

24 Allen, *Poe and the British Magazine Tradition*, pp. 70–1; see also Quinn, *Edgar Allan Poe*, p. 286.

25 Melville to Hawthorne, June 29, 1851, *The Letters of Herman Melville*, ed. Merrell R. Davis and William H. Gilman (New Haven, Conn.: Yale Univ. Press, 1960), p. 133; *Moby-Dick*, p. 310. The secret motto is the diabolical perversion of the Latin used by Captain Ahab to baptize the harpoon with which he plans to kill Moby Dick.

26 "New Notes on Edgar Poe" (1857), trans. Lois and Francis Hyslop, in *The Recognition of Edgar Allan Poe*, ed. Carlson, p. 52.

27 For Poe's revisions of the original version (*Burton's Gentleman's Magazine* for October 1839) to its final version (*Broadway Journal* for August 30, 1845), see Marc Leslie Rovner, "What William Wilson Knew: Poe's Dramatization of an Errant Mind," *The Library Chronicle* (Univ. of Pennsylvania), 41 (Spring 1976), 73–82; my interpretation of the significance of these changes differs from Rovner's.

28 Auden, in *The Recognition of Edgar Allan Poe*, ed. Carlson, p. 222.

29 Donald B. Stauffer, "Style and Meaning in 'Ligeia' and 'William Wilson,'" *Studies in Short Fiction*, 2 (Summer 1965), 324.

30 Virgil Grillo, *Charles Dickens' "Sketches By Boz": End in the Beginning* (Boulder, Colorado: The Colorado Associated Univ. Press, 1974), p. 75 n.11.

31 Poe to John Neal, [October–November, 1829,] quoted in Lease, *That Wild Fellow John Neal*, p. 130.

32 Allen, *Poe and the British Magazine Tradition*, p. 84; Edgar Johnson, *Charles Dickens: His Tragedy and Triumph* (New York: Simon and Schuster, 1952), I, 163.

33 "The Black Veil," *Sketches By Boz: Illustrative of Every-Day Life and Every-Day People* (London: Chapman and Hall, 1850), pp. 227–33. The quoted passage is on p. 232; the quotation from this sketch that follows is on p. 233.

34 Benjamin Franklin Fisher IV, "Dickens and Poe: *Pickwick* and 'Ligeia,'" *Poe Studies*, 6 (1973), 16; the quotations that follow are on pp. 15, 16.

35 While I differ with some of his critical assessments, I am indebted here to Laurence Senelick, "Charles Dickens and 'The Tell-Tale Heart,'" *Poe Studies*, 6 (1973), 12–14.

36 *The Letters of Charles Dickens*, ed. Madeline House and Graham Storey (Oxford: Clarendon Press, 1969), II, 380–2.

37 Details and quotations in this and the paragraph that follows are

drawn from *Letters of Charles Dickens*, ed. House and Storey, III, 106–7, 384–5 and the copious accompanying notes. See also Gerald Grubb, "The Personal and Literary Relations of Dickens and Poe," *Nineteenth-Century Fiction*, 5 (1950), 19–22.

38 Dickens to James McCarroll, February 28, 1862; quoted in Grubb, "Personal and Literary Relations," p. 22. Grubb says that Dickens must have been unaware of the publication by Putnam of Poe's *Tales* on both sides of the Atlantic in 1845; but Dickens may have been concerned only with Poe's publication by a British firm.

39 Johnson, *Charles Dickens*, II, 1085.

40 The review, dealing with five recently-published volumes of American poetry, is in *The Foreign Quarterly Review*, 32 (January 1844), 291–324; Poe is discussed on pp. 321–2, Emerson on pp. 311–12. The pertinent passages in Poe's letters to Lowell are in *The Letters of Edgar Allan Poe*, ed. J. R. Ostrom, I, 246–7, 254, 258. For Lowell's letter, Poe's concerns over the *Foreign Quarterly* piece, and the evidences for Forster's authorship, see *Letters of Charles Dickens*, ed. House and Storey, III, 106–7 n.6. Details about the Dickens–Forster friendship are in Johnson, *Charles Dickens*, I, 261–2, 428.

41 *Main Currents in American Thought*, 3 vols. in 1 (New York: Harcourt, Brace, 1930), II, 58.

42 *American Renaissance: Art and Expression in the Age of Emerson and Whitman* (New York: Oxford Univ. Press, 1941), p. xii n.3.

43 Quoted in Linda Welshimer Wagner, *The Prose of William Carlos Williams* (Middletown, Conn.: Wesleyan Univ. Press, 1970), p. 65; in this paragraph and the one that follows I have drawn heavily on Wagner's valuable study, esp. pp. 65–77.

44 William Carlos Williams, *In the American Grain* (New York: Albert & Charles Boni, 1925), pp. 220, 216; the emphasis is Williams'. The quotations that follow are on pp. 227, 222–3, 226.

45 "Editorial Miscellany," *The Broadway Journal*, 2 (Oct. 4, 1845), 199–200; this revealing piece, about ninety lines in length, has been neglected because it was omitted from the Harrison edition of Poe's works.

46 Review of *Calavar*, *Southern Literary Messenger*, 1 (February 1835), 315.

47 Paulding to T. W. White, December 7, 1835? *The Letters of James Kirke Paulding*, ed. Aderman, p. 171.

48 Paulding to T. W. White, March 3, 1836, *ibid.*, p. 174; the "Burlesque of 'Blackwood'" refers to "Loss of Breath, A Tale Neither In Nor Out of 'Blackwood,'" which had appeared in the *Southern Literary Messenger* of September 1835.

49 Neal, *American Writers*, ed. F. L. Pattee, p. 30.

50 Paulding to T. W. White, March 3, 1836, *The Letters of James Kirke Paulding*, ed. Aderman, p. 174.

51 *The Critic* (London), N.S., 2 (Sept. 6, 1845), 379.

52 "American Romance," London *Literary Gazette*, January 31, 1846; in *The Recognition of Edgar Allan Poe*, ed. Carlson, p. 19.

53 "The American Library," *Blackwood's Magazine*, 62 (November 1847), 582; the commentary on "The Man of the Crowd" referred to in the

following sentence is on pp. 583–5. For Smith's authorship of this omnibus review of works by W. G. Simms, Margaret Fuller, Poe and Hawthorne, see *The Wellesley Index to Victorian Periodicals, 1824–1900*, ed. Walter E. Houghton (Toronto: Univ. of Toronto Press, 1966), I, 82.

54 "The House of Poe," in *The Recognition of Edgar Allan Poe*, ed. Carlson, p. 277.

6: *Hawthorne and Our Old Home*

1 Randall Stewart, Introduction, *The English Notebooks by Nathaniel Hawthorne*, ed. Randall Stewart (New York: Modern Language Association of America, 1941), p. 49; Stewart's quoted comment refers to Hawthorne's North Adams journal but accurately describes them all.

2 *The Centenary Edition of the Works of Nathaniel Hawthorne* (Columbus: Ohio State Univ. Press, 1962–); subsequent quotations in this chapter, with parenthetical volume and page references in the text, are from this edition.

3 Hawthorne to Horace L. Conolly, June 17, 1850; quoted in Manning Hawthorne, "Hawthorne and 'The Man of God,'" *Colophon*, N.S., 2 (Winter 1937), 281.

4 For a detailed account, see Lease, "Hawthorne and 'A Certain Venerable Personage'": New Light on "The Custom-House," *Jahrbuch für Amerikastudien*, 15 (1970), 201–7; and Lease, "Salem vs. Hawthorne: An Early Review of *The Scarlet Letter*," *New England Quarterly*, 44 (1971), 110–17.

5 See Lease, "Hawthorne and *Blackwood's* in 1849: Two Unpublished Letters," *Jahrbuch für Amerikastudien*, 14 (1969), 153. The articles cited are [Charles Neaves,] "Blackwood and Copyright in America," *Blackwood's Magazine*, 63 (1848), 128; [Arthur Cleveland Coxe,] "American Copyright," *Blackwood's Magazine*, 62 (November 1847), 543. For William Henry Smith's critique of Hawthorne, see "The American Library," *Blackwood's Magazine*, 62 (November 1847), 590, 589.

6 Hawthorne's borrowings from the Salem Athenaeum included volumes 1–7 (1817–20) and 12–18 (1822–5); see Marion Kesselring, *Hawthorne's Reading, 1828–1850* (New York: The New York Public Library, 1949), p. 45. These known borrowings continued until 1839.

7 R. Stewart, Introduction, *The English Notebooks*, ed. R. Stewart, p. xxii.

8 Entry of October 2, 1855, *The English Notebooks*, ed. R. Stewart, p. 250.

9 Stewart, Introduction, *ibid.*, p. xxii.

10 Randall Stewart, *Nathaniel Hawthorne: A Biography* (New Haven, Conn.: Yale Univ. Press, 1948), p. 11.

11 Lease, "Hawthorne and *Blackwood's* in 1849," p. 154. Seven months later, reports about Hawthorne's involvement with *Blackwood's* were still being circulated; a writer for the *Literary World* (on February 2, 1850, p. 108) asserted that Hawthorne is "invited, we see it stated, by

the editor of Blackwood's Magazine to become a regular contributor."
(I am indebted to Professor Hans-Joachim Lang for calling my
attention to this item.)

12 Melville to Hawthorne, June 1?, 1851, *The Letters of Herman Melville*,
ed. Davis, p. 130.

13 Lawrance Thompson, *Young Longfellow (1807–1843)* (New York:
Macmillan, 1938), pp. 65–6.

14 *Ibid.*, p. 72.

15 Stewart, *Nathaniel Hawthorne*, pp. 29–30; according to Stewart, two
stories survived: "Alice Doane's Appeal" and (probably) "The Hollow
of Three Hills."

16 Hawthorne to Bridge, April 13, 1850; quoted in Stewart, *Nathaniel
Hawthorne*, pp. 98–9.

17 *Ibid.*, p. 95.

18 *The English Notebooks*, ed. R. Stewart, p. 225.

19 "The Genius of Nathaniel Hawthorne," *North American Review*, 129
(1879), 208; the quotations from this essay that follow are on pp. 209,
210, 212–13, 213, 210.

20 Review of *The Scarlet Letter*, *Graham's Magazine*, 36 (May 1850); in
Hawthorne: The Critical Heritage, ed. J. Donald Crowley (London:
Routledge & Kegan Paul, 1970), p. 162.

21 Sören Kierkegaard, *The Concept of Irony*, trans. Lee M. Capel (Bloomington and London: Indiana Univ. Press, 1968), p. 336.

22 Melville to Evert A. Duyckinck, March 3, 1849, *Letters of Herman
Melville*, ed. Davis, p. 79.

23 Hawthorne, review of W. G. Simms' *Views and Reviews in American
History* (1846); in Stewart, "Hawthorne's Contributions to *The Salem
Advertiser*," pp. 331–2.

24 Stewart, *Nathaniel Hawthorne*, p. 112.

25 "The Genius of Nathaniel Hawthorne," p. 214.

26 Quoted in George C. Woodberry, *Nathaniel Hawthorne* (Boston and
New York: Houghton, Mifflin and Company, 1902), p. 73.

27 Review of *The Blithedale Romance*, *The Athenaeum* (July 10, 1852),
pp. 741–3.

28 Quoted in Woodberry, *Nathaniel Hawthorne*, p. 73.

29 *New Monthly Magazine* for June 1853, quoted in Hans-Joachim Lang,
"*The Blithedale Romance*: A History of Ideas Approach," in *Literatur
und Sprache der Vereinigten Staaten* (Heidelberg: Carl Winter, 1969),
p. 88; *The Critic* (London), August 2, 1851, p. 401.

30 Quoted in Lang, "*Blithedale Romance*: History of Ideas," p. 89.

31 Horatio Bridge, *Personal Recollections of Nathaniel Hawthorne* (New
York: Harper & Bros., 1893), pp. 130–1.

32 Whipple, quoted in *Hawthorne: The Critical Heritage*, ed. Crowley,
p. 258; Chorley, review of *Blithedale*, p. 741; Dickinson to T. W.
Higginson, December 1879, *The Letters of Emily Dickinson*, ed. Thomas
H. Johnson (Cambridge, Mass.: The Belknap Press of Harvard Univ.
Press, 1958), II, 649.

33 Bridge, *Personal Recollections*, p. 131; Claude M. Simpson, Introduction

to *The Marble Faun*, Centenary Edition, IV, xix; Stewart, *Nathaniel Hawthorne*, pp. 146, 149.

34 Quoted in Stewart, *Nathaniel Hawthorne*, p. 180; Hawthorne's observation on Trollope, included in a letter to James T. Fields dated February 11, 1860, is quoted in Randall Stewart, Introduction to *The American Notebooks of Nathaniel Hawthorne*, ed. Randall Stewart (New Haven, Conn.: Yale Univ. Press, 1932), p. xcii n.148.

35 Edward H. Davidson, Introduction to *Hawthorne's "Doctor Grimshawe's Secret"* (Cambridge: Harvard Univ. Press, 1954), p. 4.

36 *American Pantheon*, ed. Daniel Aaron and Sylvan Schendler (New York: Delacorte Press, 1966), p. 98.

37 Quoted in James T. Fields, *Yesterdays With Authors* (Boston: Osgood, 1872), p. 74.

38 Entry of October 9, 1854, *English Notebooks*, ed. R. Stewart, p. 92.

39 Entry of June 22, 1855, *ibid.*, p. 124.

40 The quotations from *The Ancestral Footstep* and *Doctor Grimshawe's Secret* appear in Stewart, Introduction to *English Notebooks*, p. xxxix.

41 Entry of September 7, 1855, *English Notebooks*, ed. R. Stewart, p. 204.

42 Quoted in Robert Cantwell, *Nathaniel Hawthorne, The American Years* (New York: Rinehart & Company, 1948), p. 59.

43 Claude M. Simpson, "Explanatory Notes," *The American Notebooks*, Centenary Edition, VIII, 653.

44 *Ibid.*, p. 650.

45 Carlyle to E. W. Forster, June 11, 1853; quoted in *The Correspondence of Emerson and Carlyle*, ed. Joseph Slater (New York and London: Columbia Univ. Press, 1964), p. 495 n. 6.

46 Quoted in Vivian C. Hopkins, *Prodigal Puritan: A Life of Delia Bacon* (Cambridge, Mass.: The Belknap Press of Harvard Univ. Press, 1959), p. 200.

47 (London: Gombridge and Sons, 1857).

48 "The Authorship of Shakespeare's Plays," *The Saturday Review*, May 16, 1857, p. 457; for other hostile British reviews, see Hopkins, *Prodigal Puritan*, pp. 240–1, 245–6.

49 Hopkins, *ibid.*, p. 217.

50 *English Notebooks*, ed. R. Stewart, p. 134.

51 Hopkins, *Prodigal Puritan*, pp. 200–61 *passim*.

52 "The Genius of Nathaniel Hawthorne," p. 207.

53 Entry of August 25, 1855, *English Notebooks*, ed. R. Stewart, p. 197.

54 *The Works of Nathaniel Hawthorne*, ed. G. P. Lathrop (Boston and New York: Houghton, Mifflin and Company, 1882), vol. XIII, *Doctor Grimshawe's Secret*, p. 199.

55 *The Works of Nathaniel Hawthorne*, ed. Lathrop, XI, 489.

56 Review of *Transformation*, *The Athenaeum*, March 3, 1860, p. 297.

57 "The Genius of Nathaniel Hawthorne," p. 221.

58 Stewart, *Nathaniel Hawthorne*, p. 111.

59 Newton Arvin, *Hawthorne* (Boston: Little, Brown, 1929), pp. 261–262.

60 The quoted phrase about Kenyon is used, in another context, in

Hyatt Waggoner, *Hawthorne: A Critical Study* (Cambridge, Mass.: The Belknap Press of Harvard Univ. Press, 1955), p. 196.

61 Quoted in Nathalia Wright, *American Novelists in Italy* (Philadelphia: University of Pennsylvania Press, 1965), p. 149.

62 Stewart, *Nathaniel Hawthorne*, pp. 212, 123.

63 [E. B. Hamley,] "Hawthorne on England," *Blackwood's Magazine*, 94 (Nov. 1863), 611, 615.

64 Letter to Fields dated October 18, 1863; quoted in *Our Old Home*, Centenary Edition, p. xxxvi.

65 Quoted in *Our Old Home*, p. xxxiii.

66 *Hawthorne's Last Phase* (New Haven: Yale Univ. Press, 1949), pp. 11–12.

67 *English Notebooks*, ed. R. Stewart, pp. 432–3.

7: *Crosscurrents: Melville's England and America*

1 *Journal of a Visit to London and the Continent by Herman Melville 1849–1850*, ed. Eleanor Melville Metcalf (Cambridge, Mass.: Harvard Univ. Press, 1948), p. 18.

2 References, by volume and page number in the text, are to *The Works of Herman Melville* (London: Constable and Company, 1922–4).

3 *Melville's Early Life and Redburn* (New York: New York Univ. Press, 1951), pp. 136–7.

4 Quoted in Jay Leyda, *The Melville Log: A Documentary Life of Herman Melville, 1819–1891* (New York: Harcourt, Brace and Company, 1951), I, 92.

5 *Journal of a Visit to London*, E. Melville Metcalf, p. 23; Frederick Hardman, "Across the Atlantic," *Blackwood's Magazine*, 66 (November 1849), 567–80.

6 Letter dated June 1?, *The Letters of Herman Melville*, ed. Davis, p. 128.

7 *Bentley's Miscellany*, 26 (November 1849); quoted in Hugh W. Hetherington, *Melville's Reviewers: British and American, 1846–1891* (Chapel Hill: Univ. of North Carolina Press, 1961), p. 140.

8 *Journal of a Visit to London*, ed. Eleanor Melville Metcalf, pp. 70–1.

9 *Ibid.*, p. 75; Raymona Hull, "London and Melville's *Israel Potter*," *Emerson Society Quarterly* (2nd Quarter, 1967), 78.

10 Leon Howard, *Herman Melville: A Biography* (Berkeley: Univ. of California Press, 1967), pp. 150–2.

11 Leslie Howard Meeks, *Sheridan Knowles and the Theatre of His Time* (Bloomington, Ind.: The Principia Press, Inc., 1933), esp. pp. 52–4. "From 1843, the year of Knowles's last published play, most accounts date the beginning of his work as a preacher," observes Meeks; Knowles was ordained as a Baptist minister in 1845.

12 Leyda, *The Melville Log*, I, 487.

13 *Our Old Home*, Centenary Edition, v, 13.

14 *Journal of a Visit to London*, ed. E. Melville Metcalf, p. 25.

15 *Our Old Home*, Centenary Edition, v, 15.

16 *The Letters of Herman Melville*, ed. Davis, pp. 109, 128–9, 133.

17 Melville applies the quoted adjectives to a letter from Hawthorne (now lost) conveying appreciation of *Moby-Dick*; Melville to Hawthorne, November 17?, 1851, *The Letters of Herman Melville*, ed. Davis, p. 141.

18 See Michael Davitt Bell, "Melville and 'Romance': Literary Nationalism and Fictional Form," *American Transcendental Quarterly*, 24 (1974), 57; the quoted passage from "Hawthorne and His Mosses" is in *Moby-Dick*, Norton Critical Edition, p. 542.

19 *The Letters of Herman Melville*, ed. Davis, p. 80.

20 Bell, "Melville and 'Romance,'" p. 57; the quotations from "Hawthorne and His Mosses" are in *Moby-Dick*, pp. 546, 543.

21 The following paragraph draws on Michael T. Gilmore, "Melville's Apocalypse: American Millenialism and *Moby-Dick*," *ESQ*, 21 (1975), 154–61.

22 *Moby-Dick*, Norton Critical Edition, p. 160. Subsequent quotations are from this edition and will be cited parenthetically in the text.

23 *Billy Budd, Sailor*, ed. Milton R. Stern (Indianapolis: Bobbs-Merrill, 1975), p. 2; subsequent quotations are from this edition and will be cited parenthetically in the text.

24 Melville's sentiments about the Revolution, however, are couched in terms that convey some reservations: "During those years not the wisest could have foreseen that the outcome of all would be *what to some thinkers apparently* it has since turned out to be, a political advance along nearly the whole line for Europeans" (p. 98; italics added). Melville's narrator seems more interested in providing a historic backdrop for the drama to be enacted on the decks of the *Bellipotent* than in making a conservative or liberal pronouncement.

25 *Green Hills of Africa* (New York: Charles Scribner's Sons, 1935), p. 20; the comment about *Huckleberry Finn* that follows is on p. 22.

26 The letter is reproduced in Hans Bungert, "William Faulkner on *Moby-Dick*: An Early Letter," *Studi Americani*, 9 (1963), 373.

27 *Faulkner at Nagano*, ed. Robert A. Jelliffe (Tokyo: Kenkyusha Ltd, 1956), p. 42; Bungert, "William Faulkner on *Moby-Dick*," p. 374, presents evidence that Faulkner first read *Moby-Dick* in 1922.

28 *Faulkner in the University: Class Conferences at the University of Virginia, 1957–1958*, ed. F. L. Gwynn and J. L. Blotner (New York: Vintage Books, 1965), pp. 15, 143.

29 *Ibid.*, p. 67.

30 *The Concept of Irony*, trans. Capel (1968), p. 336.

31 C. Merton Babcock, "*The Vocabulary of Moby Dick*," *American Speech*, 27 (1952), 96–7.

32 Melville to Evert A. Duyckinck, February 24, 1849, *The Letters of Herman Melville*, ed. Davis, p. 77.

33 Melville to Hawthorne, June 1?, 1851, *ibid.*, p. 129.

34 Hayford and Parker, "The Text: History, Variants and Emendations," in *Moby-Dick*, Norton Critical Edition, p. 475.

35 The first reference to this important addition to the American text occurs in William S. Ament, "Bowdler and the Whale," *American Literature*, 4 (1932), 42; it is discussed at greater length in Lease,

"Melville's 'Gally,' 'Gallow,'" *American Speech*, 25 (1950), 186. The long footnote was first incorporated into an American edition of *Moby-Dick* by Luther S. Mansfield and Howard P. Vincent in 1952.

36 For Lowell's advocacy of this view both before and after *Moby-Dick*, see his introductory essays to *The Biglow Papers* (1848); 2nd ser. (1867). For a modern refutation of the view that American English is an archaic inheritance, see George Philip Krapp, *The English Language in America* (New York: Frederick Ungar, 1966), I, esp. 49–52.

37 William S. Ament, "Some Americanisms in Moby Dick," *American Speech*, 7 (1932), 366–7.

38 Melville, *Typee: A Peep at Polynesian Life*, ed. H. Hayford and others (Evanston and Chicago: Northwestern Univ. Press, 1968), p. 8; Leon Howard, Historical Note, *Typee*, pp. 285, 289.

39 Quoted in *Moby-Dick as Doubloon: Essays and Extracts (1851–1970)*, ed. Parker and Hayford (New York: W. W. Norton, 1970), pp. 24, 9, 72.

40 Melville to Richard Bentley, April 16, 1852; in *Letters of Herman Melville*, ed. Davis, p. 150. Bentley's reply, dated May 5, is quoted on p. 151n.

41 Howard, *Herman Melville*, p. 316; Leyda, *The Melville Log*, II, 784.

42 Billson's letter is quoted in E. Melville Metcalf, *Herman Melville: Cycle and Epicycle* (Cambridge, Mass.: Harvard Univ. Press, 1953), pp. 266–7; for details about Billson's life, see *The Letters of Herman Melville*, ed. Davis, p. 275 n. 9.

43 *The Letters of Herman Melville*, ed. Davis, p. 277.

44 Leyda, *The Melville Log*, II, 787, 792; *The Letters of Herman Melville*, ed. Davis, pp. 278–9.

45 Mather, review of Lewis Mumford's biography of Melville (1929), quoted in *The Recognition of Herman Melville*, ed. Hershel Parker (Ann Arbor: Univ. of Michigan Press, 1970), p. 154; Metcalfe, *Cycle and Epicycle*, pp. 293–4.

46 *Moby-Dick as Doubloon*, ed. Parker and Hayford, pp. 131–2, 125–6, 124, 126, 130, 134, 152.

8: *God's ambassador: Harriet Beecher Stowe and Old England*

1 Forrest Wilson, *Crusader in Crinoline: The Life of Harriet Beecher Stowe* (Philadelphia: J. B. Lippincott, 1941), pp. 294–5, 256–67; Charles Edward Stowe, *Life of Harriet Beecher Stowe* (Boston: Houghton, Mifflin and Company, 1889), pp. 148–9. At different times, the author gave different versions of the origin of *Uncle Tom's Cabin*, but she sees herself as God's instrument in all of them.

2 Wilson, *Crusader in Crinoline*, pp. 259–60.

3 Quoted in Charles Edward Stowe, *Life of Harriet Beecher Stowe*, pp. 164–5.

4 Annie Fields, *Authors and Friends* (Boston: Houghton, Mifflin and Company, 1924), p. 167.

5 Annie Fields, *Life and Letters of Harriet Beecher Stowe* (Boston: Houghton, Mifflin and Company, 1897), p. 135.

6 *Ibid.*, pp. 22, 23, 28; the quotation that follows is on p. 37.

7 *Ibid.*, pp. 38–9; Stowe was thirteen years old at the time of Byron's death (in April 1824) but mistakenly says that she was eleven.

8 Charles Edward Stowe, *Life of Harriet Beecher Stowe*, pp. 33–4.

9 *Uncle Tom's Cabin*, ed. Kenneth S. Lynn (Cambridge, Mass.: The Belknap Press of Harvard Univ. Press, 1962); my references are to this edition.

10 Quoted in G. Wilson Knight, *Lord Byron: Christian Virtues* (New York: Barnes & Noble, Inc., 1967), p. 170.

11 Conversation with Dr James Kennedy, August 10, 1823, in *His Very Self and Voice: Collected Conversations of Lord Byron*, ed. Ernest J. Lovell, Jr (New York: Macmillan, 1954), p. 407.

12 *Sunny Memories of Foreign Lands* (Boston: Phillips, Sampson, and Company, 1856), II, 325.

13 Charles Edward Stowe, *Life of Harriet Beecher Stowe*, pp. 159–60; quotations from the letter to Lord Carlisle in the paragraph that follows are on pp. 166–7.

14 Quoted in Forrest Wilson, *Crusader in Crinoline*, p. 342.

15 Charles Edward Stowe, *Life of Harriet Beecher Stowe*, p. 204.

16 *Sunny Memories*, I, 18.

17 "Public Meeting in Dundee–April 22 [1853]," Introductory, *Sunny Memories*, I, xxxvi–xxxviii; the introductory section is edited and annotated by Calvin E. Stowe.

18 Forrest Wilson, *Crusader in Crinoline*, p. 341.

19 Mrs Stowe's letter to her father is in *Sunny Memories*, p. 34; for the episode involving Professor Stowe, see Forrest Wilson, *Crusader in Crinoline*, pp. 379–80.

20 Quoted in Catherine Gilbertson, *Harriet Beecher Stowe* (New York: D. Appleton-Century, 1937), p. 160.

21 *Sunny Memories*, II, 264.

22 *Ibid.*, I, p. xli.

23 *Ibid.*, II, 264–5.

24 The account of Lord Denman's criticisms of Dickens that follows draws on Harry Stone, "Charles Dickens and Harriet Beecher Stowe," *Nineteenth-Century Fiction*, 12 (1957), 190–7.

25 Dickens' criticisms are in two letters quoted in Stone, "Dickens and Stowe," p. 193.

26 Stone, *ibid.*, pp. 193–7.

27 Forrest Wilson, *Crusader in Crinoline*, p. 364.

28 Quoted in Stone, "Dickens and Stowe," p. 200.

29 *Sunny Memories*, I, 23–4.

30 Stone, "Dickens and Stowe," p. 190 n.6.

31 *Sunny Memories*, I, 92.

32 *Ibid.*, 131–8, 69.

33 *Ibid.*, I, 103–4; II, 106–7.

34 *Ibid.*, II, 424, 432.

35 Harriet Beecher Stowe, *Lady Byron Vindicated: A History of the Byron Controversy, from its beginning in 1816 to the present time* (Boston: Fields, Osgood, & Co., 1870), p. 212; unless otherwise indicated, the account of the Stowe–Byron relationship and the Byron controversy that follows draws on this book, esp. pp. 212–55.

36 Teresa Guiccioli, *My Recollections of Lord Byron* (New York: Harper & Brothers, 1869), p. 516; John Paget, Review of *Recollections of Lord Byron, Blackwood's Edinburgh Magazine*, 106 (July 1869), 24–33. Forrest Wilson claims in *Crusader in Crinoline*, pp. 550–1, that Mrs Stowe did not see the *Blackwood's* review until after she wrote her defense of Lady Byron; for a decisive refutation of Wilson, see Charles H. Foster, *The Rungless Ladder: Harriet Beecher Stowe and New England Puritanism* (Durham, N. C.: Duke University Press, 1954), pp. 223–4.

37 Fields, *Life and Letters*, pp. 238, 243–4; the quotations from a letter to Lady Byron that follow are on p. 27.

38 "Lord Byron and his Calumniators," *Blackwood's Edinburgh Magazine*, 107 (January 1870), 123–38.

39 Quoted in Stone, "Dickens and Stowe," pp. 201–2.

40 Quoted in Wilson, *Crusader in Crinoline*, p. 545, and in Edward Wagenknecht, *Harriet Beecher Stowe: The Known and the Unknown* (New York: Oxford Univ. Press, 1965), p. 85.

41 My comments on the publication of *Lady Byron Vindicated* draw on Wagenknecht, *Harriet Beecher Stowe*, p. 84; Mrs Stow's observations about her book are from a conversation with her biographer Florence Thayer McCray, summarized *ibid.*, p. 88.

42 Fields, *Life and Letters*, pp. 241–2, 238–41.

43 *Ibid.*, pp. 117–19.

44 *Ibid.*, p. 173.

45 *The May Flower and Miscellaneous Writings* (Boston: Houghton, Mifflin and Company, 1882); the quotation from "Uncle Lot" is on p. 9.

46 Coventry Patmore, "American Novels," *North British Review*, 19 (November 1853), 53–4.

47 *Sunny Memories*, II, 29–30; Foster, *The Rungless Ladder*, p. 15, discusses the possible influence of Defoe's *Journal* on *Uncle Tom's Cabin*.

48 *A Journal of the Plague Year,* ed. Louis Landa (London: Oxford Univ. Press, 1969), p. 69; the quotation that follows is on the same page.

49 Kingsley's criticism of *Uncle Tom's Cabin* is quoted in Foster, *The Rungless Ladder*, p. 48.

9: *Emerson, Carlyle and "the two Englands"*

1 *The Journals and Miscellaneous Notebooks of Ralph Waldo Emerson,* ed. William H. Gilman and others (Cambridge, Mass.: The Belknap Press of Harvard University Press, 1960–), III, 301.

2 Joseph Slater, Introduction, *The Correspondence of Emerson and Carlyle* (New York: Columbia University Press, 1964), pp. 608; for the title and date of Emerson's sermon, see *Young Emerson Speaks: Unpublished*

Discourses on Many Subjects, ed. Arthur Cushman McGiffert, Jr (Boston: Houghton, Mifflin and Company, 1938), p. 269.

3 *The Works of Thomas Carlyle,* Centenary Edition (New York: AMS Press, 1969), XXVIII, 42.

4 *Journals and Notebooks,* ed. Gilman *et al.,* IV, 45, 52–3.

5 Landor: *The Letters of Ralph Waldo Emerson,* ed. Ralph L. Rusk (New York: Columbia University Press, 1939), I, 378, 381–3; Coleridge: *The Complete Works of Ralph Waldo Emerson,* Concord Edition (Boston: Houghton, Mifflin and Company, 1903), V, 14; Wordsworth: Emerson, *Works,* V, p. 24.

6 *Journals and Notebooks,* ed. Gilman *et al.,* IV, 219–21.

7 *Letters,* ed. Rusk, I, 394–5; *Works,* V, 17–18.

8 Slater, *Correspondence of Emerson and Carlyle,* pp. 14, 12.

9 *Journals and Notebooks,* ed. Gilman *et al.,* IV, 78–9, 81.

10 *Ibid.,* IV, 236, 80–1, 84.

11 *Young Emerson Speaks,* ed. McGiffert, Jr, p. 191.

12 *Ibid.,* p. 200.

13 "The Uses of Natural History" and "The Naturalist"; in *The Early Lectures of Ralph Waldo Emerson,* ed. Stephen E. Whicher and Robert E. Spiller (Cambridge, Mass.: Harvard University Press, 1959), I, 6, 16–17, 24, 72, 75.

14 *The Correspondence of Emerson and Carlyle,* ed. Slater, pp. 98–100.

15 *Ibid.,* pp. 103–5.

16 *Ibid.,* pp. 110, 122–7, 289.

17 *Ibid.,* pp. 106, 147–8, 120, 317.

18 Slater, *Correspondence of Emerson and Carlyle,* pp. 16–29.

19 *Ibid.,* 16–17.

20 Emerson, *Uncollected Writings: Essays, Addresses, Poems, Reviews and Letters* (New York: Lamb Publishing Company, 1912), pp. 26–7.

21 Emerson, *Works,* XII, 279–91.

22 *Ibid.,* I, 3, 73–4; III, 18.

23 *The Melville Log,* II, 648–9; shortly before his second voyage to England, Melville asked his father-in-law, Lemuel Shaw, to write Emerson for a letter of introduction that the American novelist could present to Carlyle. No evidence has survived of response from Emerson – or of a visit to Carlyle by Melville.

24 *Correspondence of Emerson and Carlyle,* ed. Slater, pp. 349–50, 370–1.

25 *Ibid.,* pp. 372–3.

26 *Ibid.,* p. 413 and n.5.

27 Emerson, *Works,* III, 10; IX, 120.

28 *Correspondence of Emerson and Carlyle,* ed. Slater, p. 416.

29 *Ibid.,* p. 172.

30 Quoted in *The Works of Thomas Carlyle,* ed. H. D. Traill (New York: AMS Press, 1969), XI, 109, 115.

31 *A Correspondence Between John Sterling and Ralph Waldo Emerson,* ed. Edward Waldo Emerson (Boston: Houghton, Mifflin and Company, 1897), pp. 37 n.1, 45, 61–2.

32 *Ibid.,* p. 45.

33 Emerson, *Works*, II, 208–9.
34 *Letters of Thomas Carlyle*, ed. Alexander Carlyle (New York: Frederick A. Stokes Company, 1923), pp. 245–6; Emerson, *Works*, II, 208.
35 *A Correspondence Between John Sterling and Ralph Waldo Emerson*, ed. E. W. Emerson, pp. 45–6.
36 Carlyle, *Works*, XI, 195–6.
37 *A Correspondence Between John Sterling and Ralph Waldo Emerson* ed. E. W. Emerson, pp. 74–7; Emerson's evaluation of Channing is quoted in Ralph L. Rusk, *The Life of Ralph Waldo Emerson*, (New York: Columbia University Press, 1949), p. 298.
38 *A Correspondence Between John Sterling and Ralph Waldo Emerson*, ed. E. W. Emerson, p. 85.
39 *Ibid.*, pp. 86–91; *The Correspondence of Emerson and Carlyle*, ed. Slater, pp. 365–6, 372.
40 Townsend Scudder III, "Emerson's British Lecture Tour, 1847–1848" (pt I), *American Literature*, VII (1935–6), 15–16; *Letters*, ed. Rusk, III, 380, 379 n.39; *Correspondence of Emerson and Carlyle*, ed. Slater, pp. 419, 425.
41 Quoted in James Elliot Cabot, *A Memoir of Ralph Waldo Emerson* (New York: AMS Press, 1965), II, 495.
42 *Letters*, ed. Rusk, III, 407 n. 37, 407; *Works*, V, 26, 33.
43 Townsend Scudder III, *The Lonely Wayfaring Man: Emerson and some Englishmen* (London: Oxford Univ. Press, 1936), p. 64; Scudder, "Emerson's British Lecture Tour" (pt II), p. 178 and n.41.
44 *A Correspondence Between John Sterling and Ralph Waldo Emerson*, ed. E. W. Emerson, p. 46.
45 Scudder, "Emerson's British Lecture Tour" (pt II), pp. 171–2.
46 Quoted in William J. Sowder, *Emerson's Impact on the British Isles and Canada* (Charlottesville: Univ. Press of Virginia, 1966), p. 8.
47 Scudder, "Emerson's British Lecture Tour" (pt II), pp. 173–6.
48 *Ibid.*, p. 179.
49 *Letters*, ed. Rusk, III, 454.
50 *The Correspondence of Emerson and Carlyle*, ed. Slater, pp. 35–6; Townsend Scudder III, "Emerson in London and the London Lectures," *American Literature*, VIII (1936–7), 26–8, 34–5.
51 Quoted in *Correspondence of Emerson and Carlyle*, ed. Slater, pp. 42, 38.
52 Emerson, *Works*, V, 273–6.
53 *Correspondence of Emerson and Carlyle*, ed. Slater, pp. 341, 469.
54 *Ibid.*, p. 460.
55 Emerson, *Works*, IV, 6–7, 36–7, 290.
56 Carlyle, *Works*, V, 77.
57 *Ibid.*, p. 13.
58 Mathew Arnold, *Discourses in America* (New York: The Macmillan Co., 1896), p. 145.
59 "The Emerson Mania," quoted in Sowder, *Emerson's Impact*, pp. 8–9;
60 *The Critic* (July 15, 1851), pp. 326–7.
61 *Journals and Notebooks*, ed. Gilman *et al.*, XI, 214.
   Ibid., p. 214 n.92.

62 Quoted in *Correspondence of Emerson and Carlyle*, ed. Slater, p. 471 n.5.

63 *Correspondence of Emerson and Carlyle*, ed. Slater, pp. 470–1, 476; *Journals and Notebooks*, ed Gilman *et al.*, XI, 448–9.

64 *Correspondence of Emerson and Carlyle*, ed. Slater, p. 367; Anne Kimball Tuell, *John Sterling, Representative Victorian* (1941); quoted in Albert J. La Valley, *Carlyle and the Idea of the Modern* (New Haven: Yale Univ. Press, 1968), p. 315 n.2.

65 *Emerson–Clough Letters*, ed. H. F. Lowry and R. L. Rusk (Folcroft, Penn.: The Folcroft Press, 1969), letter 29; *Correspondence of Emerson and Carlyle*, ed. Slater, p. 517.

66 Emerson, *Works*, V, 153, 105, 252.

67 *Ibid.*, pp. 178–9.

68 *Ibid.*, pp. 41, 288.

69 *Correspondence of Emerson and Carlyle*, ed. Slater, pp. 486, 489.

70 Emerson's letter is quoted in *Leaves of Grass*, ed. Sculley Bradley and Harold W. Blodgett (New York: W. W. Norton & Company, 1973), pp. 731–2; *Correspondence of Emerson and Carlyle*, ed. Slater, p. 509.

71 *Emerson–Clough Letters*, ed. Lowry and Rusk, letter 29.

72 *The Saturday Review*, October 4, 1856, pp. 509–10; July 7, 1860, p. 20.

73 *Correspondence of Emerson and Carlyle*, ed. Slater, p. 470.

74 Carlyle, *Works*, XI, 106.

75 *Correspondence of Emerson and Carlyle*, ed. Slater, pp. 45–7.

76 *Ibid.*, p. 551.

77 *Ibid.*, pp. 554–5, 555 n. 3, 557 n. 1, 559.

78 *Ibid.*, pp. 581–2, 587–8.

79 Rusk, *Life of Emerson*, pp. 452–3; James Elliot Cabot, *A Memoir of Ralph Waldo Emerson* (New York: AMS Press, Inc., 1965), II, 653–5, 703–9.

80 Cabot, *A Memoir*, II, 658, 662–3.

81 *Correspondence of Emerson and Carlyle*, ed. Slater, pp. 57–8.

82 *Ibid.*, p. 89; Cabot, *A Memoir*, II, 663–4.

83 *Correspondence of Emerson and Carlyle*, ed. Slater, pp. 533–4; Emerson, *Works*, VI, 313, 325.

84 Journal entry quoted in *Works*, VI, 428.

85 Hawthorne, *Works*, Centenary Edition, I, 145; Poe, *Works*, III, 242.

86 Leyda, *The Melville Log*, II, 715; *The Letters of Herman Melville*, ed. Davis, p. 79.

87 This passage, from the first printed version of "The Hall of Fantasy," was later deleted by Hawthorne; quoted in Marjorie J. Elder, *Nathaniel Hawthorne: Transcendental Symbolist* (Athens, Ohio: Ohio University Press, 1969), p. 46.

88 Bellow, "Where Do We Go from Here: The Future of Fiction," in *Saul Bellow and the Critics*, ed. Irving Malin (New York: New York University Press, 1967), p. 220.

89 Emerson, *Works*, I, 24–30.

90 *Ibid.*, III, 5, 33.

91 *Ibid.*, II, 367–8.

92 *Ibid.*, III, 37–8, 40–1.

93 Frost, "On Emerson," *Selected Prose of Robert Frost*, ed. Hyde Cox and Edward Connery Lathem (New York: Holt, Rinehart and Winston, 1966), pp. 112–13.
94 Emerson, *Works*, IV, 168.
95 See above, pp. 140–1 and 277 n.36.
96 Quoted in Mathiessen, *American Renaissance*, pp. 36–6.
97 Quoted in Elaine Barry, *Robert Frost on Writing* (New Brunswick, N.J.: Rutgers Univ. Press, 1973), p. 97.

10: *A Brother's house: Thoreau's resurrection ode*

1 Henry Seidel Canby, *Thoreau* (Boston: Houghton, Mifflin and Company, 1939), pp. 110–28; for a judicious review of the uncertainties surrounding this version of Thoreau's relationship with Ellen Sewall, see Perry Miller, *Consciousness in Concord* (Boston: Houghton, Mifflin and Company, 1958), esp. pp. 82–9.
2 F. B. Sanborn, *The Life of Henry David Thoreau* (Boston: Houghton, Mifflin and Company, 1917), p. 216.
3 *Ibid.*, pp. 201–13; Canby, *Thoreau*, pp. 28, 68–9; *Remembrances of Concord and the Thoreaus: Letters of Horace Hosmer to Dr. S. A. Jones*, ed. George Hendrick (Urbana: Univ. of Illinois Press, 1977), pp. 70–6.
4 Canby, *Thoreau*, pp. 177–9; letter of Thoreau to Isaiah T. Williams, March 14, 1842, *The Correspondence of Henry David Thoreau*, ed. Walter Harding and Carl Bode (New York: New York Univ. Press, 1958), p. 66.
5 *The Letters of Ralph Waldo Emerson*, ed. Rusk, III, 3, 4, 6.
6 *The Correspondence*, ed. Harding and Bode, pp. 66–7.
7 Henry D. Thoreau, *Early Essays and Miscellanies*, ed. Joseph J. Moldenhauer and Edwin Moser (Princeton, N.J.: Princeton Univ. Press, 1975), pp. 106–8.
8 *The Writings of Henry David Thoreau* (Boston: Houghton, Mifflin and Company, 1906), VII, 62.
9 *Ibid.*, XVI, 150–1.
10 *The Correspondence*, ed. Harding and Bode, p. 67.
11 *Writings*, II, 108–9.
12 Miller, *Consciousness in Concord*, p. 53; for a discussion of Thoreau's Byronism, see pp. 50–4; *Writings*, II, 21.
13 William Ellery Channing, *Thoreau the Poet–Naturalist* (Boston: Charles E. Goodspeed, 1902), p. 50.
14 Walter Harding, *The Days of Henry Thoreau* (New York: Alfred A. Knopf, 1966), pp. 64–5.
15 For persuasive evidence, see Gerry H. Brookes, *The Rhetorical Form of Carlyle's Sartor Resartus* (Berkeley: Univ. of California Press, 1972), pp. 81–2 and n. 3.
16 *Writings*, IV, 347–8.
17 *Ibid.*, II, 4.
18 Carlyle, *Works*, I, 48–9; Thoreau, *Writings*, II, 24–5.
19 *Writings*, IV, 332.

20 *Ibid.*, 334; VII, 336.
21 *Early Essays and Miscellanies*, ed. Moldenhauer and Moser, pp. 178–9; Thoreau's quotation is from a contemporary account.
22 *Ibid.*, pp. 187–91.
23 *Ibid.*, pp. 211–12.
24 *Ibid.*, pp. 212–14.
25 *Ibid.*, pp. 207–8, 194–5.
26 *Writings*, I, 177–8.
27 Thoreau's lecture, "Walking, or the Wild," was revised shortly before his death and published posthumously; *Writings*, V, 218, 219–20, 223–4.
28 *Writings*, V, 224, 231; VIII, 97; V, 231–2, 237.
29 *Ibid.*, VIII, 451.
30 *Ibid.*, V, 245–8.
31 *Ibid.*, I, 2.
32 *Ibid.*, 3–6.
33 *Ibid.*, 189–98.
34 *Ibid.*, 420.
35 *Ibid.*, II, 351.
36 *Ibid.*, I, 307–8.
37 *Ibid.*, II, 64.
38 *Ibid.*, 78–9.
39 *Correspondence of Emerson and Carlyle*, ed. Slater, p. 521.
40 *Writings*, I, 54.
41 *Ibid.*, II, 202–3.
42 *Ibid.*, 232–3.
43 *Ibid.*, 324–8.
44 *Ibid.*, 335–51.
45 *Ibid.*, 366–7.
46 *Ibid.*, 170.
47 Joseph Jones, "Walden and Ultima Thule: A Twin-Centennial," *Library Chronicle of University of Texas*, V (1954), 14–17.
48 Harding, *The Days of Henry Thoreau*, p. 347; *Writings*, XIII, 64–5.
49 *The Correspondence*, ed. Harding and Bode, p. 350; Emerson, *Letters*, IV, 479.
50 *The Correspondence*, ed. Harding and Bode, pp. 364–5, 370.
51 *Ibid.*, pp. 387, 403, 388, 397–9.
52 *Ibid.*, pp. 435–7.
53 *Ibid.*, pp. 448–55.
54 *Ibid.*, p. 483.
55 Andrew Schiller, "Thoreau and Whitman: The Record of a Pilgrimage," *New England Quarterly*, 28 (1955), 190–1.
56 *Writings*, II, 242–3.
57 Schiller, "Thoreau and Whitman," pp. 190, 191.
58 *The Correspondence*, ed. Harding and Bode, pp. 480–3.
59 Sanborn, *Thoreau*, pp. 310–11.
60 Sanborn, "Thoreau and His English Friend Thomas Cholmondeley," *Atlantic Monthly*, 77 (1893), 755.

61 *The Correspondence*, ed. Harding and Bode, pp. 531, 547.
62 *Writings*, VI, 162.
63 *Ibid.*, 37.
64 *Ibid.*, XV, 205.
65 *The Correspondence*, ed. Harding and Bode, p. 399.
66 *Writings*, VI, 236; Sanborn, *Thoreau*, pp. 310–11.
67 *The Correspondence*, ed. Harding and Bode, pp. 364, 370.
68 Leyda, *The Melville Log*, I, 259.
69 Melville, *Works*, VI, 502–4.
70 The manner in which Cholmondeley shaped his letters for the word "Mothers" (he omitted the apostrophe) makes Thoreau's misreading an understandable one. A further study of the letter, however, has led me to question Harding and Bode (*The Correspondence*, p. 364) in their transcription of the word as "Mothers." Cholmondeley's letter is in the Alfred Hosmer Collection, Concord Free Public Library; I am grateful to Marcia E. Moss, Curator of the Library, for sending me a photocopy. (Mrs Moss reads the word as "Brothers.")
71 *Writings*, II, 59–60.

11 : *"Leaves of Grass": England and the outsetting bard*

1 Gay Wilson Allen, *The Solitary Singer: A Critical Biography of Walt Whitman* (New York: The Macmillan Company, 1955), p. 242.
2 Floyd Stovall, *The Foreground of Leaves of Grass* (Charlottesville: University Press of Virginia, 1974), pp. 184–8.
3 Stovall, *The Foreground*, p. 117.
4 Walt Whitman, *Prose Works 1892*, ed. Floyd Stovall (New York: New York Univ. Press, 1963–4), II, 522, 490, 388.
5 Thomas L. Brasher, *Whitman as Editor of the Brooklyn "Daily Eagle"* (Detroit: Wayne State Univ. Press, 1970), pp. 189, 190.
6 Walt Whitman, *The Gathering of the Forces*, ed. Cleveland Rodgers and John Black (New York: G. P. Putnam's Sons, 1920), II, 298–9.
7 Fred Manning Smith, "Whitman's Debt to Carlyle's *Sartor Resartus*," *Modern Language Quarterly*, 3 (1942), 51.
8 *Leaves of Grass*, ed. Harold W. Blodgett and Sculley Bradley (New York: New York Univ. Press, 1965), p. 730.
9 *The Gathering of the Forces*, ed. Rodgers and Black, II, 290–1.
10 *Ibid.*, 293.
11 *The Uncollected Poetry and Prose of Walt Whitman*, ed. Emory Holloway (Garden City, N.Y.: Doubleday, Page & Company, 1921), II, 83.
12 Smith, "Whitman's Debt," p. 52; the following comparison of passages from *Sartor* and Whitman's "I Sit and Look Out" draws on Smith, p. 55.
13 Carlyle, *Works*, I, 15–17.
14 *Leaves of Grass*, ed. Blodgett and Bradley, pp. 272–3.
15 See Albert J. LaValley, *Carlyle and the Idea of the Modern* (New Haven, Conn.: Yale Univ. Press, 1968), esp. p. 107.

16 Carlyle, *Works*, I, 9–10.
17 *Ibid.*, 17–18.
18 *Leaves of Grass*, ed. Blodgett and Bradley, pp. 38–9.
19 Carlyle, *Works*, I, 238.
20 *Leaves of Grass*, ed. Blodgett and Bradley, p. 85.
21 *Ibid.*, p. 89.
22 *Ibid.*, p. 89.
23 *Ibid.*, p. 55.
24 Carlyle, *Works*, V, 83.
25 *Ibid.*, 189, 191.
26 Gregory Paine, "The Literary Relations of Whitman and Carlyle with Especial Reference to Their Contrasting Views on Democracy," *Studies in Philology*, 36 (1939), 550, 556.
27 Whitman, *Prose Works 1892*, ed Stovall, II, 375.
28 *Ibid.*, 369–70.
29 *Leaves of Grass*, Facsimile of First Edition (New York: Eakins Press, 1966), p. 47.
30 *Prose Works 1892*, ed. Stovall, I, 250–1.
31 *Walt Whitman: The Critical Heritage*, ed. Milton Hindus (New York: Barnes & Noble, 1971), p. 79; the reviewer has been variously identified as William Howitt or William J. Fox.
32 Harold Blodgett, *Walt Whitman in England* (Ithaca, N.Y.: Cornell Univ. Press, 1934), pp. 14–17, 20, 22.
33 *Prose Works 1892*, I, 332–3 n. 88.
34 Horace Traubel, *With Walt Whitman in Camden* (New York: Mitchell Kennerley, 1914), III, 303–4, 305.
35 *Poems by Walt Whitman*, p. [v].
36 *The Correspondence of Walt Whitman*, ed. Edwin H. Miller (New York: New York Univ. Press, 1961–9), II, 16; in later years, Whitman changed his view and expressed regret that he had consented to Rossetti's *Selection*: "In a day and month and year of weakness, I yielded to the idea that the English reader could not stand a full dose of Walt Whitman": Traubel, *With Walt Whitman in Camden*, II, 266.
37 Blodgett, *Walt Whitman in England*, p. 105.
38 *Ibid.*, pp. 105–6.
39 *Anne Gilchrist: Her Life and Writings*, ed. Herbert H. Gilchrist (London: T. Fisher Unwin, 1887), pp. 177, 179.
40 *The Letters of Anne Gilchrist and Walt Whitman*, ed. Thomas B. Harned (Garden City, N.Y.: Doubleday, Page & Company, 1918), p. xxx.
41 *Anne Gilchrist*, ed. Herbert Gilchrist, pp. 292–3, 306, 299–301.
42 *The Correspondence of Walt Whitman*, ed. Miller, II, 91.
43 *Anne Gilchrist*, ed. Herbert Gilchrist pp. 207, 210–11.
44 *The Correspondence of Walt Whitman*, ed. Miller, II, 131; Traubel, *With Walt Whitman in Camden*, III, 376–7.
45 *The Correspondence of Walt Whitman*, ed. Miller, II, 134–38.
46 *Ibid.*, p. 140.
47 *Ibid.*, pp. 141–2.
48 *Ibid.*, pp. 164, 161.

49 *Ibid.*, p. 170, pp. 170–1 n. 87; *Anne Gilchrist*, ed. Herbert Gilchrist, p. 86.
50 *Ibid.*, pp. 192, 199.
51 *Ibid.*, pp. 220–1 n. 85.
52 *Ibid.*, p. 225.
53 *Anne Gilchrist*, ed. Herbert Gilchrist, pp. 91–3.
54 *The Correspondence of Walt Whitman*, ed. Miller, II, 234–5.
55 *Anne Gilchrist*, ed. Herbert Gilchrist, pp. 96–7.
56 *Ibid.*, p. 119.
57 *The Correspondence of Walt Whitman*, ed. Miller, II, 336.
58 *Anne Gilchrist*, ed. Herbert Gilchrist, pp. 129, 139, 141.
59 *The Correspondence of Walt Whitman*, ed. Miller, III, 31; *Anne Gilchrist*, ed. Herbert Gilchrist, p. 149.
60 Emory Holloway, *Free and Lonesome Heart: The Secret of Walt Whitman* (New York: Vantage Press, 1960), pp. 181–2.
61 *Ibid.*, p. 182; Blodgett, *Walt Whitman in England*, p. 98.
62 *Anne Gilchrist*, ed. Herbert Gilchrist, pp. 230, 234, 236–7.
63 *The Letters of Anne Gilchrist and Walt Whitman*, ed. Harned, pp. 161–2; *Anne Gilchrist*, ed. Herbert Gilchrist, pp. 245, 249, 251–2.
64 *Anne Gilchrist*, ed. Herbert Gilchrist, pp. 338–9.
65 See Joseph Beaver, *Walt Whitman–Poet of Science* (New York: Octagon Books, 1974), pp. 9–14.
66 Blodgett, *Walt Whitman in England*, pp. 89–90.
67 *Leaves of Grass*, p. 525.
68 *Anne Gilchrist*, p. 355.
69 *Leaves of Grass*, ed. Blodgett and Bradley, p. 730; Traubel, *With Walt Whitman in Camden*, II, 130.
70 Blodgett, *Walt Whitman in England*, pp. 141–2.
71 *Ibid.*, pp. 201–3.
72 *Letters of William Michael Rossetti*, ed. Clarence Gohdes and Paull Franklin Baum (Durham, N.C.: Duke Univ. Press, 1934), p. 106.
73 Traubel, *With Walt Whitman in Camden*, I, 244–5.
74 J. Johnston and J. W. Wallace, *Visits to Walt Whitman in 1890–1891* (New York: Egmont Arens, 1918), p. 18.
75 *Ibid.*, pp. 17–19.
76 *Ibid.*, p. 274.
77 Blodgett, *Walt Whitman in England*, p. 212.
78 Phillips' unsigned review is reprinted (without attribution) in *Walt Whitman: The Critical Heritage*, ed. Hindus, pp. 100–1; for evidence of his authorship and further information about him, see Stovall, *The Foreground*, pp. 132 n. 92, 4 and n. 6, 8 and n. 17.
79 *Letters to Edward Dowden* (London: J. M. Dent & Sons, 1914), p. 40.
80 Blodgett, *Walt Whitman in England*, p. 46.
81 Traubel, *With Walt Whitman in Camden*, I, 134.
82 Edward Dowden, *Studies in Literature, 1789–1877* (London: C. Kegan Paul & Co., 1878), pp. 470–1, 472, 473.
83 *Ibid.*, pp. 475–89, 490, 491, 494, 495 –6.
84 *Ibid.*, pp. 491, 498–9.

85 *Ibid.*, pp. 501, 502, 506, 521–2.
86 *Ibid.*, pp. 470–1.
87 D. H. Lawrence, *The Symbolic Meaning: The Uncollected Versions of "Studies in Classic American Literature,"* ed. Armin Arnold (New York: Viking Press, 1961), p. 16.
88 *Ibid.*, p. 27.
89 *Ibid.*, p. 30.
90 Armin Arnold in Lawrence, *The Symbolic Meaning*, pp. 6–7, 229–30.
91 Lawrence, *The Symbolic Meaning*, pp. 230–1.
92 *Ibid.*, pp. 232–5.
93 *Ibid.*, pp. 236–9.
94 *Ibid.*, p. 240.
95 D. H. Lawrence, *Studies in Classic American Literature* (Garden City, N.Y.: Doubleday and Company, 1953), pp. 174–91; at the close of the Whitman chapter – and the book – are the words *"Lobo, New Mexico."*
96 *The Collected Letters of D. H. Lawrence*, ed. Harry T. Moore (New York: The Viking Press, 1962), II, 856.
97 Introduction, D. H. Lawrence, *Apocalypse* (New York: The Viking Press, 1966), p. xxix.
98 Lawrence, *Apocalypse*, pp. 199–200.

Afterword: Ave Mark Twain!

1 Thoreau, *Writings*, V, 233.
2 Dennis Welland, *Mark Twain in England* (Atlantic Highlands, N.J.: Humanities Press, 1978), p. 125.
3 Walter Blair, *Mark Twain & Huck Finn* (Berkeley: Univ. of California Press, 1962), p. 376.
4 George Stuart Gordon, quoted in Blair, *Mark Twain & Huck Finn*, p. 377.
5 Quoted in Welland, *Mark Twain in England*, p. 220.
6 *The Autobiography of Mark Twain*, ed. Charles Neider (New York: Harper & Row, 1959), pp. 348–9.
7 Welland, *Mark Twain in England*, p. 53.
8 *The Autobiography*, pp. 322–3.
9 Welland, *Mark Twain in England*, pp. 169–70.
10 *Mark Twain–Howells Letters*, ed. Henry Nash Smith and William M. Gibson (Cambridge, Mass.: The Belknap Press of Harvard Univ. Press, 1960), II, 663.
11 *Mark Twain Speaking*, ed. Paul Fatout (Iowa City: Univ. of Iowa Press, 1976), p. 556.
12 *Mark Twain Speaking*, pp. 561–2.
13 Hamlin Hill, *Mark Twain: God's Fool* (New York: Harper & Row, 1973), p. 175.
14 Howard G. Baetzhold, *Mark Twain and John Bull: The British Connection* (Bloomington: Indiana Univ. Press, 1970), pp. 244, 246.

Index

289

AAD-4853